21世纪英语专业系列教材

# Interpreting
## for General Purposes (Third Edition)

# 通用口译教程
## （第三版）

主编　梅德明

编者　梅德明　吴赟　李梅　贾丹　曹磊

图书在版编目 (CIP) 数据

通用口译教程 / 梅德明主编. —3 版. —北京：北京大学出版社，2021.5
21 世纪英语专业系列教材
ISBN 978-7-301-32127-0

Ⅰ. ①通… Ⅱ. ①梅… Ⅲ. ①英语—口译—高等学校—教材 Ⅳ. ① H315.9

中国版本图书馆 CIP 数据核字 (2021) 第 065372 号

| | |
|---|---|
| 书　　　名 | 通用口译教程（第三版）<br>TONGYONG KOUYI JIAOCHENG（DI-SAN BAN） |
| 著作责任者 | 梅德明　主编 |
| 责 任 编 辑 | 郝妮娜 |
| 标 准 书 号 | ISBN 978-7-301-32127-0 |
| 出 版 发 行 | 北京大学出版社 |
| 地　　　址 | 北京市海淀区成府路 205 号　100871 |
| 网　　　址 | http://www.pup.cn　　新浪微博：@北京大学出版社 |
| 编辑部邮箱 | pupwaiwen@pup.cn |
| 总编室邮箱 | zpup@pup.cn |
| 电　　　话 | 邮购部 010-62752015　发行部 010-62750672　编辑部 010-62759634 |
| 印 刷 者 | 河北滦县鑫华书刊印刷厂 |
| 经 销 者 | 新华书店<br>787 毫米 ×1092 毫米　16 开本　16.25 印张　516 千字<br>2007 年 4 月第 1 版　2014 年 9 月第 2 版<br>2021 年 5 月第 3 版　2023 年 8 月第 4 次印刷 |
| 定　　　价 | 58.00 元 |

未经许可，不得以任何方式复制或抄袭本书之部分或全部内容。
**版权所有，侵权必究**
举报电话：010-62752024　电子信箱：fd@pup.pku.edu.cn
图书如有印装质量问题，请与出版部联系，电话：010-62756370

# 总　序

　　北京大学出版社自2005年以来已出版《语言学与应用语言学知识系列读本》多种,为了配合第十一个五年计划,现又策划陆续出版《21世纪英语专业系列教材》。这个重大举措势必受到英语专业广大教师和学生的欢迎。

　　作为英语教师,最让人揪心的莫过于听人说英语不是一个专业,只是一个工具。说这些话的领导和教师的用心是好的,为英语专业的毕业生将来找工作着想,因此要为英语专业的学生多多开设诸如新闻、法律、国际贸易、经济、旅游等其他专业的课程。但事与愿违,英语专业的教师们很快发现,学生投入英语学习的时间少了,掌握英语专业课程知识甚微,即使对四个技能的掌握并不比大学英语学生高明多少,而那个所谓的第二专业在有关专家的眼中只是学到些皮毛而已。

　　英语专业的路在何方？有没有其他路可走？这是需要我们英语专业教师思索的问题。中央领导关于创新是一个民族的灵魂和要培养创新人才等的指示精神,让我们在层层迷雾中找到了航向。显然,培养学生具有自主学习能力和能进行创造性思维是我们更为重要的战略目标,使英语专业的人才更能适应21世纪的需要,迎接21世纪的挑战。

　　如今,北京大学出版社外语部的领导和编辑同志们,也从教材出版的视角探索英语专业的教材问题,从而为贯彻英语专业教学大纲做些有益的工作,为教师们开设大纲中所规定的必修、选修课程提供各种教材。他们把英语专业教材的出版看作是第十一个五年计划期间组织出版国家"十一五"重点出版规划项目——《面向新世纪的立体化网络化英语学科建设丛书》的重要组成部分。这套系列教材要体现新世纪英语教学的自主化、协作化、模块化和超文本化,结合外语教材的具体情况,既要解决语言、教学内容、教学方法和教育技术的时代化,也要坚持弘扬以爱国主义为核心的民族精神。因此,今天北京大学出版社在大力提倡专业英语教学改革的基础上,编辑出版各种语言、文学、文化课程的教材,以培养具有创新性思维和具有实际工作能力的学生,充分体现了时代精神。

　　北京大学出版社的远见卓识,也反映了英语专业广大师生盼望已久的心愿。由北京大学等全国几十所院校具体组织力量,积极编写相关教材。这就是说,这套教材是由一些高等院校有水平有经验的第一线教师们制定编写大纲,反复讨论,特别是考虑到在不同层次、不同背景学校之间取得平衡,避免了先前的教材或偏难或偏易的弊病。与此同时,一批知名专家教授参与策划和教材审定工作,保证了教材质量。

  当然,这套系列教材出版只是初步实现了出版社和编者们的预期目标。为了获得更大效果,希望使用本系列教材的教师和同学不吝指教,及时将意见反馈给我们,使教材更加完善。

  航道已经开通,我们有决心乘风破浪,奋勇前进!

胡壮麟

北京大学蓝旗营

2007 年 2 月

# 第三版前言

《通用口译教程》自 2007 年推出第一版、2014 年推出第二版,历经 10 多年的使用,已成为口译教学领域深受师生广泛欢迎的专业教材。时至今日,编者根据时代的变化和一线教学的需求,再次修订教材并推出第三版。

《通用口译教程》是一部以口译学习者为主要对象的英汉双向口译教材。之所以取名为《通用口译教程》是因为本教材属基础型、宽领域、泛题材的教程,适合大学英语专业课堂口译教学,也可用作意欲提高自己口译水平以便从事兼职口译工作的各类人士的一本自学教程。

《通用口译教程》的取材立足当代国际社会的跨文化交际现实,与我国当代社会活动与文化生活相吻合,可满足对外交流口译工作的基本需求。教程的题材广泛、内容实用、体例规范、语言地道。除了口译导论、口译技巧、教学测评、机构名称等部分之外,教程含"迎来送往""礼仪致辞""会展活动""庆典致辞""海外学习""教育论坛""人物访谈""文化交流""饮食文化""时代潮流""业务洽谈""商务谈判""节日风俗""旅游观光""绿色城市"和"全球环境"等主题。

《通用口译教程》采用教案式教材的编写方法,即教材的项目布局充分考虑到教学的顺序,以利组织教学活动。教程有配套录音,便于教师课堂教学,也便于学生课余操练。"口译导论"部分对口译的定义、范畴、研究、教学、技能、测试等问题做了概述。"教学单元"部分围绕着 16 个特定的主题安排了内容丰富的教学活动,从对话到篇章,从主课到练习、从词语扩展到知识技巧,编排科学合理,难度循序渐进,符合教学过程的实际。"口译教学测评"简要介绍了口译教学测试方法,着重介绍了一项标准化口译水平考试,即"上海市英语口译岗位资格证书考试"中级口译考试和高级口译考试部分的考试要求和考试程序,并提供了测试样卷各三套。

《通用口译教程》的主编长期从事口译教学和口译教材的开发,参编人员均为上海外国语大学英语教师,有着丰富的口译教学与实践经验。《通用口译教程》第三版的编者在对前版的使用情况做了深入调查研究的基础上,并根据新编口译教材须与时俱进的原则,对原教程的内容做了必要的调整和更新,对主课文和配套练习反复筛选,精雕细凿,对所保留部分也做了一定程度的修改和充实。

　　编者希望《通用口译教程》第三版能对我国高校英语口译教学做出新的贡献，对本教材中的纰缪或疏漏之处，编者还祈望专家、学者、同行以及使用本教程的师生不吝指正。

梅德明<br>2020 年 1 月于上海外国语大学

# 目 录

| | |
|---|---|
| 口译导论 | 1 |
| **第1单元　迎来送往 Meeting and Seeing Off** | 1 |
| 　第1部分 | 3 |
| 　　词汇预习 | 3 |
| 　　口译实践 | 3 |
| 　　课文注释 | 4 |
| 　　词语扩展 | 5 |
| 　　口译操练 | 7 |
| 　第2部分 | 9 |
| 　　词汇预习 | 9 |
| 　　口译实践 | 9 |
| 　　课文注释 | 10 |
| 　　词语扩展 | 10 |
| 　　口译操练 | 11 |
| 　　口译常识与技巧 | 13 |
| **第2单元　礼仪致辞 Ceremonial Speeches** | 15 |
| 　第1部分 | 17 |
| 　　词汇预习 | 17 |
| 　　口译实践 | 17 |
| 　　课文注释 | 18 |
| 　　词语扩展 | 18 |
| 　　口译操练 | 20 |
| 　第2部分 | 22 |
| 　　词汇预习 | 22 |
| 　　口译实践 | 22 |
| 　　课文注释 | 23 |
| 　　词语扩展 | 23 |
| 　　口译操练 | 24 |
| 　　口译常识与技巧 | 25 |
| **第3单元　会展活动 Exhibitions** | 27 |
| 　第1部分 | 29 |
| 　　词汇预习 | 29 |
| 　　口译实践 | 29 |

    课文注释 ·········································································· 30
    词语扩展 ·········································································· 31
    口译操练 ·········································································· 32
  第 2 部分 ············································································· 35
    词汇预习 ·········································································· 35
    口译实践 ·········································································· 35
    课文注释 ·········································································· 36
    词语扩展 ·········································································· 37
    口译操练 ·········································································· 38
    口译常识与技巧 ································································ 39

第 4 单元　庆典致辞 Celebrative Speeches ·································· 41
  第 1 部分 ············································································· 43
    词汇预习 ·········································································· 43
    口译实践 ·········································································· 43
    课文注释 ·········································································· 44
    词语扩展 ·········································································· 45
    口译操练 ·········································································· 46
  第 2 部分 ············································································· 49
    词汇预习 ·········································································· 49
    口译实践 ·········································································· 49
    课文注释 ·········································································· 50
    词语扩展 ·········································································· 50
    口译操练 ·········································································· 51
    口译常识与技巧 ································································ 53

第 5 单元　海外学习 Overseas Education ·································· 55
  第 1 部分 ············································································· 57
    词汇预习 ·········································································· 57
    口译实践 ·········································································· 57
    课文注释 ·········································································· 58
    词语扩展 ·········································································· 59
    口译操练 ·········································································· 60
  第 2 部分 ············································································· 61
    词汇预习 ·········································································· 61
    口译实践 ·········································································· 61
    课文注释 ·········································································· 62
    词语扩展 ·········································································· 63
    口译操练 ·········································································· 64
    口译常识与技巧 ································································ 64

## 第 6 单元　教育论坛 On Education ····· 67
### 第 1 部分 ····· 69
　词汇预习 ····· 69
　口译实践 ····· 69
　课文注释 ····· 70
　词语扩展 ····· 71
　口译操练 ····· 72

### 第 2 部分 ····· 73
　词汇预习 ····· 73
　口译实践 ····· 73
　课文注释 ····· 74
　词语扩展 ····· 75
　口译操练 ····· 76
　口译常识与技巧 ····· 77

## 第 7 单元　人物访谈 Interviews ····· 79
### 第 1 部分 ····· 81
　词汇预习 ····· 81
　口译实践 ····· 81
　课文注释 ····· 82
　词语扩展 ····· 83
　口译操练 ····· 84

### 第 2 部分 ····· 85
　词汇预习 ····· 85
　口译实践 ····· 85
　课文注释 ····· 86
　词语扩展 ····· 87
　口译操练 ····· 88
　口译常识与技巧 ····· 88
　技巧练习 ····· 90

## 第 8 单元　文化交流 Cultural Exchange ····· 91
### 第 1 部分 ····· 93
　词汇预习 ····· 93
　口译实践 ····· 93
　课文注释 ····· 94
　词语扩展 ····· 95
　口译操练 ····· 96

### 第 2 部分 ····· 98
　词汇预习 ····· 98

| | |
|---|---|
| 口译实践 | 98 |
| 课文注释 | 99 |
| 词语扩展 | 100 |
| 口译操练 | 101 |
| 口译常识与技巧 | 102 |
| 技巧练习 | 102 |

### 第9单元　饮食文化 Culinary Culture　　105

#### 第1部分　　107

| | |
|---|---|
| 词汇预习 | 107 |
| 口译实践 | 107 |
| 课文注释 | 108 |
| 词语扩展 | 109 |
| 口译操练 | 110 |

#### 第2部分　　113

| | |
|---|---|
| 词汇预习 | 113 |
| 口译实践 | 113 |
| 课文注释 | 114 |
| 词语扩展 | 115 |
| 口译操练 | 116 |
| 口译常识与技巧 | 117 |
| 技巧练习 | 118 |

### 第10单元　时代潮流 New Trends　　119

#### 第1部分　　121

| | |
|---|---|
| 词汇预习 | 121 |
| 口译实践 | 121 |
| 课文注释 | 122 |
| 词语扩展 | 123 |
| 口译操练 | 124 |

#### 第2部分　　127

| | |
|---|---|
| 词汇预习 | 127 |
| 口译实践 | 127 |
| 课文注释 | 128 |
| 词语扩展 | 129 |
| 口译操练 | 130 |
| 口译常识与技巧 | 131 |
| 技巧练习 | 132 |

## 第 11 单元　业务洽谈 Business Talk ········· 135
### 第 1 部分 ········· 137
　　词汇预习 ········· 137
　　口译实践 ········· 137
　　课文注释 ········· 138
　　词语扩展 ········· 139
　　口译操练 ········· 140
### 第 2 部分 ········· 142
　　词汇预习 ········· 142
　　口译实践 ········· 142
　　课文注释 ········· 143
　　词语扩展 ········· 144
　　口译操练 ········· 145
　　口译常识与技巧 ········· 146

## 第 12 单元　商务谈判 Business Negotiation ········· 149
### 第 1 部分 ········· 151
　　词汇预习 ········· 151
　　口译实践 ········· 151
　　课文注释 ········· 152
　　词语扩展 ········· 153
　　口译操练 ········· 154
### 第 2 部分 ········· 156
　　词汇预习 ········· 156
　　口译实践 ········· 156
　　课文注释 ········· 157
　　词语扩展 ········· 158
　　口译操练 ········· 159
　　口译常识与技巧 ········· 160
　　技巧练习 ········· 161

## 第 13 单元　节日风俗 Festivals and Customs ········· 163
### 第 1 部分 ········· 165
　　词汇预习 ········· 165
　　口译实践 ········· 165
　　课文注释 ········· 166
　　词语扩展 ········· 167
　　口译操练 ········· 168
### 第 2 部分 ········· 169
　　词汇预习 ········· 169

		口译实践 …… 169
		课文注释 …… 170
		词语扩展 …… 170
		口译操练 …… 171
		口译常识与技巧 …… 172

### 第 14 单元　旅游观光 Sightseeing …… 175
	第 1 部分 …… 177
		词汇预习 …… 177
		口译实践 …… 177
		课文注释 …… 179
		词语扩展 …… 179
		口译操练 …… 180
	第 2 部分 …… 182
		词汇预习 …… 182
		口译实践 …… 182
		课文注释 …… 183
		词语扩展 …… 183
		口译操练 …… 184
		口译常识与技巧 …… 185

### 第 15 单元　绿色城市 Green City …… 189
	第 1 部分 …… 191
		词汇预习 …… 191
		口译实践 …… 191
		课文注释 …… 192
		词语扩展 …… 193
		口译操练 …… 194
	第 2 部分 …… 196
		词汇预习 …… 196
		口译实践 …… 196
		课文注释 …… 197
		词语扩展 …… 197
		口译操练 …… 199
		口译常识与技巧 …… 199

### 第 16 单元　全球环境 Global Environment …… 203
	第 1 部分 …… 205
		词汇预习 …… 205
		口译实践 …… 205

课文注释 …………………………………………………… 207
　　词语扩展 …………………………………………………… 207
　　口译操练 …………………………………………………… 208
　第2部分 ………………………………………………………… 210
　　词汇预习 …………………………………………………… 210
　　口译实践 …………………………………………………… 210
　　课文注释 …………………………………………………… 211
　　词语扩展 …………………………………………………… 212
　　口译操练 …………………………………………………… 213
　　口译常识与技巧 …………………………………………… 213

口译教学测评 ……………………………………………………… 216
附录一：常用国名(地区名)速记方法 …………………………… 231
附录二：常用国际机构名称英汉对照表 ………………………… 233
附录三：常见企业英文译名 ……………………………………… 236

# 口译导论

## 第一章　口译与译员培训

口译人才的培养看上去似乎是一种实践性很强的教学工作,所谓"实践出真知",能培养出"能说会译者"即可,这种观点确实代表了不少人对口译培训的基本看法。当然持有这种观点者并非犯了什么大错,因为口译培训本应培养"能说会译者",口译教学的确是一门实践课。但是,这里有一个"匠"和"师"的差别问题,即"教书匠"和"教师"的差别。"匠"者,行为者也,"帅",思想者也;"匠"者知其然,"师"者知其所以然也。编者走过了一段"匠"者之路之后,也该登上"师"者之道了,研究一下"何为口译""如何口译""如何训译""如何审译"等问题,尤其应该探讨一下口译的"定义""模式"和"培训"三个核心问题,从而以"师"导之,以"匠"行之。

### 一、口译的定义

口译隶属于翻译的范畴,翻译含笔译和口译两大类,既可指笔译,也可表示口译。"我们有些资料要翻译",这里指的是笔译;"我们有个会议要翻译",这里指的却是口译。笔译有笔译的职业要求,口译自然也有口译的职业标准。笔译有反映笔译特点的定义,口译也有体现口译特征的定义。

口译的定义似乎很简单,"口译,口译翻译者是也"。因此口译似乎可被定义为"用口头表达的方式进行翻译"。那么何谓"翻译"?"翻译、翻译,翻转解译者是也"。其实不然。无论口译还是笔译,都必须解决"两个标准"问题。第一个标准是形式上的转换标准,第二个问题是内容上的解意标准。定义蕴涵标准,定义若已确立,标准则立于其间。

那么什么是口译?口译是一种通过口头表达形式,将所感知和理解的信息准确而又快速地由一种语言形式转换成另一种语言形式,进而达到即时传递与交流信息之目的的交际行为,是现代社会跨文化、跨民族交往的一种基本沟通方式。"形变"而"意存","形转"而"意达",是口译的基本要求;"意及"而又"神似","意传"而又"迅达"是口译的职业标准。

表面上看,口译似乎是一种被动、单一、机械性的语言传达活动。其实不然,口译是一种积极的、复杂的、具有一定创造性的意义再现活动。口译所再现的话语意义不仅仅是简单的言内意义,其还涉及信息内容所包含的言外含义、话语风格、文化特征、言者精神。从这个意义上说,口译是一种集语言信息、语境信息、文化信息、心理信息等于一体的综合交际活动。

### 二、口译的模式

对口译下定义,反映了我们对口译译质的一种认识,但是这种认识无法使我们深入了解口译译质的内涵。本书在这里提出一个反映口译语用机制、口译职业特征、口译培训标准的"口译模式"。根据这个模式,口译由"译能""译技"和"译为"三个相互关联的组成部分构成。译能指的是口译能力,译技指的是口译技巧,译为指的是口译行为。

译能系译员的知识体系、语言能力、心理素质和道德意识的综合才能。知识体系含语言知识、社会知识、通用知识、专用知识等。语言能力含语言感知能力、辨析解意能力、转码处理能力、连贯表达能力等。心理素质含短时记忆素质、压力承受素质、现场应变素质、虚怀以待素质等。道德意识含忠贞意识、诚信意识、保密意识、服务意识等。

译能在一定程度上是一种天赋才能。几乎懂双语者都可以从事某种程度的口译，但是绝对做不了高级口译。一名出类拔萃的高级译员通常天资聪颖，具备常人没有的口译天分。但是口译天分不等于口译才能，译能的很大一部分不是先天赋予的，而是后天练就的。良好的译能不可能一蹴而就，而需经历一个逐步形成、渐进完善的过程。译能源自一分天资，九分努力，虽然"朽木不可雕"，但是"百炼能成钢"。"只要功夫深，铁杵磨成针。"讲的就是这个道理。

译技系译员所掌握的口译技巧体系。译技含语言知识运用的话语技巧，以及心智能力展现的认知技巧。口译成功与否在很大程度取决于口译技巧的掌握和运用。口译技巧包括耳听会意技巧、笔头速记技巧、语言表述技巧、主题借用技巧、论点预测技巧、信息归纳技巧、生词解意技巧、寓意揣摩技巧、话语转承技巧、语码重组技巧、场景利用技巧、障碍排除技巧等。

译技获得的主渠道是实践。口译实践需要苦练、实练加巧练，口译实践是一个"实践——总结——实践——提高"的过程。技巧、技巧，生而丢技，疏而弃巧。所谓"熟巧"，其道理无非就是"熟能生巧"，"巧能获技"。

译为系译员的日常口译行为。译为是口译活动的具体实践，是口译任务的实际操作。译为既是译能的体现，也是译技的展示。译为可以表现为信息的单向传译，即单一地将A语译入B语，或将B语译入A语，也可以表现为信息的双向交流，即A语和B语的交替译出或译入。

译为可分为操练性译为和真实性译为两种。操练性译为系编造性口译行为，是培养译员的主要方法，其难度和量度是可控的，内容是可知的，甚至是已知的，操作属量体裁衣式，符合"因材施教"的教学原则。真实性译为是真实场景下的口译行为，属译员的正式口译操作，其难度和量度是可变的，内容可能是可预测的，也可能变化难测的，操作时心理压力大，译员的注意力更为集中，情绪更为激动，译效持续更为久远。口译培训时，教师若能适时将操练性译为尽可能地转变为真实性译为，则教学效果更为明显。

译能、译技、译为三位一体，是口译的全部内容，是译质的综合体现。三者的特点可有如下之表现：译能是口译活动的动力，是口译译质的核能，是口译信息传递的基础，是口译水准的源泉。译技是口译活动的手段，是口译译质的协能，是口译信息传递的便道，是口译水准的保障。译为是口译活动的目的，是口译译质的效能，是口译信息传递的实现，是口译水准的刻度。

译能、译技、译为互根互用，互为依存，互为转化。三者之间的关系可有如下之表现：译能更多地存在于译员的头脑里，译技更多地存在于译员的心智中，译为更多地表现在译员的舌尖上。

译为虽然依赖译能和译技而体现，但不一定能如实展现译能。有良好的译能不一定确保每次都有良好的译为，就好比一个有良好体操能力的运动员不一定每次都有良好的体操表现。译能是静态的、稳定的，译为是动态的、变化的。译能没有例外，而译为却可表现为失常。译能差，译为一定差，而译能优却不一定保证译为优。译为以译能为基础，但可以提炼译能。译技是一系列知识运用的技巧，可以通过译为不断增加数量、提高质量。译技不断提高的过程也是译能不断完善的过程。一般说来，译为越多，译技则越高，译能也就越强。没有译为的译能可能是停留在书面上的一些口译理论知识，而没有译为的译技则是不存在的。"熟能生巧"的熟巧关系可以表明译为与译技之间的关系。

## 三、口译的培训

　　口译的译训指的是对译员的口译培训。口译培训可以分为三类,一类是对国际会议高级译员的同传或交传能力的高端培训,另一类是对通用型或专业型译员的口译职业能力的系统培训,再一类是对意欲短期兼职的口译爱好者之口译基础能力的普通培训。上述口译培训的成果鉴定往往是所获取的口译学位文凭或口译职业资格证书。

　　近年来,我国高等院校外语专业的课程设置已将口译课列为专业必修课,有条件的非外语专业的学科也在课程设置中将口译培训列为选修课。北京、上海、广州、厦门、西安等地区的高校所开展的口译教学实践表明,对大学生进行口译能力培训确实是一种提高学习者外语综合能力的有效方法。事实上,口译课已在我国高等院校和社会办学培训中成为最受学生欢迎的课程之一。

　　同任何科目的教学相似,口译培训的三大要素是教师、教材、教法。三大要素中教师是关键,教材是手段,教法是保障。

　　口译课教师应该具备两个基本条件,一是具有语言教学和翻译教学经验的双语人,二是具有丰富口译经验的职业译员,或一定经验的兼职译员或业余译员。经常承担各类口译任务的高校外语教师是理想的口译课教师人选。口译课教师首先必须具有语言教学经验和翻译教学经验,这是因为口译教学涉及教学人员的教学理念、教学原则,以及语言教学和翻译教学的方法。一个语言教学和翻译教学的外行难以成为口译教学的内行。其次,口译教师还必须具有口译工作的经验,这是因为口译工作属职业性和经验性很强的行业,有其特定的行业规范和操作方法。由于没有口译实践经验的外语教师难以在口译教学中进行内行的点拨和讲解,难以组织内行的有效训练,因而难以胜任较高层次的口译教学。

　　有人说,一个好的教师无须好的教材便能上好课,这是不符合教学事实的,也是不负责任的做法。好教师无好教材能够上课,甚至能一时上好课,但不能长久地上好课。教材是达到教学目的之不可缺的手段。好教材是好教师上好课的"炊之米"。对口译培训来说,拥有优秀的教材尤为重要。

　　口译培训教材有两类,一类为时事性的政务类和商务类讲话,另一类为系统性的专业培训教材。时事讲话具有很强的现时性和现场性,从而保证了口译培训的真实性。时事讲话通常用作同声传译的培训教材。但是时事讲话有其自身的缺点,即缺乏教学的系统性和针对性。系统教材克服了上述时势讲话所含的缺点,教材通常按培训对象的现有水平、口译教学的阶段目的、口译题材的难易程度、口译技能的训练项目等要求而系统编写,是综合培训口译能力的常用教材。系统口译教材除了具备一般教材的特点之外,还应该体现口译的特点,例如语言经典、题材广泛、情景真实、内容实用、词语通用、语言规范、技巧科学、操作容易、手段多样等。总之口译教材应该具有时代性、经典性、科学性、综合性、实用性、立体性、参阅性等特点。

　　口译教学有了优秀的师资和良好的教材,还需要一套科学的教学方法来实施口译教学的阶段性教学计划,达到终极性教学目标,即制定和实施短期目标与长期目标的计划和方法。国内高校对口译教学方法的研究目前尚处起步阶段,至今还未见一套以科学的口译教学理念为指导的较完整的教学法面世。国外的口译模式及口译教学理论如 Seleskovitch 的"释意理论"、Gile 的"认知负荷模型"和 Anderson 的"认知能力发展模式"对我国口译理论研究产生了较积极的影响,但这种影响并未对我国口译教学方法研究和我国高校口译教学方法标准的制定与实施产生有效的作用。

　　口译教学可以采用基础能力培训和应用能力培训结合、听说读写译技能教学兼容,文字声像多媒体教学手段并用的综合教学法。口译活动涉及耳听会意、话语理解、信息加工、文本翻译、笔头记录、口头表述等能力,因而口译教学旨在培养牢固掌握两种语言知识、熟练运用语用技能、精于语言翻译技巧、擅长标准口译操作的人才,旨在培养语言通才的基础上培养口译专才。在口译教学中,无论选择何种教学方法都应该明确，培养语言通才是培养口译专才的必然阶段，培养口译专才是培养语言通才的最终阶段。

虽然"眼前道路千万条，条条道路通罗马"，但是道路有曲有直，行速有快有慢，车技有高有低，效果也会有好有差。口译教学可以以综合教学法为主，以专项教学法为辅，以课堂教学为培训主体，以现场实践为职业体验，精讲泛练，点面结合，文本音像，立体教学。起点已清楚，目标亦明确，手段可定局，这就是教学方法的重要性。

# 第二章　口译理论研究的现状与展望

## 一、口译理论研究的宏观框架及研究方法

口译属于翻译的一种形式，究其实质而言，口译理论研究属于翻译理论研究的一个分支。以翻译理论研究的宏观框架为参照系，口译理论研究的宏观框架可大致分为三部分：一般口译研究、特殊口译研究和应用口译研究。

一般口译研究主要包括对口译的性质、过程、标准等根本问题的研究。其中，口译性质研究主要指对口译的定义、口译和笔译的关系、口译的目的、类型、社会功能等问题的研究。口译过程研究主要指对口译中译员的信息处理过程的研究，以及在此过程中译员的生理、心理及认知特点等问题的研究。口译标准研究主要指对口译质量的一般标准、不同口译任务的质量评估标准、评估模式及实际操作等问题的研究。此外，一般口译研究还应包括对口译员的职业素质、工作条件、工作方式、口译的价值与价格等问题的研究，以及对口译史和口译教学史的研究。

特殊口译研究主要包括对两种具体语言的对比和互译、对两种文化的对比研究，提出能指导两种具体语言互译的理论。在这方面，口译研究可借鉴翻译研究的成果。一般口译研究和特殊口译研究都属于口译基本理论性研究范畴。

应用口译研究则主要包括对口译技巧和口译教学与培训的研究。口译技巧研究包括对口译的基本技巧的一般研究和对不同口译类型特殊技巧的研究。接续口译和同声传译是最重要的两种口译形式，口译界有关这两种口译技巧的研究也是最多的。口译教学与培训研究主要指对口译教学的原则和方法、培养目标、教学内容、教资力量和设备、学员素质要求及学前水平测试等问题的研究，同时还包括对口译教学实践的各个具体环节的研究，如口译课程设置、口译教材选编、口译技能化教学及培训、口译教学评估等，以及对口译测试和口译资格认证等问题的研究。

综合口译理论研究的特点，我们认为，口译理论研究的性质仍然属于以经验研究为基础的翻译理论研究，其鲜明特征是其跨学科性。许多相关学科如翻译研究、心理学、语言学、文化研究都尝试解释真实的口译现象，并为此做出了一定的贡献。西方口译理论研究传统上主要有两大学派：一派主张用类似自然科学的方法来研究口译，强调量化分析，另一派则主张用人文科学的方法，赞成归纳性的一般理论。鲍刚将口译理论研究方法归纳为十种：经验总结法，归纳思辨法，内省法，黑箱法，现场观察法，调查法，原、译语资料分析法，口译模式设定法，实验法，跨学科借鉴法等。这些方法是相辅相成、互相补充的。目前，以认知科学为基础的跨学科借鉴法已成为口译界的占主流地位的研究方法之一。

## 二、口译理论研究现状的主要特征

口译理论研究呈现出跨学科、全方位、多视角的特点。

一方面，口译理论性研究由早期的专业译员内省式的经验谈发展为20世纪90年代后口译研究界的专家学者和研究人员借鉴相关学科和研究领域的研究成果进行具有一定理论基础和理论深度的研究，研究视角由最初的局限于口译活动本身的描述式

研究发展为进行跨学科、全方位、多视角的剖析式研究,具体表现为以下三方面:

(1) 口译过程研究由描述口译阶段过程的层面逐渐开始深入译员思维活动过程的规律。

(2) 口译标准研究由关于一般原则的比较抽象概括的经验总结上升为以有理论指导的直观、量化研究,质量评估标准更加客观、全面。

(3) 口译能力研究逐渐受到重视。20世纪90年代以前,很多人仅仅把口译当作一种纯粹的技巧。近年来,口译界逐渐意识到,口译具有自身独特的规律,要求译员掌握专门的技能,译员的口译能力包括知识能力、技能能力和心理能力。

另一方面,随着近年来对口译人才的需求逐渐升温,口译员培训和口译教学广泛兴起,应用性口译研究也得到迅速发展,由最初关于单一的口译技巧研究发展为围绕口译员培训和口译教学为中心的更加系统化、专业化的研究。经过不断的实践和积累,现在口译界已经总结出比较系统化、专业化的口译技能化训练技巧,并已经在国内高校的口译课程和培训项目中付诸实践,如口译短期记忆、口译笔记、口译笔记阅读、连续传译理解原则、言语类型分析、主题思想识别、目的语信息重组、口译应对策略、译前准备技巧、演说技巧、跨文化交际技巧等。

口译理论性研究基本上是对西方口译理论成果的评介与扩展,其中最有影响力的三大理论分别是:原巴黎高等翻译学校(ESIT)的校长Seleskovitch创立的释意理论(theorie du sens)、现执教于巴黎国立东方语言文化大学高等翻译学院的Gile提出的认知负荷模型(The Effort Models),以及Anderson提出的认知能力发展模式(Adaptive Control of Thoughts)。我们可以对这三大理论进行深入的研究,引用相关学科的研究成果对其进行实证与扩充。

**1. 释意理论**

Seleskovitch在1968年发表的《国际会议译员——言语与交际问题》标志着释意理论的诞生。后经她本人和Lederer等人的努力,该理论已发展成为国际上最有影响力的口笔译理论之一。该理论的最大特点是对译员的思维过程进行了详细描述,提出三角形翻译过程的假设,认为翻译的对象应该是源语信息的意义(sens),而不是其语言外壳,意义是语言同认知知识结合的结果。

**2. 认知负荷模型**

1995年,Daniel Gile在其《口笔译训练的基本概念与模式》(*Basic Concepts and Models for Interpreter and Translator Training*)的著作中提出了认知负荷模型。该模型以认知科学为理论基础,借用了"有限的注意力资源"和"任务的困难程度与任务实施的时限之间有很强的关联性"两个主要的认知概念,重在描述口译(尤其是同声口译)中译员如何分配精力(effort)处理听、理解、记忆、产出等几乎同时发生的任务,并根据口译工作过程的阶段性特点提出了"同声传译的口译模型""接续口译的口译模型"和"口译的理解模型"。认知负荷模型是关于口译操作制约的模型,其优势在于它有很强的可操作性,并且对分析口译过程中的错译和漏译现象具有较强的说服力。

**3. 认知技能发展模式**

Anderson的认知技能发展模式(Adaptive Control of Thoughts)最初在1982年提出。该理论认为,任何熟练的行为都要求将陈述性知识(declarative knowledge)转化为程序性知识(procedural knowledge)。由陈述性知识到程序性知识有个发展过程:认知(cognitive)、联想(associative)和自主(autonomous)阶段。在认知阶段只有陈述性知识,陈述性知识以解释(interpretative)的方式提取,速度很慢;在联想阶段,既有陈述性知识也有程序性知识,但提取速度仍不够快。自主阶段的知识完全程序化了,其提取速度极快。该模式适用于解释任何认知能力的习得,并且可以从人类各种认知技能的习得过程中找到例证,尤其是各种语言技能的习得过程。认知技能发展模式不仅可以指导译员口译能力的发展过程,而且从理论上弥补了释意理论和认知负荷模型在解释译员长期技能发展方面的不足。

### 三、口译理论研究中存在的主要问题与前景展望

西方口译研究至今为止已经历了四个阶段约50年的发展：从20世纪50年代至60年代的口译从业人员经验谈阶段，60年代至70年代初期的实验心理学研究阶段，70年代初到80年代中期的从业人员理论研究阶段，一直到80年代后半期开始至今的跨学科和实证研究阶段，形成了四种最有影响的口译研究视角：信息处理范式、释意派理论、神经生理学研究和跨学科实证研究，主要围绕五大研究主题，即口译训练、语言问题、认知问题、质量问题和从业问题，并且已经形成多个有影响的口译研究中心。

与西方相比，我国对口译研究起步较晚，且主要围绕口译的特点及技巧进行论述，属于经验交流和问题陈述。口译研究缺乏理论体系，多从经验出发。尽管口译理论研究中存在诸多困难，我们仍对口译理论研究的前景充满希望。一方面，在口译理论性研究方面，有些学者的研究成果已具有一定程度的理论创新，如刘和平的"推理教学法"、厦门大学口译训练模式、陈菁的交际法口译测试量化评估等等。当然，理论创新不是一朝一夕就能完成，而是需要许多人长期不懈的努力，口译研究者正朝着这一目标迈进。

## 第三章 口译认证考试

外语口译认证考试火爆中国大陆，吸引了越来越多的赶考者，其中包括港澳台地区的考生。但是外语口译难考，也是不争的事实。

那么口译难考，究竟难在哪里呢？主要原因在于口译是一种技能，而不是一种技巧，因此口译考试考的是口译能力，而不是口译窍门。

口译能力是一种综合能力，考生必须具有扎实的双语功底。这种双语能力不仅指通晓基本语言知识，如语音语调、句法结构、词法语义等知识的掌握，更重要的是指运用语言知识的能力（如听、说、读、写、译）。

考生应该了解语言的不同语体风格和语用功能，掌握一定数量的习语、俚语、术语、谚语、委婉语、略语、诗句等词语的翻译方法。

考生必须具备清晰、流畅、达意的表达能力。口译时，语速不急不缓，音调不高不低，吐字清晰自然，表达干净利落，择词准确恰当，语句简明易解，译语传神传情。

考生必须具有良好的心理承压能力、短时记忆能力、笔头速记能力、信息组合能力、逻辑思维能力、辨析解意能力和应变反应能力。

考生还应该具有广博的知识，对时事要闻、政经知识、人文知识、科技知识、商贸知识、法律知识、史地知识、国际知识、民俗知识、生活常识等等，都要略窥门径。

考生必须明白，口译不是一种机械地将信息的来源语符号转换为目标语符号的语言活动，而是一种积极地、始终以交流信息意义为宗旨的、具有一定创造性的语言交际活动。因此，口译不是孤立地以词义和句子意义为转换单位的单一性语言活动，而是兼顾交际内容所涉及的词语意义、话语上下文意义、语体含义、民族文化含义等信息的综合性语言活动。从这个意义上说，口译不仅仅是语言活动，还是文化活动、心理活动和社交活动。

考生必须明白，口译考试质量有两条基本衡量标准：一是"准确"，二是"流利"。首先，口译必须准确。不准确的口译可能是"胡译"，可能是"篡译"，也可能是"误译"。准确是口译的灵魂，是口译的生命线。具体说来，口译的准确涉及口译时的主题准确、精神准确、论点准确、风格准确、词语准确、数字准确、表达准确、语速准确以及口吻准确等方面。准确的译语应该同时保持源语的意义和风格。"流利"体现了口译的特点，是考生必须遵循的另一标准。考生在准确口译的前提下，应该迅速流畅地传译。口译的

现场性、现时性、即席性、限时性、交互性等因素要求口译过程宜短,节奏宜紧。口译是交际的工具,工具的价值在于效用和效率。工具首先得有效用,否则就不成其为工具,但高效用而低效率的工具不是一件好工具。口译考试要求考生具有较快的信息感知速度、意义解析速度、重新编码速度,以及正常的译语表达速度。

考生还应该了解口译考试时的基本过程。口译的基本过程是输入、解译、输出,即从信息的感知开始,经过信息加工处理,再将信息表达出来,具体表现为信息的接收、解码、记录、编码和表达这五个阶段。

考生对信息的接收有被动接收和主动接收两种,被动接收表现为孤立地听入单词和句子,注意力过分集中在信息的语言形式上。主动接收是指译员在听入时重信息的意义。考生应该采取主动听入的方法。

解码是指考生对接收到的信息码进行解意,获取语言和非语言形式所包含的各种信息。来源语信息码是多方面、多层次的,有语言码,如语音、句法、词汇等信息,也有非语言码,如文化传统、专业知识、信息背景、表达风格、神态表情等信息,也有介于两者之间的,如双关语、话中话、语体意义等信息。

记录,或者叫作暂存,是指将感知到的语码信息暂时储存下来。当以某一种语码形式出现的信息被感知后,在转换成另一种语码前,须暂时储存下来。由于口译内容转瞬即逝,良好的记录显得十分重要。口译的信息记录可采用"脑记"加"笔记"方法。无论采用"脑记"还是"笔记",考生记录的内容主要是信息的概念、主题、论点、情节、要点、逻辑关系、数量关系等。一般宜采用网状式的整体记忆法,避免点状式的局部记忆法。

编码是指将来源语的信息解码后,赋以目标语的表达形式。考生在编码时要排除来源语语言结构的干扰,使重新编码的信息不仅在语言形式上符合目标语的表达规范,而且在内容上也保持信息的完整性,并尽可能在风格上保持不变。

表达是指将听入的来源语信息以目标语口头传译出来。表达是口译考试的最后一道环节,也是口译考试成败的关键。口译表达要求考生口齿清楚、吐字干脆、音调准确、择词得当、语句通顺、表达流畅。

有人说,口译才能是天赋的,也有人说,口译才能是练就的。这两种说法虽都不全面,但有一点是肯定的,口译才能的天赋至多为一分,而精心锤炼却占九分以上。

迎来送往

# Meeting and Seeing Off

# 第1单元 迎来送往 Meeting and Seeing Off

# 第1部分 Section 1

 **Vocabulary Work**

| | | | |
|---|---|---|---|
| marketing department | 营销部 | send regards (to) | 致意 |
| fruitful cooperation | 合作愉快 | pick up (sb.) | 接人 |
| reception dinner | 接风晚宴 | shipment | 货物 |
| hospitality | 热情款待 | rewarding | 有收获的 |

 **Text Interpreting**

Interpret the following conversation alternatively into Chinese and English:

### Meeting at the Airport

Mr. Moore: Excuse me, but are you from Fusheng Trading?
王先生: 是的,您是GE进出口公司的吗?
Mr. Moore: Yes, I am Daniel Moore, Executive Director of the Marketing Department of GE Import and Export Company. Our general manager, Mr. Defoe asked me to come and meet you because he is chairing a meeting at this moment. He sends his warmest regards.
王先生: 谢谢,很高兴见到您。我是公司的翻译。请让我介绍陈先生。这位是陈先生,福生贸易公司总经理;这是莫尔先生,GE进出口公司销售部主任。
陈先生: 您好,莫尔先生。
Mr. Moore: How do you do! I hope you had a pleasant flight.
陈先生: 很愉快。天气很好。
Mr. Moore: Good! You see, we are all very glad that you've come to New York. We are looking forward to our fruitful cooperation.
陈先生: 这也是我们的愿望。
Mr. Moore: For your convenience and comfort, we accommodate you in one of the company's villas for overseas visitors. It is located by the beach, overlooking the sea. It is only 20 minutes' drive from our company. I am sure you will like it.

陈先生： 好极了。我喜欢视野开阔的房子。
Mr. Moore： I'm glad to hear it. Just to confirm—you know that tomorrow's meeting is set for 9:30 a.m. at our office. Is that all right for you?
陈先生： 我没问题。
Mr. Moore： Then I'll pick you up at 8:50 tomorrow morning.
陈先生： 很好,莫尔先生,谢谢。
Mr. Moore： It's my pleasure. Tomorrow evening at 7:00 we will host a reception dinner in your honor. By the way, are there any sights you'd like to see while you are here? I'd be glad to show you around.
陈先生： 看情况吧。如果一切顺利如愿的话,我很想留出一天时间观光。我一直想看看现代艺术博物馆和林肯表演艺术中心。我对艺术特别感兴趣。
Mr. Moore： That's no problem. I'll make some arrangements for this tour around.
陈先生： 谢谢!
Mr. Moore： You are welcome. I hope you will enjoy your stay here. See you tomorrow!

## Seeing off at the Airport

陈先生： 我的行李都进去了,看来该说再见了。
Mr. Moore： I know you must be excited to go home after such a long business trip.
陈先生： 那当然。这次我们谈得很成功,我也很高兴。我们能在一个月内收到你们的第一批货,对吧?
Mr. Moore： Yes, that's right. You won't be disappointed.
陈先生： 这一点我相信。我真的很感激你们的热情款待,也感谢你陪我在市内观光。这次旅行非常有意义,也非常有收获。
Mr. Moore： I'm glad to hear it.
陈先生： 再次感谢你们使这次旅行如此成功。过圣诞节的时候,如果你有空,欢迎到上海来。我可以带你看看我们的城市。
Mr. Moore： Thanks for the invitation. I will think about it.
陈先生： 这是最后一次登机广播了。我们得说再见了。
Mr. Moore： Good bye and have a nice flight!

## 课文注释  Notes on the Text

1. 一些常用头衔的翻译:

首席长官称谓常以"总"表示,与之相对应的英语词有: chief, general, head, managing 等。例如:

  总工程师 chief engineer
  总代理 general agent
  总教练 head coach

汉语中表示副职的头衔常以"副"字表示,与之对应的英语词有: vice, associate, assistant, deputy 等。例如:

  副总统/大学副校长 vice president
  副教授 associate professor

## 第 1 单元 迎来送往 Meeting and Seeing Off

  副总经理 assistant/deputy general manager
  副市长 deputy mayor

学术头衔除了有"正""副"级别外,还有"助理"级,英语中常用 assistant 一词。例如:

  助理工程师 assistant engineer
  助理编辑 assistant editor

汉语的"代理"一词,英语可以用 acting:

  代理市长 acting mayor
  代理主任 acting director

汉语的"常务"一词,一般可翻译为 managing:

  常务理事 managing director
  常务副校长 managing vice president

汉语的"执行"一词可以用 executive:

  执行主席 executive chairman

汉语的"名誉",可译为 honorary:

  名誉主席 honorary chairman

2. ...a pleasant flight:译成"旅途愉快"较合适。
3. ... our fruitful cooperation:fruitful 原意为"富有成效的,有果实的",按照汉语习惯简单译成"合作成功"。
4. For your convenience and comfort:for 也可译为"为了你们的方便和舒适",不如译为"考虑到……"更符合汉语的习惯。
5. ...host a reception dinner in your honor:host 为动词,含有"以主人的身份招待宾客"之意。
   in your honor 或 in the honor of... 是比较正式的欢迎辞短语,用于外事接待场合。
6. 如果一切如愿的话:译成 If everything comes out good and satisfactory。good and... 短语表示"非常……",如:This road is good and long.(这条路很长。)
7. 看来该说再见了:译成 I am all set to go,意指:一切都准备妥当了。
8. 表达"祝你们一路平安"等良好愿望的常用说法有:
   Have a nice trip! / Wish you a pleasant journey! / Bon voyage!
   若给乘飞机的人送行,可说:Have a nice flight!

## 词语扩展 *Developing Vocabulary and Expressions*

- Welcome to... 欢迎来……
- Thank you very much for coming all the way to meet me. 谢谢您专程来接我。
- It is with great pleasure that I... / I have the great pleasure to... / It gives me great pleasure... 我为能……而深感荣幸。
- It is my pleasure to welcome you all here today. 我很高兴今天在这里欢迎你们大家。
- I hope you will have a very enjoyable stay. 希望您在这里过得愉快。

- I am delighted to welcome you to... 我很高兴欢迎你们来到……
- I'd like to introduce you to/ I would like you to meet/May I introduce you to... 我想把您介绍给……
- I don't think you have met before. 我想你们未曾见过面。
- I am glad to have the honor of introducing... 我很高兴能有此殊荣向诸位介绍……
- I take great pleasure in introducing our guest Professor Black. 我很高兴向各位介绍我们的客人布莱克教授。
- Allow me to introduce myself. I am..., the interpreter. 请允许我介绍一下自己。我叫……,是翻译。
- Excuse me, I haven't had the honor of knowing you. 对不起,我还没有请教阁下的尊姓大名呢。
- You must be our expected guest, Mr. Thompson from CI Oil Company. 您一定是我们期盼的客人,CI 石油公司的汤普逊先生吧。
- I am delighted to make your acquaintance. 我很高兴能与您结识。
- I'm glad/happy/delighted to have the pleasure of meeting you in my hometown. 很高兴能在我的家乡接待您。
- I would like to show you our tentative itinerary. 我想向您介绍一下我们初步拟定的活动日程。
- I'd like to take a few minutes to tell you about your schedule here. 我想花几分钟介绍一下各位在这里的行程。
- We have a tight schedule for your short/brief visit/stay. I hope you don't mind. 您此次短暂访问/逗留期间,我们为您安排的日程很紧,希望您不要介意。
- Wish your visit a complete success. 祝您的访问圆满成功。
- Wish you all the best in your tour/visit. 祝您的旅途/参观一切顺利。
- I'm sure you'll enjoy yourselves. If there's anything I can do to help, please let me know. 我相信你们会玩得很愉快!如果有需要我帮忙的地方,请直说。
- Don't hesitate to ask if you need anything. 有什么需要我帮忙的,请直说。
- Let me know if you need anything. 有什么需要我帮忙的,请直说。
- One thing you should remember is... 千万记住一点……
- It gives me so great a pleasure on behalf of... to extend a warm welcome to... 我非常高兴能代表……向来访的……表示热烈的欢迎。
- I would like to express my heartfelt thanks to you. 我谨向您表示衷心的感谢。
- I am looking forward to visiting your country in the near future. 我期待在不久的将来访问贵国。
- Thank you very much for such a thoughtful arrangement for us. 感谢你们为我们所做的如此精心的安排。
- No words can fully express our gratitude to the leadership of this company for their great kindness and thoughtful consideration for us during our stay here. 贵公司领导在我们逗留期间给予无微不至的关照,千言万语也道不尽我们的感激之情。
- I am looking forward to the opportunity of hosting you again here. 期待有机会能再次作为东道主接待您。
- It's very kind of you to come all the way to see me off. 谢谢你们专程来送别。
- Take care, and have a pleasant trip. 保重!祝您一路平安。
- Good luck, and enjoy your flight. 祝您好运(保重)。祝您一路平安。
- Bon voyage! 一路平安!
- Remember me to.../ Say hello to... for me. 代我向……问好。

## 第 1 单元 迎来送往 Meeting and Seeing Off

## 译操练 *Interpreting Practice*

### 1. 听译 ▶▶ Listening Interpreting

A. Listen to the sentences and interpret them into Chinese.
   Sentences 1—10

B. Listen to the paragraphs and interpret them into Chinese.
   Paragraphs 1—2

### 2. 视译 ▶▶ Sight Interpreting

A. **Interpret the following sentences into Chinese：**
   (1) It gives me such a great pleasure to meet you and your family here in Shanghai and I am very glad that you will be working with us for the next three months.
   (2) If you should encounter any inconveniences in your life and work here, do not hesitate to let me know and I'll be very glad to help you out.
   (3) Our general director will host a reception banquet in your honor at 7:00 tonight, and we would like you and your family to come.
   (4) I would like to avail myself of this opportunity to extend my warm welcome to you all.
   (5) Permit me first of all, to thank our host, for your extraordinary arrangements and hospitality.
   (6) It is in the spirit of friendly cooperation, mutual promotion and common prosperity that I extend to you the warmest welcome and convey to you the most gracious greetings from all the employees of the CB Corporation.
   (7) Mr. Jackson, the rest of the staff of the school will join with us in extending to you our sincerest welcome.
   (8) The generous/gracious hospitality of our host will remain in our memory forever.
   (9) It would be both an honor and a pleasure to have your presence.
   (10) It gives me great pleasure to express once again to our host my deep appreciation for the grand reception and boundless and generous hospitality we enjoy here.

B. **Interpret the following paragraphs into Chinese：**
   (1) Ministers and other distinguished delegates, first of all, let me welcome you to Sydney. While brief, I hope our time in Sydney will be highly productive. I also hope you take the opportunity while you are here to enjoy a small taste of what Australia's major city has to offer.
   (2) 40 years ago, the great statesmen of our two countries used the small ping-pong ball for a big undertaking: the resumption of contact between the two countries. The ship of China-US relations, moored for so long, again set sail, braving the wind and waves. Today, NBA player Yao Ming has become a star popular among the people of both

countries. From the ping-pong ball to the basketball, it is not just a change in diameter. Rather, it reflects the enormous progress in depth and breadth of China-US relations over the short span of 30 years.

### 3. 情景练习 ▶▶ Situational Interpreting

**Interpret the following conversation alternatively into Chinese and English:**

> **Roles**
> Mr. Feng: a Chinese
> Steven: an American
> Miss Chen: an interpreter

Steven: Mr. Feng. Great to see you again!
Feng: 我也很高兴再次见到你!旅途还顺利吗?
Steven: Good! The flight was comfortable. I was able to take a nap on the way over.
Feng: 那就好!会不会还不太适应时差?
Steven: No, not now. I adjusted to the time difference while I was in Japan and Singapore, so I'll be all right.
Feng: 那太好了。我每次旅行都很难适应时差。
Steven: I heard you had a dust storm recently.
Feng: 是的,但只是轻度沙尘暴。天气预报说未来几天天气很好,我们大可不必担心。
Steven: Wonderful! I was hoping to do some jogging every day and go sightseeing. Will we have enough time?
Feng: 当然。你的时间安排得很灵活。明天一天看厂房,后天上午去公司和几个客户见见面,吃顿午餐。其他时间你可以自由支配。
Steven: Excellent! Last time I only had time to visit the Great Wall and Ming Tomb.
Feng: 这次我们可以去故宫博物院,再去天安门广场看看。
Steven: Sounds very exciting!
Feng: 你回去之前,我们还可以去逛街买东西。也许你可以给夫人和女儿买点有趣的礼物呢。
Steven: Great! I just can't wait. Feng, it is really good to see you again.
Feng: 好好休息,明天见。

# 第2部分 Section 2

 **Vocabulary Work**

| 欢迎辞 | welcome speech | 华盛顿奇才队 | Washington Wizard |
| 职务相当的人 | counterpart | 全明星队运动员 | all-star (n.) |
| 地震重建项目 | earthquake recovery project | 象征性地 | symbolically |
| 表演赛 | exhibition game | 双边关系 | bilateral relationship |

 **Text Interpreting**

Interpret the following speech into English:

### 向来访的美国篮球队代表团致欢迎辞

尊敬的各位来宾：

晚上好！

感谢各位来宾和华盛顿奇才篮球队代表团的全体成员，感谢你们在周六晚上抽出时间前来参加欢迎会。我知道奇才队的队员们度过了一个非常繁忙的白天，去都江堰看了地震重建项目，参观了学校，并与电子科技大学进行了篮球表演赛。感谢你们大家的参与。我希望这不仅仅是一个招待会，同时还是一个庆祝会。

你们很多人都知道，奇才队来华是为了庆祝我们两国重建外交关系三十周年，同时也是为了纪念美国篮球队首次访华三十周年，当时奇才队还叫华盛顿子弹队。

我们常常记得尼克松总统与中国领导人曾把"乒乓外交"作为重建两国关系的第一步。此后不久，应邓小平的邀请，华盛顿子弹队以他们特殊的"篮球外交"形式，成为第一支访华的美国NBA篮球队。在重建两国关系的日子里，我们看到了美中两国人民能够通过体育运动的共同兴趣和热情走到一起。在三十年里程碑式的时刻，观看了今天下午举行的表演赛后，我想冒昧地说这至今仍然是不变的真理。

奇才队代表团包括了它三十年前历史性访华以来的每十载中的至少一位球星。其中，韦斯·昂塞尔德是NBA五十巨星之一，也是首次访华代表团成员，乔治·穆雷桑是NBA历史上身材最高的队员，还有卡隆·巴特勒，奇才队的现役队员，他两次入选NBA全明星队。

今晚，在这里值得强调的是，奇才队象征性地让我们回顾了过去这些年以及许多方面的变迁。从那个时候起，美中关系得到了极大的发展，成为当今世界上最重要的双边关系。在贸易、环保合作以及教育和文化交流等众多领域中，我们两国之间已建立起越来越庞大的关系网络。无可置疑,美国和中国西南地区也共享了这种特殊的关系。

今晚,我们庆祝奇才队访华,尤其是在成都这个特别重要的一站。我们也借此机会庆祝美中外交关系和友谊的三十周年纪念,我们在今后的岁月中将继续共享成果。

现在请和我一起对奇才队及他们所代表的历史性访问表示热烈的欢迎。

让我们愉快地分享今晚的聚会。谢谢。

## 课文注释  Notes on the Text

1. 感谢各位来宾和华盛顿奇才篮球队代表团的全体成员,感谢你们在周六晚上抽出时间前来参加欢迎会:I want to thank all of you, dear guests and members..., for taking the time on a Saturday evening to come to this welcome reception. 此处使用 thank sb. for doing sth. 的结构,既能一一反映原句信息,又简化了原句结构。另外,译文中增加了 all of you,把"各位来宾和华盛顿奇才篮球队代表团的全体成员"处理为 all of you 的同位语,避免造成句子冗长而累赘。

2. ……当时奇才队还叫华盛顿子弹队:... then known as the Washington Bullets, shortly thereafter. 原句中出现三个篮球队的名字:奇才队、美国篮球队、华盛顿子弹队。译者需准备必要的背景常识,才能避免歧义。1979 年,中美两国正式建立外交关系。同年 8 月,获得 NBA 总冠军的华盛顿子弹队访问中国,成为第一支访华的美国 NBA 篮球队。1997-1998 赛季子弹队改为现在的华盛顿奇才队。因此,译文采用过去分词结构 known as 做定语修饰 their basketball team。

3. 我们常常记得尼克松总统与中国领导人曾把"乒乓外交"作为重建两国关系的第一步:We often remember "ping pong diplomacy" as one the first steps taken by President Nixon and his Chinese counterparts as they worked to reestablish the relationship. 此句的处理和原句句式结构不同,译文突出了"乒乓外交"。另外,注意"counterpart"的使用,可以表示同等或职务对应的人,避免重复表述。例如:The secretary of defense met with his counterparts in Asia to discuss the nuclear crisis.(这位国防部长与亚洲各国国防部长会晤商讨核危机问题。)

4. 其中,韦斯·昂塞尔德是 NBA 五十巨星之一……两次入选 NBA 全明星队:注意汉语和英语句式结构不同。原文由多个句子构成,译成英文时没有必要译成完整的句子,可以采取平列结构、同位语等形式简化句型,更加符合英文的表达习惯,例如:... including Wes Unseld, one of the NBA's top 50 All-Time players and a member of the original delegation that travelled to China; Gheorghe Muresan, ...

## 词语扩展  Developing Vocabulary and Expressions

- ❖ 欢迎辞      welcome speech / welcome address
- ❖ 告别辞      farewell speech / farewell address
- ❖ 外宾      foreign guests / overseas visitors
- ❖ 贵宾      distinguished guests
- ❖ 外国专家      foreign experts / foreign specialists
- ❖ 接待      to host / to receive
- ❖ 接待单位      the host organization

## 第 1 单元 迎来送往 Meeting and Seeing Off

- 接待人员     reception personnel
- 受到友好接待     to be cordially received /to get a friendly reception
- 设宴洗尘     to give a banquet in somebody's honor
- 举行盛大招待会     to hold a grand reception
- 答谢招待会     a reciprocal reception
- 冷餐招待会     buffet reception
- 感谢热情招待     to thank you for your kind hospitality
- 不辞辛劳远道来访     to come in spite of the long and tiring journey
- 短暂的访问     brief visit
- 请允许我介绍……     May I present...? /Allow me to introduce...
- 专程赶来     to come all the way
- 亲自接待     to meet in person
- 若有不便     to encounter any inconveniences
- 排忧解难     to help you out
- 活动日程     itinerary of a visit
- 初步拟订的活动日程     tentative itinerary
- 紧凑的活动安排     tight schedule/busy schedule
- 精心的安排     thoughtful arrangements
- 期待已久     long-expected
- 合作共事     to work as your colleague
- 与某人结识     to make the acquaintance of somebody
- 文化交流     cultural exchange
- 促进友谊     to promote friendship
- 加强合作     to enhance cooperation
- 有此殊荣     to have the honor of doing something
- 很高兴做某事     to have the pleasure in doing something
- 祝您/你们参观顺利     Wish you a pleasant visit.
- 祝您/你们访问圆满成功     Wish your visit a complete success.
- 祝您/你们万事如意     Wish you all the best.
- 期待再次来访     Look forward to your visit again.
- 希望再次相会     Hope to see each other again soon.
- 代我向……问好     Say hello to... for me/Remember me to...
- 保持联系     Keep in touch.
- 与……取得联系     to get into touch with.../to establish contact with...

### 译操练  *Interpreting Practice*

**1. 听译 ▶▶▶ Listening Interpreting**

    **A.** Listen to the sentences and interpret them into English.
        Sentences 1—10

    **B.** Listen to the paragraphs and interpret them into English.
        Paragraphs 1—2

## 2. 视译 ▶▶▶ Sight Interpreting

**A. Interpret the following sentences into English：**

（1）我衷心地希望你们一如既往，继续巩固和强化我们的友谊和合作。

（2）20世纪60年代第一届残奥会举办以来，在国际社会共同努力下，残奥会已经成为增进人民相互了解和友谊、促进人类文明发展的重要文化体育盛事。

（3）我感谢总统先生的邀请，怀着愉快的心情，对美国进行正式访问，我带来了伟大的中国人民对伟大的美国人民的诚挚问候和良好祝愿。

（4）回顾过去，展望未来，感受到的是自豪和鼓舞。

（5）各国之间的竞争，说到底，是人才的竞争，是民族创新能力的竞争。

（6）我高兴地得知，总统先生将于明年访问中国，我期待在北京与您再次见面。

（7）我的访问是良好诚意的象征，我们怀着这种良好的诚意，希望能在友谊的基础上建立和加强文化交流关系。

（8）这是我第三次来到香港。每次来，都对这座城市的发展活力和独特魅力有新的感受。

（9）接下来，我们将请中国国家交响乐团为大家准备一场中西结合、轻松美妙的音乐会。

（10）最后，祝大家工作顺利，阖家幸福，万事如意。谢谢大家！

**B. Interpret the following paragraphs into English：**

（1）我来到英国后，已经会见了英国朝野一些人士，听到最多的话就是"中英要加强相互了解"。据我了解，在今年1月英国议会的一次对华政策辩论中，议员们发出的最强烈声音也是"双方要努力了解对方"。那么了解从什么地方开始？我认为，要从我们各自的语言和文化开始。

（2）近年来，中非青年交往日益密切。越来越多的非洲青年渴望了解中国，走进中国，迄今已有两万多名非洲青年学生获得中国政府奖学金赴华学习，他们中很多人已成为非洲国家建设的栋梁。一批批中国青年也来到非洲，同当地民众朝夕相处，同甘共苦，参与非洲经济社会发展，成为中非友好的使者。

## 3. 情景练习 ▶▶▶ Situational Interpreting

**Interpret based on the information given. Add any information when necessary.**

> **Roles**
> 董先生：北京文化交流中心的代理主任
> Edward Williams：美国GE家具公司海外部经理
> 陈小姐：翻译

欢迎Williams先生和夫人来访北京。根据Williams先生和夫人在电子邮件中提到的要求，为他们预订了"唐寓"酒店的套房，该酒店从设计到装潢都体现了唐朝的建筑风格。安排他们参观家具厂、家具销售店，与三家家具公司进行业务洽谈，到闻名遐迩的中餐馆用餐。

Williams夫人对旗袍非常感兴趣，希望能定做两套带回美国。Williams先生则想买一些有民族特色的装饰品带回去送朋友。

# 第 1 单元 迎来送往 Meeting and Seeing Off

双方都希望这次合作成功。

## 译常识与技巧  *Interpreting Tips and Skills*

**口译的特点**（The Characteristics of Interpretation）

口译是一项很特殊的语言交际活动,有其自身的特殊性:

第一,口译是一种具有不可预测性的即席双语传言活动。口译人员需要在准备有限的情况下,即刻进入双语语码切换状态,进行现时现场的口译操作。在有些口译场合,如记者招待会和商务谈判,口译话题千变万化,往往难以预测。此外,交际各方都希望能连贯表达自己的思想,并能迅速传递给对方。但是由于在语言不同的交际双方之间介入了一个传言人,这在一定程度上影响了信息传达的连贯性和接受的快捷性。因而,交际双方都希望作为交际中介的译员不要过多地占用他们的交谈时间,尽可能做到捷达高效。这就要求译员具有高超的即席应变能力和流利的现时表达能力。

第二,口译是一个现场气氛压力极大的工作。口译场面有时非常严肃庄重,如国际会议和外交谈判。正式场合的严肃气氛会让经验不足的译员产生较大的心理压力,紧张情绪会影响译员的自信,怯场心态会使译员口误频生。瞬息万变的现场气氛会使译员反应迟钝,从而影响口译水平的正常发挥。这就要求译员有优良的心理素质。

第三,口译基本属个体性操作,译责重大。通常,译员在整个口译过程中基本上是孤立无援的。译员必须随时独立处理可能碰到的任何问题。有些问题属语言类,更多的属社会科学类,与译员的社会、文化、国情、时事等方面的基本知识有关。译员无法回避面临的任何一个问题,只有正视每一道难题,及时处理。在口译过程中,译员不可能查询工具书或有关参考资料,也不能频频打断发言人,要求对方重复自己所讲的内容,解释其中的难点。作为个体劳动者,译员要求对自己的口译负责。

第四,口译是一种综合运用视、听、说、写、读等知识和技能的语言操作活动。"视"是指译员具有观察捕捉说话人的脸部表情、手势体姿、情绪变化等非语言因素的能力。"听"是指译员能够耳听会意各种带地方口音以及不同语速的说话的能力。"说"指译员能用母语和外语进行流利而达意地表达的能力。"写"是指译员在口译过程中能进行快速笔记的能力。"读"是指译员在视译时能进行快速阅读和理解的能力。口译属一种立体式、交叉型的信息传播方式。

第五,在口译过程中,信息交流的内容包罗万象。职业译员的口译范围没有界限,内容可以上至天文,下至地理,无所不涉,无所不包。由于口译的服务对象是各界人士,他们来自各个阶层、各行各业,有不同的教育背景和文化背景,在交际过程中他们会有意或无意地将自己所熟悉的专业知识表达出来,这是译员无法回避的现实。当然,无人能精通百家,博晓万事。但是,口译内容的繁杂无限却是不争的事实。坐在翻译席上的译员,自然而然地被视为既是一名精通语言的专家,同时又是一名通晓百事的杂家。

第 2 单元 礼仪致辞

Unit 2 Ceremonial Speeches

# 第2单元 礼仪致辞 Ceremonial Speeches

# 第1部分 Section 1

 **Vocabulary Work**

| | | | |
|---|---|---|---|
| kickstart | 开启 | prospects | 前景 |
| boost | 促进 | transition | 转折,改变 |
| harness | 利用 | de-escalate | 降低 |
| resolve | 解决 | prosperous | 繁荣的 |

 **Text Interpreting**

Interpret the following speech into Chinese:

### Speech at a Forum

Honored guests, ladies and gentlemen,

　　Good morning! Let me begin by expressing my appreciation to you for inviting me to speak at this great forum.

　　Last night, when I was coming into town from Pudong Airport, I crossed the beautiful Huangpu River on the Lupu Bridge. This reminded me of China's talent in making bridges and made me think of three other important bridges.

　　Bridge number one: 40 years ago, China started to build a "bridge to the world" by opening its economy and by kickstarting reforms that have changed the lives and prospects of hundreds of millions of people—here and beyond China.

　　By transforming itself—through trade, hard work, and learning from others — China has also helped to transform the global economy. Progress in this country has played a significant role in boosting productivity, innovation and living standards in countries around the world.

　　Bridge number two: China is building a "bridge to prosperity" by rebalancing its economy towards consumption-led growth, rather than export- and investment-led growth.

　　Building that bridge is well underway. In the first three quarters of this year, consumption contributed 78 percent to China's GDP growth, up from 50 percent only 5 years ago.

　　This transition—which is symbolized by the China International Import Expo—

is good for China, especially in terms of rising standards of living for the Chinese people, and good for the world, including all those who see China as a vital and vibrant market for their goods and services.

Bridge number three: China is building a "bridge to the future" by harnessing the power of international cooperation, especially on trade.

On behalf of the IMF, I have called on all countries to de-escalate and resolve the current trade disputes and to fix the global trade system, not destroy it. To achieve these goals, we need more international cooperation, not less.

The French philosopher Montesquieu once said that "wherever there is good citizenship, there is trade, and wherever there is trade, there is good citizenship." In other words, trade has the capacity to boost innovation, foster not only prosperity but also peace within countries and among nations.

So, in Shanghai, the city of 12 bridges, let's start this cooperation towards more peace and more prosperous future.

Thank you.

## Notes on the Text

1. … by kickstarting reforms that have changed the lives and prospects of hundreds of millions of people…:原文中的 kickstart 原意为"脚踏启动",在此句中可以译为"启动,开创"。

2. … by rebalancing its economy towards consumption-led growth, rather than export- and investment-led growth…:原文中三处单词 consumption-led, export- and investment-led 均为名词加过去分词 led 构成的复合形容词,可根据上下文分部译为"消费带动"和"出口和投资驱动的"。

3. …especially in terms of rising standards of living for the Chinese people…:原文中 in terms of 字面意思是"依据;按照;在……方面",在此处根据上下文可灵活处理,不一定译出来。

4. … by harnessing the power of international cooperation…:原文中 harness 原意为"将(两只动物)拴在一起;套;驾驭",在此句中根据上下文可译为"利用"。

5. On behalf of the IMF, I have called on all countries to de-escalate and resolve the current trade disputes and to fix the global trade system, not destroy it. 原文中 on behalf of 是常用的礼仪性会议口译词汇,意思是"代表",如:On behalf of all my colleagues, I'd like to extend my greetings to you. 另外,原文中的 de-escalate 是 escalate 的反义派生词,可译为"降温,缓和"。

6. Montesquieu:夏尔·德·塞孔达,孟德斯鸠男爵(1689年1月18日—1755年2月10日),法国启蒙运动时期思想家、律师,西方国家学说以及法学理论的奠基人,与伏尔泰、卢梭合称"法兰西启蒙运动三剑侠"。孟德斯鸠是一位百科全书式的学者。在学术上取得了巨大成就,得到了很高的荣誉。

## Developing Vocabulary and Expressions

❖ Respected Mr. Prime Minister 尊敬的首相
❖ Your Highness Prince… 尊敬的……王子/亲王殿下

# 第 2 单元 礼仪致辞 Ceremonial Speeches

- Your Excellency Respected and Dear... 敬爱的……阁下
- Your Excellency Respected... 尊敬的……阁下
- Your/His/Her Excellency 阁下
- Your/His/Her Imperial Majesty 皇帝陛下
- Your/His/Her Majesty 陛下
- Your/His/Her Royal Highness 殿下
- luncheon 午餐会;宴客午餐
- cocktail party 鸡尾酒会
- buffet supper 自助晚餐
- formal dinner 正式宴会
- barbecue 烧烤性野宴
- I now propose a toast, to the health of the President and Mrs.... Cheers! 现在，我提议让我们为……总统和夫人的身体健康干杯！
- I wish to invite you to join me in a toast to the health of all our distinguished guests. Cheers! 让我们共同举杯，为所有贵宾的身体健康干杯！
- Finally, please allow me to propose a toast. To the good working relationship between us and to the success of the PB Project, *Gan Bei*! 最后，请允许我提议，为我们的友好合作关系，为 PB 项目的成功，干杯！
- We'll do a virtual toast, to the peace and prosperity of the world. Cheers! 让我们象征性地干杯，祝愿全世界和平、繁荣，干杯！
- It is my privilege and great pleasure to host this banquet in honor of... and other distinguished guests. 我为能在此设宴招待……以及其他贵宾而深感荣幸和愉快。
- In closing, I would like you to join me in a toast! 在我结束讲话之际，我请各位与我一起举杯！
- It gives us a feeling of special joy to have the opportunity of entertaining our distinguished guests from China. 我们特别高兴能有机会招待我们的中国贵宾。
- On the occasion of this reception, I wish Mr. Mayor and all our Chinese friends present here tonight good health. 请允许我借此机会，祝愿市长先生，祝愿出席今晚招待会的所有中国朋友，身体健康！
- This is a very happy and memorable occasion for me personally and the members of the Board to host you here in New York. 对我本人以及董事会的全体成员来说，能在纽约接待您是非常愉快和令人难忘的。
- It is a great pleasure for me to preside at this dinner in honor of Chairman Wang. 我能为在此为王董事长主持晚宴而深感愉快。
- Glasses have been distributed to everyone. When all are ready, we shall call for a toast. 酒杯都已分送到每一位的手上，准备就绪之后，我们将一起干杯。
- Gentlemen, I ask you to drink a toast to Mr. A. 先生们，我请你们为 A 先生干一杯。
- Let us drink to the health of Mr. A. 让我们为 A 先生的健康干一杯。
- Gentlemen, I would like to propose a toast of the evening. 先生们，我想提议大家为今晚干一杯。
- I drink to the health of all the guests present. 我为全体来宾们的健康干杯。
- May I ask you to join me in a toast to the friendship and cooperation between our two cities. 请允许我请各位与我一起举杯，为我们两市的友谊与合作干杯！
- I have the honor to express this warm welcome on behalf of the staff of the company to the delegation from P&L Corporation. 我很荣幸地代表我们公司的全体员工向来自 P&L 公司的代表团表示热烈的欢迎。

❖ Allow me to express my warm welcome and gracious greetings to our distinguished guests coming from afar. 请允许我向远道而来的贵宾表示热烈的欢迎和亲切的问候。

## 口译操练 *Interpreting Practice*

### 1. 听译 ▶▶ Listening Interpreting

A. Listen to the sentences and interpret them into Chinese.
   Sentences 1—10

B. Listen to the paragraphs and interpret them into Chinese.
   Paragraphs 1—2

### 2. 视译 ▶▶ Sight Interpreting

A. Interpret the following sentences into Chinese：
   （1）All the guests here tonight prove the vitality of the relations of our two companies. The range of those relations is impressive.
   （2）I take great pleasure to welcome you and thank you for attending tonight's dinner in honor of all those who have taken part in the PB Project.
   （3）It is in the spirit of friendly cooperation, mutual promotion and common prosperity that I extend to you the warmest welcome and convey to you the most gracious greetings from all the employees of our Petrol-Chemical Group Corporation.
   （4）I am certain that this exhibition will strengthen our economic cooperation and contribute directly to our further trade expansion.
   （5）The municipal government's commitment to building an information technology infrastructure will enable the city to compete on an equal footing with other major cities of the world.
   （6）Our goal is to help improve access to information technology and to incorporate the Internet into the educational process.
   （7）Through these efforts, young people will not only improve their education by using the Internet, they will also learn skills that are critically needed to help China achieve its information technology and E-commerce.
   （8）As in the past, our company remains a leader in infrastructure projects so vital to growing economics.
   （9）For 100 years, BC Company has led the industry and maintained a fine reputation built on trust, quality, and reliability.
   （10）Today, all of our company's major businesses are active in China and many are actively involved in joint ventures with Chinese partners.

B. Interpret the following paragraphs into Chinese：
   （1）On behalf of all your American guests, I wish to thank you for the incomparable hospitality. I particularly want to pay tribute, not only to

those who prepared the magnificent dinner, but also to those who have provided the splendid music. Never have I heard American music played better in a foreign land.

(2) I wish to take this opportunity to thank you on behalf of all my colleagues for your warm reception and incomparable hospitality. The past five days in Beijing have been truly pleasant and enjoyable, and most memorable. Here, I particularly want to pay tribute to our Chinese partners whose effort has made possible the successful conclusion of the cooperative agreements. May I ask all of you present here to join me in raising your glasses, to the lasting friendship and cooperation between our two companies.

## 3. 情景练习 ▶▶ Situational Interpreting

**Interpret the following speech into Chinese:**

> **Roles**
> Seamus Heaney: the Nobel Prize winner
> Miss Chen: an interpreter

Your Majesties, Your Royal Highnesses, Ladies and Gentlemen,

Today's ceremony and tonight's banquet have been mighty and memorable events. Nobody who has shared in them will ever forget them, but for the laureates these celebrations have had a unique importance. Each of us has participated in a ritual, a rite of passage, a public drama which has been commensurate with the inner experience of winning a Nobel Prize. The slightly incredible condition we have lived in since the news of the prizes was announced a couple of weeks ago has now been rendered credible. The mysterious powers represented by the words Nobel Foundation and Swedish Academy have manifested themselves in friendly human form. For me, it has been a great joy and a great reassurance to come to Stockholm and to meet at every turn people of such grace, such intelligence and such good will. It is another way of saying that the whole week has not only been ceremonially impressive: it has also felt emotionally true, and it is the sense of something personally trustworthy at the center of the great event that I finally value most, and cherish and give you thanks for. It has helped more than anything else to bring home to me the reality of the great honour I have received. Oscar Wilde once said that the only way to survive temptation was to yield to it. So here and now, I happily and gratefully yield to the temptation to believe that I am indeed the winner of a Nobel Prize.

Thank you very much.

\* Seamus Heaney(谢默斯·希尼,1939—    )—winner of the Nobel Prize for Literature in 1995. He has been described as "the most important Irish poet since Yeats."

# 第 2 部分 Section 2

 **Vocabulary Work**

| 全面的 | all-round | 姐妹城市 | sister-city |
| 暂时地 | temporarily | 赞颂 | pay tribute to |
| 搁置 | shelve | 奉献 | dedication |
| 人力资源 | human resources | 各界人士 | people from all walks of life |

 **Text Interpreting**

**Interpret the following speech into English:**

### 答谢致辞

市长先生，女士们，先生们：

  我谨代表我们一行的全体成员，对你们热情接待以及无与伦比的款待表示感谢。在纽约度过的这六天，的确令人愉快，令人难以忘怀。我们强烈地感受到了纽约这座城市的活力，我们感受到了纽约市民的高度礼貌和诚挚的友情。我很高兴地看到我们这两座城市终于踏上了一条通往建立真诚友好与合作的道路。

  我们双方一致同意建立面向 21 世纪的姐妹城市友好关系。为了实现这个目标，我们已经在以下三个原则上取得共识：

  第一，我们要充分运用已经确立的全面对话合作机制，拓展双方在各个领域、各个层次、各个渠道的交流与合作；加强双方领导人和各界人士之间的交往，增进信任，扩大共识，加强友谊。

  第二，我们要本着优势互补、互利互惠的原则，把双方经贸、科技合作摆到重要地位；加强在资源、技术、市场、金融、信息、人力资源开发以及投资等领域的合作，以利于相互促进，共同发展。

  第三，通过平等友好协商，处理彼此间存在的一些分歧和争议，寻求问题的逐步解决。有些分歧一时解决不了，可以暂时搁置，求同存异，而不要影响双方互信伙伴关系的建立和发展。

  我特别要赞颂我们的美国合作伙伴，没有他们的努力我们是无法成功地达成合作协议的。我在此敬请各位与我一起举杯，为我们两座城市永久的友谊与合作，为我们美国同仁的身体健康，干杯！

### 圣诞晚会致谢

董事长先生，女士们，先生们：

  各位圣诞快乐！

我谨代表我们一行的全体成员,感谢董事长先生盛情邀请我们参加如此欢快的圣诞晚会。

圣诞节是一年中的良辰佳时。它让我们感受到人间的温暖、关怀、团聚、融洽和奉献。晚会组织得完美无缺,令人尽兴尽致。这里的美酒佳肴、美味的烤火鸡和美妙的音乐真是令人难忘。更为重要的是,我喜欢同你们聚会,同你们交谈,增进了解,共度好时光。

今年对我们所有人来说都是一个好年度。我们合资企业的销售额有显著的增长。希望我们能保持这种务实的合作关系,使明年的业绩更加辉煌。

让我们在这年终岁末之际,共同举杯,祝贺这喜庆佳节。

我再一次祝各位圣诞快乐!

 **Notes on the Text**

1. 我们要充分运用已经确立的全面对话合作机制,拓展双方在各个领域、各个层次、各个渠道的交流与合作:在汉语里,全句是用逗号隔开的两个小句,看似两个平行结构,实际上,后一小句表达目的。在译成英语时,可用英语中习惯的不定式结构表示,译为:. . . make the best use of the existing mechanism of all-round dialogue and cooperation to broaden our exchanges and cooperation . . . 后一句也做同样处理。

2. 有些分歧一时解决不了,可以暂时搁置,求同存异,而不要影响双方互信伙伴关系的建立和发展:这一句与注释1提到的情况相同。汉语重"神似",结构看似松散。在翻译时,译者一定要理清小句间的关系,加上适当的词、词组或连词将整个句子有序地连接起来。该句可用定语结构 that cannot be solved . . . ,介词短语 on the basis of . . . 和目的状语连词 so that . . .

3. 我在此敬请各位与我一起举杯:敬酒语的译法可用 May I . . . ! 还可译为:Permit me/ Allow me . . .

4. 它让我们感受到人间的温暖、关怀、团聚 ……:顺延前一句的译文 Christmas is a wonderful time . . . It is a time of . . .

5. 晚会……令人尽兴尽致:汉语习惯用类似"令人……"的句式,译文应视情景而定。此句可译为 I enjoy every minute of it. "令人难忘"可用形容词 memorable 或 can never be forgotten 等。

……使明年的业绩更加辉煌:用 fruitful 表达"硕果累累""业绩辉煌"很生动,也很贴切。

 **Developing Vocabulary and Expressions**

❖ 承蒙/应……的盛情邀请 at the gracious invitation of . . .
❖ 荣幸地答谢你们给予我们的热情招待 have the honor of reciprocating your warm reception
❖ 愉快地答谢您热情洋溢的欢迎词 have the pleasure in replying to your gracious speech of welcome
❖ 随同贸易代表团来访的商界朋友们 friends from the business community accompanying the trade delegation
❖ 增进我们彼此之间的理解和友谊 increase/strengthen/promote/expand our

- mutual understanding and friendship
- 促进我们之间的友好合作关系 promote /facilitate/enhance/strengthen/advance our friendly relations of cooperation
- 符合我们双方的共同利益 accord with/agree with/ conform to/meet the common interests of our two parties
- I'd like to take a moment to offer my sincere thanks to... 我想占用各位一点时间,向……表示我诚挚的感激。
- Allow me a moment to express my sincere thanks to... 我想占用各位一点时间,向……表示我诚挚的感激。
- I'd like to take this time to say thank you to... 我想占用各位一点时间,向……表示我诚挚的感激。
- Permit me first to thank our hosts for your extraordinary arrangements and hospitality. My wife and I, as well as our entire party, are deeply grateful. 首先,请允许我对主人十分出色的安排和款待表示感谢。我和夫人以及全体随行人员都深为感动。

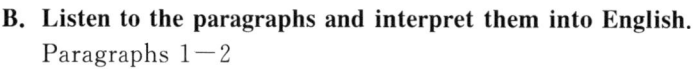

### 1. 听译 ▶▶▶ Listening Interpreting

A. Listen to the sentences and interpret them into English.
   Sentences 1—10

B. Listen to the paragraphs and interpret them into English.
   Paragraphs 1—2

### 2. 视译 ▶▶▶ Sight Interpreting

A. Interpret the following sentences into English:
   (1) 我谨代表总经理以及公司的全体同仁,感谢各位从百忙之中抽出时间光临我们的新年晚会。
   (2) 今晚我们请到了从美国纽约远道而来的贵宾与我们共度中国的传统节日中秋佳节,我为此深感自豪与荣幸。
   (3) 回顾过去,展望未来,我认为一种新型伙伴关系必须建筑在相互尊重和平等互利的基础上。
   (4) 让我们求同存异,增进理解和信任,加强交流与合作。
   (5) 我们已经一致同意建立董事会来监管运作,并以平等的伙伴关系分享权利,承担义务。
   (6) 我们的友好合作关系将会十分广泛,会深入到我们城市生活的方方面面:商业、文化、教育,以及科学交流。
   (7) 我们过去建立的友好合作关系是建立在相互尊重和平等互利的基础上的。
   (8) 通过对话和相互信任以消除分歧、增强我们的合作关系,这是我们的共同愿望。
   (9) 我们在贵市度过了非常愉快的时光,很高兴我们的访问能在如此融洽的气氛中结束。
   (10) 贵市的现代化建设给我们留下了深刻的印象。这一雄心勃勃的伟业,使我们的合作前景一片光明。

## 第 2 单元 礼仪致辞 Ceremonial Speeches

B. **Interpret the following paragraphs into English：**
（1）在这个明月当空、举国同庆的夜晚,我谨代表公司的全体成员,感谢各位光临我们的中秋晚会。我希望各位中外同事共度一个轻松、欢快的夜晚。我愿外国来宾能尽情品尝中国的传统佳肴和美酒。我希望这次晚会能使我们有机会彼此沟通、增进友谊。最后我提议为我们的身体健康、事业有成干杯。

（2）今天我们聚会在一起,在平等互利的基础上,就广阔领域里建立合作伙伴关系交换我们彼此的看法。这是一次具有历史意义的开拓性会议,它反映了我们希望进行交流与合作、增进相互理解和信任的共同愿望。我深信这次会议将对我们的双边关系和多边关系产生积极的影响。我愿借此机会,向会议的东道主表示衷心的感谢。最后,让我们为会议的成功,干杯!

### 3. 情景练习 ▶▶▶ Situational Interpreting

Interpret based on the information given. Add any information when necessary.

> Roles：
> Mr. Stanley: an American
> Miss Chen: an interpreter

- 美国 GE 公司代表团来上海参观,受到热情的款待；
- 共计三天；
- 参观了许多工厂,会见了很多老朋友；
- 看到了许多新的成就,印象深刻；
- 希望进行真诚的、富有成效的合作；
- 为高科技领域的合作成功,干杯。

## 译常识与技巧  Interpreting Tips and Skills

**口译的标准（The Criteria of Interpretation）**

衡量口译优劣有两条基本标准:一是准确,二是流利。

首先,口译必须"准确"。准确是口译的灵魂,是口译的生命线。准确要求译员将原语一方的信息完整无误地传达给目的语一方。具体说来,口译的准确性涉及口译时的主题准确、精神准确、论点准确、风格准确、词语准确、表达准确、语速准确以及口吻准确等方面。归根结底,准确的译语应该同时保持原语意义和风格。准确的口译不仅是双语成功交际的保障,而且也是译员职业道德和专业水平的集中表现。准确的口译不仅是对交际活动的尊重和负责,而且也体现了译员对交际双方的尊重和负责。必须指出,我们所讲的准确性并非是那种机械刻板的"模压式"口译或"盖章式"口译。例如,对原语者明显的口吃,不可妄加模仿。如法炮制说话人的语疾不是忠实翻译,而是人身侮辱。对交际一方过快或过慢的语速、明显的口误或浓重的口音,译员也不可模压炮制,鹦鹉学舌般地如数传递给另一方。

谈到翻译的"准确性",我们不得不考虑由于文化差异或特定场合引起的翻译困难,如何灵活机动地处理这些问题。看下面的例子:

两位中国女士在谈论衣服:

A:你的英语讲得真好。
B:哪里！哪里！

25

B的回答是中国人对于别人的赞扬显示谦虚的典型表达方式。翻译时则应该译成"Thank you",而不是"Where? Where?"

　　再如,在教室里,老师准备放幻灯片了,他对一学生喊道:Lights! Please! 则可译为"请关灯!"因此,翻译时还需考虑文化的得体性,特定场合所需的得体性。我们把这种翻译原则叫作"**语用对等**"原则。

　　"流利"是译员必须遵循的另一大标准。译员在确保"准确"口译的前提下,应该迅速流畅地将一方的信息传译给另一方。口译的现场性、现时性、即席性、交互性等因素要求口译过程宜短不宜长,节奏宜紧不宜松。口译是交际工具。工具首先得有效用,否则就不成其为工具,但有效用而无效率(或低效率)的工具绝不是好工具。

　　那么,口译的流利程度如何来衡量呢？口译的流利程度包括译员对原语信息的感知速度和解析速度,以及用目的语进行编码和表达的速度。通常,口译时译员对母语信息的感知速度和解析速度快于对外语的感知速度和解析速度,同时,用母语编码和表达的速度也快于用外语编码和表达的速度。在口译场合,译员对信息的感知和解析受到"现实""限刻"的制约,无法"自由自在"地调解速度,所以必须同步加工。而在编码和表达阶段,由于译员可以自我控制速度,所以目标语为母语的口译所需要的时间相对少于目标语为外语的口译所需要的时间。当然,口译的类型、内容、场合、对象、风格等因素都会对口译的速度产生影响,用同一把尺子来衡量不同类别的口译是不合理的。一般说来,我们可以依据译员所用的口译时间是否同发言者的讲话时间大体相等来衡量口译是否流利。以两倍于原语发言者的讲话时间进行口译者显然不能被视为流利。

会展活动

# Unit 3 Exhibitions

# 第1部分 Section 1

## Vocabulary Work

| | | | |
|---|---|---|---|
| electric toy | 电动玩具 | electronic toy | 电子玩具 |
| intellectual toy | 智力开发玩具 | plush toy | 长毛绒玩具 |
| reverse | (车辆)倒车 | altitude | 高度 |
| maneuver | (技巧)动作 | trick flying | 特技飞行 |
| plush stuffed toy | 长毛绒填充玩具 | fabric | 织物,布料 |
| fillings | 填充物 | commission | 佣金 |

## Text Interpreting

**Interpret the following speech into Chinese:**

### Introducing Goods

Ladies and Gentlemen,

Welcome to E & P Toys exhibition hall. We specialize in toys for children. Our company is one of the leaders in the toy industry and we provide a unique collection of machine toys, electric toys, electronic toys, and intellectual toys for markets both at home and abroad. And of course there's an extensive choice of plush toys of all sorts, which are the cutest you've ever seen.

Well, the toys on the right are machine toys, electric toys, electronic toys, and intellectual toys, suitable for children from the age of five and upwards. They are cute, aren't they? What I'd like to tell you is we have just brought out some new models. It's a choice variety of toys which you can get nowhere other than from us. After arduous research work, we have developed a new processing technique, which makes the machine toys, electric toys and electronic toys safer to play and which has enabled them to reduce the prices at no sacrifice of quality. Now, I would like to recommend specially a new model of racing cars to you. You press this button and it starts to go. You see it's now turning around the corner. And it can reverse and change its routes and directions. It is very easy to operate. The only thing you have to do is to press the green buttons here. And I have something more interesting to show you, a toy plane. It is a remote control plane. We have two buttons to control the movement and altitude. It also has two selectable speed controls. The most exciting thing about it is its skillful maneuver. When it flies to a certain height, it can do trick flying. It's a shame that I can't show you how it works here in this showroom. All boys love it, and of course many girls love it, too.

And here on the left are plush stuffed toys. Teddy bears, Mickey Mouse, Snoopy, giraffes, deer, sheep, kangaroos, tigers, dinosaurs, pandas, and what you have. Don't you think they are lovely? Our products are very popular in many parts of the world, because we are very particular about the fabric and the fillings. All these are made of beautiful fabric and filled with best plush. Please have a closer look at them and you know I'm telling the truth. What's more, our toys are easy to care. Most of them are machine washable and tumble driable. What's the age range for our toys? A good question. We have two groups, and the recommended age for one group is 24 months to 3 years and the other belongs to 5 to 7 age range. Of course, they are all suitable for adults who like toys.

And finally, we have been on good terms with many of you. And of course some of you are new here but that makes no difference. So, to you, we will not only make concessions in price, but also offer good commissions. This is our overall philosophy in doing business. We can allow you a ten per cent commission for an order exceeding $10,000 and 15 per cent for an order over $30,000. I'm sure the commission we offer is really very favorable.

And here are our brochures and quotations, and we can have a closer look at them. If you have any questions, just come to me.

Thank you.

## 课文注释  Notes on the Text

1. We specialize in toys for children:我们专营儿童玩具。specialize (in) 是"专门生产/经营"或"专攻(某一学科)"的意思。例如,The company specializes in (producing) personal computers.(这家公司专门生产个人电脑。);My brother specializes in science.(我哥哥专攻理科。);He decided to specialize in children diseases.(他决定专攻儿童疾病。)当然,"这家公司专门生产个人电脑"也可以翻译为 The company is a professional personal computer manufacturer.

2. ... and we provide a unique collection of machine toys, electric toys, electronic toys, and intellectual toys for markets both at home and abroad:我们的产品包括一系列独特的机械玩具、电动玩具、电子玩具、智力开发玩具。我们的产品畅销国内,也远销国外。

我们看到,这里说"我们的产品包括……"要比直译"我们提供……"更为地道。口译中要特别注意这一点,不然,翻译出的句子会很"欧化",有时会影响理解。

另外,英语句子有时候会比较长,书面语和在比较正式的场合使用的口语体特别如此;但是,汉语的特点是句子比较短小。因此,在翻译过程中,要学会把一个比较长的英文句子处理成两个或者多个汉语句子。例如,把这一句翻译为"我们为国内外市场提供一系列独特的机械玩具、电动玩具、电子玩具、智力开发玩具",就不是很好,不如翻译为两句更符合汉语讲话习惯的句子:"我们的产品包括一系列独特的机械玩具、电动玩具、电子玩具、智力开发玩具。我们的产品畅销国内,也远销国外。"

3. ... suitable for children from the age of five and upwards:适合五岁以上的小孩。upwards 为美国英语用词,英国人用 upward。

4. It is very easy to operate. The only thing you have to do is to press the green buttons here:操作起来也非常方便,只要按这几个绿色按钮就行了。
　　我们把两句英文合译为一句汉语,即简洁又地道。

5. When it flies to a certain height, it can do trick flying:飞行到一定的高度,它就可以做特技动作。
　　汉语的习惯是省略句子和句子之间的连接手段(transitions);因此,在英译汉的过程中,我们要学会省略英文的连接手段,但在汉译英时,我们则要不断去添加一些连接手段,以便保持意思的连贯性。

6. It's a shame that I can't show you how it works here in the showroom:很可惜我不能在展室里给你们演示。其中,shame 一词的意思是"可惜"或"遗憾",而不是"羞愧";这个含义是口语用法,常常用在句型 it's a shame that ... 中。例如,It's a shame that you have to leave so early.(很遗憾,你这么快就要走了。)

7. ... because we are very particular about the fabric and the fillings:因为我们很注重布料和填充物的质量。particular（about）的意思是"讲究的""挑剔的""吹毛求疵的"。例如,She's very particular about her food and clothes.（她很讲究吃穿。）

8. Most of them are machine washable and tumble driable:绝大部分都可以机洗、烘干。其中 machine washable 的意思是"可以用洗衣机洗的";类似的说法还有 machine-readable(可机读的)。

9. What's the age range for our toys? 你问玩具适用的年龄范围? 其中 age range 意思是"年龄范围"或"年龄段",例如,pre-school age range(学龄前年龄段)和 11 to 15 age range(11 至 15 岁)。类似的说法还有 price range(价格段)。

# 词语扩展  *Developing Vocabulary and Expressions*

- commodity fair　　　　　　　　　　　　商品交易会
- organizing committee　　　　　　　　　组委会
- organizer　　　　　　　　　　　　　　主办商
- exhibitor　　　　　　　　　　　　　　参展商
- registration　　　　　　　　　　　　　注册
- buying group　　　　　　　　　　　　采购团
- booth(number)　　　　　　　　　　　展位(号)
- display counter/shelf　　　　　　　　展示柜/架
- brochure　　　　　　　　　　　　　　(产品)宣传手册
- catalogue　　　　　　　　　　　　　产品目录
- exhibition cost　　　　　　　　　　　参展费用
- exhibit　　　　　　　　　　　　　　展览品
- finished product　　　　　　　　　　成品
- semi-finished product　　　　　　　　半成品
- brand-consciousness　　　　　　　　品牌意识
- quoted company　　　　　　　　　　上市公司
- reference price　　　　　　　　　　参考价格
- ruling price　　　　　　　　　　　　现行价格
- retail price　　　　　　　　　　　　零售价

- office supplies　　　　　　　　　　　　办公用品
- aquatic product　　　　　　　　　　　　水产品
- livestock product　　　　　　　　　　　畜牧产品
- plastic ware　　　　　　　　　　　　　塑料制品
- glassware　　　　　　　　　　　　　　玻璃器皿
- foodstuff exhibition hall　　　　　　　　食品展厅
- jewelry exhibition hall　　　　　　　　　珠宝展厅
- high-tech product　　　　　　　　　　　高科技产品
- feminine hygiene　　　　　　　　　　　女性卫生用品
- exhibition hall of electronics　　　　　　电子产品展厅
- exhibition hall of consumer goods　　　　日用品展厅
- textile and garment exhibition hall　　　　纺织品与服装展厅
- exhibition hall of agricultural products　　农产品展厅
- exhibition hall of handcrafts　　　　　　工艺品展厅
- exhibition hall of household electronic appliances　　家用电器展厅

## 口译操练 Interpreting Practice

### 1. 听译　Listening Interpreting

A. Listen to the sentences and interpret them into Chinese.
Sentences 1—10

B. Listen to the paragraphs and interpret them into Chinese.
Paragraphs 1—2

### 2. 视译　Sight Interpreting

**A. Interpret the following sentences into Chinese:**

(1) Our computers should have been sold for better prices for their top quality.

(2) I'd like to specially recommend a newly developed model of digital camera to you.

(3) You have looked around our showroom. Is there anything in particular you are interested in?

(4) We are a well-established firm in the industry, and we enjoy good relations with wholesalers, chain stores and distributors in China.

(5) Our designers attach great importance to both comfort and beauty, and they always maintain a perfect balance between the two.

(6) Our products are competitive in quality and enjoy a very good reputation in both domestic and international markets.

(7) The design is exaggerated. That's why it is very popular among youngsters.

(8) Here are our brochures and relevant publicity materials which may help you make a good decision.

(9) This model is available in gray and pink.

(10) Here are the most favorite products on display. All of them are local or national prize products.

**B. Interpret the following paragraphs into Chinese：**

（1）These are newly developed models. They've been on the market only for a few months, but they are already very popular among teenagers, who love to seek for novel things and new experience. I'm very glad that some parents have become our consumers simply because their sons and daughters are crazy about these models. You know they are both decorative and practical. Yes, they are more expensive than similar products, but only because of its top quality and our after-sales service.

（2）Well, I'm much impressed by your showroom. Most of the models are new to our customers in America, but I believe some have potential markets there. I've already seen some items we'd like to order, and I know you will give us a favorable discount for the first possible order, which of course cannot be a large one. I'll talk to my office about the size of the order and we have to study it a bit further. I'll probably let you know by the next Monday.

## 3. 情景练习 ▶▶▶ Situational Interpreting

**Interpret the following conversation alternatively into English and Chinese. Add any information when necessary.**

Roles
Mr. Zhou：a Chinese
Mr. Anderson：an American businessman
Miss Chen：an interpreter

Mr. Anderson： Good morning. I'm in the line of textile business. I wonder if you have the time to show me around your showroom?
Mr. Zhou： 我很乐意。我们经营多种纺织品。
Mr. Anderson： What a spacious showroom!
Mr. Zhou： 我们的展室是不小,共分四个部分:纺织品、男女服饰、鞋帽和纺织机械。
Mr. Anderson： Oh, there are so many new products that I have never seen in other showrooms. Let me have a good look.
Mr. Zhou： 我们最近推出了不少新产品。质量上乘,价格也不是很高。也许你有兴趣看看衣架上的这些人造丝织品。我们上个月才推出的新品,别的地方肯定见不到。
Mr. Anderson： They're quite attractive. And they feel great! I guess Americans will love them. Do you have catalogues or something that will tell us all about them?
Mr. Zhou： 有的。这些产品目录中有很完整的介绍。
Mr. Anderson： Thank you. I'm honored to have the opportunity of seeing

|  | your samples in the showroom. Please give us time to study them a bit further. I'll probably be able to let you know our decision in a few days. |
|---|---|
| Mr. Zhou: | 你对我们的产品有兴趣,我很高兴。那我就等您的回音。 |

# 第3单元 会展活动 Exhibitions

# 第2部分 Section 2

 **Vocabulary Work**

| 两门汽车 | two-door car | 传动系统 | transmission |
| 行李箱/后备箱 | trunk | 净空高度 | headroom |
| 立体音响系统 | stereo system | 活动式座椅 | reclining seat |
| 气囊 | air bag | 着色的 | tinted |
| 钢边轮胎 | steel-belted tire | 车垫 | floor mat |
| 天窗 | sunroof | 上班族 | office worker |
| 经济实用型款式 | economy model | 方向盘 | steering wheel |

 **Text Interpreting**

Interpret the following conversation alternatively into English and Chinese:

**汽车展厅**

A：早上好！我很乐意为您效劳。

B：Good morning. This is a great showroom. I'm looking for some two-door cars—something nice, but not too expensive. Would you recommend some to me?

A：当然可以。这些是我们新推出的或者改进型的款式。大部分都是经济实用型的。操作系统有自动型和手动型两种。

B：What's the price difference?

A：嗯，自动操作的当然要贵一些。你必须考虑维修费用。自动操作的汽车维修费用当然要比手动的高一点。

B：I see. Is that one over there one of your latest models? It looks great! Does it have a manual transmission?

A：是的。它后备箱空间很大，头顶空间也不小，还有一个带AM/FA立体收音机的DVD播放器。这个款式刚刚上市约半年时间，就很受东南亚客户的青睐。这种车在那里的大城市很受欢迎，因为你知道那里不少人每天必须在家和工作单位之间奔波。有了这样一部车，就意味着早上不必很早就起床，而且，当然晚上也可以早点上床睡觉了。

B：It sounds nice. What else does it have?

35

A: 其他的特点包括:空调、旅程动力车窗、倾斜方向盘、自动车门锁和防死锁刹车功能。当然,还有安全气囊。

B: An air bag is especially useful. It protects the driver and passengers in an accident.

A: 确实如此。这款车还有着色玻璃、钢边轮胎、车垫和天窗。此外,它的汽油里程率为一加仑可行驶20英里,相当不错。

B: Excellent! I'm sure this car will be a favorite in Beijing, especially with young office workers, who don't have money to burn. Something economic you know. A Benz or Cadillac is for businessmen who are richer.

A: 为像你这样的人?我可没有开奔驰,也没有开卡迪拉克。

B: I'll certainly own a Benz if you grant me a favorable discount, say 50%.

A: 你开玩笑!那样的话,我会被解雇的。这种手动型的每部5000美元,自动的6000。说实话,我最多能给你9折。超过9折就超出了我的谈判限度。不要忘了这些都是新产品,我们在设计和生产上投入了大量的研究工作。上面的指示是我不能让步,但我们还是可以想办法达成共识。

B: I see. You mean you have to talk to your office. Your price is too dear, compared with those of others. My suggestion is 20%, which will make it easier for us to promote your cars in our area. What about the color? Are they available in blue, white, and yellow?

A: 有好几种颜色:红色、蓝色、白色、灰色和粉红色,但是目前还没有黄色。你知道,这种款式针对的是年轻人,但现在年轻人不喜欢黄色。黄的汽车在美国和欧洲市场销路最近不是很好。

B: Many people in Beijing do love yellow cars. There are differences between people with different cultural backgrounds. Anyway, I was greatly impressed by your showroom, and we'll study your catalogues further and let you know our decision as early as possible.

A: 谢谢!我期待你们的回音。

## 课文注释  Notes on the Text

1. 这些是我们新推出的或者改进型的款式:Here are our new or modified models. "改进型的"英文常用 modified。例如,modified precision radar(改进型精密雷达)。

2. 自动操作的汽车维修费用当然要比手动的高一点:Cars with automatic transmission are generally more expensive to service. 介词 with 可表示某种事物或者人有某种特征,例如 a room with a veranda(有阳台的房间),a book with a green cover(绿色封面的书)和 a table with three legs(三条腿的桌子)。

3. 这个款式刚刚上市约半年时间,就很受东南亚客户的青睐:It has been on the market only for about six months, but it has become a great favorite with customers in Southeast Asian countries. "上市"的英文是 go/appear/be on the market,例如 Watermelons have appeared on the market.(西瓜上市了。)

4. ……不少人每天必须在家和工作单位之间奔波:... many people have to commute from home to work every day. 英文词 commute 指的是 regularly travel a long distance to get to work,也就是"在家和工作单位之间奔波"。

5. What else does it have? 这款车还有什么特点?按照字面意思,这句话是"这款车上还有什么?"为了地道起见,我们可将之意译为"这款车还有什么特点?"

6. ...who don't have money to burn. 没有太多的钱可以挥霍。have money to burn 是口语说法,意思是"钱多得花不完"。

## 词语扩展  Developing Vocabulary and Expressions

| | |
|---|---|
| ❖ 产品推广 | product promotion |
| ❖ 畅销国内外 | sell well both at home and abroad |
| ❖ 订货量大 | large/heavy order |
| ❖ 缺货 | be out of stock |
| ❖ 有现货供应 | be available from stock |
| ❖ 有销路 | have a ready market |
| ❖ 热销产品 | hot-selling product |
| ❖ 库存有限 | have limited stock |
| ❖ 符合国际标准 | live up to international standards |
| ❖ 卫生标准 | sanitary standard |
| ❖ 独家代理 | sole agent |
| ❖ 上市公司 | quoted company |
| ❖ 公司形象 | corporation image |
| ❖ 商会 | chamber of commerce |
| ❖ 竞争力 | competitive power |
| ❖ 老客户 | regular customer |
| ❖ 特色产品 | featured product |
| ❖ 享受优惠价格 | enjoy favorable prices |
| ❖ 享有良好声誉 | enjoy a good reputation |
| ❖ 不含有害化学物质 | free from harmful chemicals |
| ❖ 优等产品 | choice product |
| ❖ 质量保证书 | product warranty |
| ❖ 质量管理体系 | quality control system |
| ❖ 质量规格 | quality specification |
| ❖ 资格证书 | qualification certificate |
| ❖ 子公司 | subsidiary corporation |
| ❖ 上市 | enter a market |
| ❖ 供不应求 | production/supply falls behind demand, production/supply fails to meet demand, demand exceeds/outstrips supply |
| ❖ 供过于求 | supply exceeds/outstrips demand, have an excess of supply over demand |
| ❖ 有巨大的市场潜力 | show great market potential |
| ❖ 报最低价 | quote the lowest/best price; give the lowest/best quotation |
| ❖ 价格优惠 | be competitive in price |
| ❖ 给出优惠的折扣 | grant/give/allow a profitable discount |
| ❖ 不能再作让步 | can't make any concessions |
| ❖ 在价格上各让一步 | split the difference in price |

## 口译操练 Interpreting Practice

### 1. 听译 Listening Interpreting

A. Listen to the sentences and interpret them into English.
   Sentences 1—10

B. Listen to the paragraphs and interpret them into English.
   Paragraphs 1—2

### 2. 视译 Sight Interpreting

A. Interpret the following sentences into English:
（1）我们公司专门生产儿童服装,这套春秋系列是我们的特色产品。
（2）我们的设计理念既讲求以人为本,又强调美观大方。
（3）这些热销的电子产品在你们当地一定会有市场潜力。
（4）在这个信息时代,电脑日新月异,老的产品注定要被淘汰。
（5）我们在生意上有多年的往来。不知我们可否成为你们的产品在我国的独家代理?
（6）你们的产品给我留下了很深的印象,品种多样,具有独创性。我相信在我地很有市场潜力。
（7）如果订货量大,我们就在折扣上给予优惠。
（8）只要价格合理,高质量的产品在中国是有市场的。
（9）若对此事或其他未及事宜有疑问,请随时跟我联系。
（10）我希望这个报价令你们满意。

B. Interpret the following paragraphs into English:
（1）如果你们愿意,可以在2月份任何一天的上午9点至下午5点到我们的展厅来。我们的新产品和改进型产品在展厅内都有展示,其中包括你们特别感兴趣的我们的特色产品双门无霜冰箱。另外,你们也会看到其他的类似产品。我相信它们也会在你地有一定的市场潜力。
（2）不同厂家的产品有时候在设计、质量和做工上不具有可比性。你说得对,我们的新产品价格高得多。你知道,新产品的成本比较高。我们不可能以低于其实际价值的价格出售。另外,我们的产品质量上乘,理应售价较高。

### 3. 情景练习 Situational Interpreting

Interpret based on the information given. Add any information when necessary.

Roles:
李先生:北京电脑公司销售部主任
George Smith:美国 Star 电脑公司经理
王小姐:翻译

Smith 先生在北京电脑公司的展室里。他对一款新型电脑很感兴趣。李先生对其介绍该款电脑的特点和价格。

- 为该公司的特色产品,内存量大,运行速度快,外形美观大方,携带方便;
- 因其独特的设计和良好的性能获得10项国家和国际大奖;
- 零售价399美元,批发价379美元;
- 订货量500台佣金8%;每增加150台增加2%佣金。

## 译常识与技巧  Interpreting Tips and Skills

**口译的类型（Types of Interpretation）**

口译按其操作形式可以分为以下四种:

交替口译（alternating interpretation） 交替口译是指译员同时以两种语言为操不同语言的交际双方进行交替式口译。这是最常见的口译方式。交替口译的场合很广,可以是一般的非事务性的交谈,可以是正式的政府首脑会谈,也可以是记者招待会。这种口译要求译员不停地转换语码,在交谈双方或多方之间频繁穿梭,来回传递语段简短的信息。

接续口译（consecutive interpretation） 接续口译,又称交传,是指一种以句子或段落为单位传递信息的单向口译形式。接续口译多用于演讲、祝词、授课、高级会议、新闻发布会等。译员往往是以一段接一段的方式,在发言人的自然停顿间隙,将信息一组接一组地传译给听众。

同声传译（simultaneous interpretation） 同声传译,又称同步传译,是指译员在不打断发言人的情况下,不停顿地将其讲话内容传译给听众的一种口译形式。同声传译时,译员的口译与讲话者的发言几乎同步进行,因而,可保证发言人作连贯发言,不影响或中断发言者的思路,有利于听众对发言全文的通篇理解。同声传译是国际会议最基本的口译手段,有时也用于学术报告、授课讲座等场合。

耳语口译（whispering interpretation） 耳语口译是指译员将一方的讲话内容用耳语的方式轻轻地传译给另一方的口译形式。它与同声传译一样,属于不停顿的连续作战口译活动。不过,它的服务对象往往是个人,如接见的外宾、参加会晤的国家元首或高级政府官员。

口译按其获取语源的方式可分以下两种:

听译（listening interpretation） 听译是以听的方式接受来源语信息,以口头方式传出信息的口译方式。这是口译的典型方式。

视译（sight interpretation） 视译是以看的方式接受来源语信息,以口头方式传出信息的口译方式。视译的内容通常是一篇准备好的讲稿或文件。发言人可以在场发言,这样译员可以边听边看边口译。发言者也可以不在场,译员就需根据演讲稿用另一种语言来宣读讲稿。与同声传译和耳语口译一样,视译同属不间断的连贯式口译活动。

口译按其操作内容可以大致分为以下五种:

导游口译（guide interpretation） 其范围包括接待、陪同、参观、游览、购物等活动。

礼仪口译（ceremony interpretation） 其范围包括外宾迎送、开幕式、闭幕式、招待会、合同签字等活动。

宣传口译（information interpretation） 其范围包括机构介绍、政策宣传、广告宣传、促销展销、授课讲座、文化交流等活动。

会议口译（conference interpretation） 其范围包括国际会议、记者招待会、商务会议、学术讨论会等活动。

谈判口译（negotiation interpretation） 其范围包括国事会谈、双边会谈、外交谈判、商务谈判等活动。

以上我们对口译进行了粗略的分类。但是，必须认识到，在实际工作中，口译类别的划分并非如此分明。许多场合的翻译往往不是单一性的，而是混合性的。因此，一名优秀的译员应该能胜任各种类型的口译工作。

# 第 4 单元 庆典致辞

## Unit 4 Celebrative Speeches

# 第4单元 庆典致辞 Celebrative Speeches

# 第1部分 Section 1

## 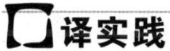 Vocabulary Work

| | | | |
|---|---|---|---|
| ethnicity | 族裔 | sanitation facilities | 卫生设施 |
| the most vulnerable | 最弱势群体 | marginalised | 边缘化 |
| governance | 治理 | resilient | 具复原力的 |

##  Text Interpreting

**Interpret the following speech into Chinese:**

### UN Secretary-General's Message on World Water Day

Water is vital for survival and, alongside sanitation, helps protect public and environmental health. Our bodies, our cities and our industries, our agriculture and our ecosystems all depend on it.

Water is a human right. Nobody should be denied access. This World Water Day is about upholding this right for all, leaving no one behind.

Today, 2.1 billion people live without safe water due to factors such as economic status, gender, ethnicity, religion and age. Growing demands, coupled with poor management, have increased water stress in many parts of the world. Climate change is adding dramatically to the pressure. By 2030, an estimated 700 million people worldwide could be displaced by intense water scarcity.

We must encourage cooperation to tackle the global water crisis and strengthen our resilience to the effects of climate change to ensure access to water for all, especially for the most vulnerable. These are vital steps towards a more peaceful and prosperous future. As we strive to achieve the Sustainable Development Goals, we must value water resources and ensure their inclusive management if we are to protect and use this vital resource sustainably for the benefit of all people.

### Message from Ms. Audrey Azoulay, Director-General of UNESCO, on the Occasion of World Water Day

Access to safe water is a human right and—along with access to sanitation facilities—drives forward development.

Yet, nearly a third of the global population do not use safely managed drinking water services and only two fifths have access to safely managed sanitation services.

That is why the theme of this year's World Water Day is "leaving no-one behind", echoing the bold promises of the United Nations Sustainable Development Agenda.

This aspiration to reach even the most vulnerable is increasingly important: the intensification of environmental degradation, climate change, population growth and rapid urbanisation — among other factors — pose considerable challenges to water security.

Nevertheless, water and sanitation can significantly contribute to the achievement of the broad set of goals of the 2030 Agenda for Sustainable Development: from food and energy security, to economic development and environmental sustainability.

Given the wide-ranging impact of access to water, this year's, United Nations World Water Development Report — published by UNESCO, in collaboration with the whole UN Water Family — focuses on the theme of tackling the barriers to water access, particularly for the most disadvantaged.

The report advocates for a boost to international political will to reach those marginalised and to tackle the existing inequalities — whether they be socio-economic, gender-based, due to the particular challenges of urban or rural settings, or any other factor.

This need for increased international solidarity is especially prominent in certain regions such as sub-Saharan Africa and South Asia, where access to basic services such as water supply and sanitation, remains largely limited.

In an increasingly globalised world, the impact of water-related decisions crosses borders and affects everyone, therefore advocating for a comprehensive water governance.

This World Water Day, UNESCO reaffirms its commitment to support governments in their efforts towards achieving universal access to water and sanitation for all, without discrimination.

By prioritizing those most in need, we can build more resilient communities, more equal societies and a more peaceful, sustainable world.

## 课文注释 Notes on the Text

1. 本文基于联合国秘书长安东尼奥·古特雷斯和教科文组织总干事奥德蕾·阿祖莱于 2019 年 3 月所做的世界水日致辞。
2. 安东尼奥·古特雷斯,1949 年 4 月 30 日出生于葡萄牙里斯本。1995 年 10 月至 2002 年任葡萄牙总理。2005 年 6 月至 2015 年 12 月执掌联合国难民署。2017 年 1 月 1 日,古特雷斯开始正式任职联合国秘书长,任期五年。
3. 奥德蕾·阿祖莱,1972 年出生于法国,2017 年 11 月出任教科文组织总干事,成为前任伊琳娜·博科娃以来教科文组织历史上第二位女性总干事。
4. This aspiration to reach even the most vulnerable is increasingly important: the intensification of environmental degradation, climate change, population growth and rapid urbanisation — among other factors — pose considerable challenges to water security. 这一长句翻译是要注意语序的处理和适当添加体现逻辑的衔接

词,既要完整达意,又要符合汉语表达习惯:让最弱势群体也从中受益,这一志愿的重要性正与日俱增,因为环境恶化加剧、气候变化、人口增长和快速城市化等因素对水安全构成了巨大挑战。

# 词语扩展  Developing Vocabulary and Expressions

- theme 主题
- reaffirm its commitment 重申致力于
- aspiration 抱负
- inauguration 就职典礼
- acceptance speech 受奖致辞/总统候选人所做的提名演讲
- awarding speech 颁奖致辞
- awarding ceremony 颁奖典礼
- business-opening ceremony 开业典礼
- celebration remarks 庆典致辞
- celebration meeting 庆祝大会
- closing ceremony 闭幕式
- closing remark/speech/address 闭幕辞
- commencement 毕业典礼
- farewell speech/address,valediction 告别辞
- festival celebration 节日庆典
- festival greetings 节日致辞
- formality remarks 礼仪致辞
- inaugural address 就职演说
- inauguration ceremony (for a building) (建筑物)落成典礼
- opening ceremony 开幕式
- opening remark/speech/address 开幕致辞
- propose a toast 提议祝酒
- radio address 广播献辞
- signing ceremony 签字仪式
- school-opening ceremony 开学典礼
- video message 电视献辞
- welcome speech/address, speech of welcome 欢迎致辞
- declare...open 宣布……开幕
- distinguished guest 贵宾
- gracious hospitality 友好款待
- host country 东道国
- anniversary 周年纪念
- in the name of 以……名义
- in the spirit of 本着……精神
- official invitation 正式邀请
- on the occasion of 值此……之际
- heartfelt congratulations 衷心的祝贺
- in conclusion/closing 最后
- celebrity 名人

## 口译操练 Interpreting Practice

### 1. 听译 ▶▶ Listening Interpreting

A. **Listen to the sentences and interpret them into Chinese.**
Sentences 1—10

B. **Listen to the paragraphs and interpret them into Chinese.**
Paragraphs 1—2

### 2. 视译 ▶▶ Sight Interpreting

A. **Interpret the following sentences into Chinese:**

(1) It is in the spirit of friendly cooperation, mutual promotion and common prosperity that I extend to you the warmest welcome and convey to you the most gracious greetings from all the employees of our ABC Corporation.

(2) I am pleased to join the honorable Mayor of New York as well as other dignitaries here today for this exciting event.

(3) I would like to extend my genuine thanks to you for taking time to join this party to celebrate with us the establishment of this new office.

(4) Today, I know all of you here as honored as I do of this new building to house the Management Graduate Institute at A University. It is an important step for the Management Institute, the university, and the whole nation.

(5) We are here as world leaders and world citizens. And now is the time and today is the day for a new beginning to give renewed impetus to peace, cooperation, development, security and stability in the world.

(6) Never before have the leaders of so many nations come together in a single Assembly. This is a unique event. A unique opportunity. And therefore a unique responsibility.

(7) Time has changed its rhythm. A new world has emerged in the space of a single generation. A world that still bears the scars of the past and where crises and conflicts still persist. But a world that is already in the future.

(8) We must breathe life into an ethic for the 21st century to serve mankind, human dignity and human rights. This ethical combat is above all the combat for peace and democracy.

(9) These are all critical issues for the inhabitants of our planet and we can only make progress on them together, in a spirit of shared responsibility.

(10) Thank you and good evening. On behalf of the 55,000 Merrill Lynch employees in 45 countries around the world, I am honored to accept the Marco Polo Award.

B. **Interpret the following paragraphs into Chinese:**

(1) Welcome to the official launch of ABC company. I regard it a great

# 第 4 单元 庆典致辞 Celebrative Speeches

honor that you are here with us at this important occasion. May I take this opportunity to outline our history, the market strategy of our company and our objectives for future business dealings in China. Our company would like to share our success with Chinese customers and we are looking forward to a long-term relationship with our clients.

（2）The shape of the world is changing almost as dramatically as this city's skyline. Today the cold war is over. The risk of the global nuclear conflict has been greatly reduced and the free flow of goods and ideas is bringing to life the concept of a global village. But just as all nations can benefit from the promise of this new world, no nation is immune to its perils. We all have a stake in building peace and prosperity, and in confronting threats that respect no borders—terrorism and drug trafficking, disease and environmental destruction.

## 3. 情景练习 ▶▶ Situational Interpreting

**Interpret the following conversation alternatively into English and Chinese. Add any information when necessary.**

> **Roles**
> Mr. Thomas: an American
> Mr. Rong: a Chinese
> Miss Chen: an interpreter

Mr. Rong:
女士们,先生们,各位朋友,我很荣幸能够出任美国H&C医疗器械公司北京分公司的经理。今天,在这样一个隆重的场合,我很荣幸地请公司董事长Thomas先生来参加开业典礼并致贺辞。有请Thomas先生!

Mr. Thomas:
Thank you, Mr. Rong, and all the friends here. It is my great pleasure to be here in Beijing to witness and address the official launch of our branch company. On behalf of the board of directors, I'd like to extend my genuine thanks and warm welcome to all the guests here for your gracious presence at this historical moment in H&C Medical Instruments Corporation's development.

H&C was first set up with a staff of only 5 medical graduates ten years ago in the US. At that time, they were inspired by Michael Jackson's song "Heal the World," and they worked with a similar passion like the singer's by giving birth to H&C, whose name means "Heal and Care." Today, this name rings almost everywhere in the world. The staff has grown into a number 1000 times more than the original. And with the development of modern technology and strategies of management, H&C has greatly quickened its pace. That's how we are here in Beijing today.

Beijing is a very special place for our investment and development. It is a mixture of both modernity and antiquity. I can foresee a new chapter in H&C's legendary story with the very wisdom of traditional Chinese medicine and its medical instrument manufacturing.

Mr. Rong has worked for about 5 years in H&C's parent company. His training and his experience there will make him a capable and qualified manager, of course, with the support of all the company members and friends here.

Thank you!

# 第4单元 庆典致辞 Celebrative Speeches

# 第2部分 Section 2

## 词汇预习 Vocabulary Work

| 代言人 | be one's voice | 思考 | ponder over |
|---|---|---|---|
| 智识群体 | intellectual community | 牢靠的 | secure |
| 社会行为 | civic conduct | 灯塔 | beacon of light |
| 拱顶石 | keystone | 与日俱增 | flourish with the days |
| 树立 | fashion | 百年校庆 | centennial anniversary celebration |

## 口译实践 Text Interpreting

Interpret the following speech into English:

### 在百年校庆典礼上的致词

校长先生,女士们,先生们:

感谢校长先生的盛情邀请和贵校的热情接待。能前来参加贵校宏大的百年校庆,是我的荣幸。我谨代表来自国内各大学的所有客人,也以我个人的名义,向校长先生和全体师生表达我们最为热烈的祝贺,祝愿贵校"苟日新、又日新、日日新!"

由于我是今天在此派有代表的国内各大学中建校历史最久的大学的副校长,我被推选来代表他们讲话。我很高兴作为大家的代言人,送上我们衷心的祝贺。

在11世纪,由于人类文明的发展,大学产生了。十个世纪之后,我们在贵校相聚,继续思考我们的生活,继续探究无涯的知识。

我们这些大学在全世界形成一个很大的智识群体。科学无国籍,知识属于每一个人。

我们这些大学创造了新的知识。我们传授这些知识,也传授其他大学所创造的新知识,传授先辈们所发现、试验和积累的伟大知识宝库中的真知灼见。

所有的大学都在为国家的繁荣和成功添砖加瓦。同时,这些大学也在为保护本国文明所特有的文化和遗产而贡献力量。但是,大学的作为不止于此。唯有付出艰辛,通过对准确性、理性和真实性进行独立验证的知识,才是真知灼见。因此,当我们给学生传授技能时,我们也是在给他们传授各种价值观。一方面,我们传授个人行为和社会行为方面的价值观。另一方面,这些价值观强调个人独立思考的必要性。独立思考是人类创造力的源泉。

大学的上述任务赋予大学高度的责任感。这些任务根植于诚实的态度、自由无畏的探究和独立性三者构成的伟大优良传统之中。每一所大学都是自己社会里的一座灯塔。通过和兄弟大学的联络,该大学所创造的知识和价值得以广泛传播。

传统不易树立,也不能在顷刻间树立。在过去的一百年里,贵校形成了自己的传统。贵校今天和将来的成员们!我们希望看到你们的传统得以发展和巩固。我们希望看到你们成为知识界的一块拱顶石。随着你们的成员越来越多地参与兄弟大学的活动,在你们的第二个百年中,我们希望看到你们会对整个国际学术运动做出贡献。

再次向贵校表示衷心的祝贺和最良好的祝愿!愿我们的友谊与日俱增!

谢谢大家!

 **Notes on the Text**

1. 苟日新,又日新,日日新:演讲者经常喜欢引经据典,此句出于《礼记·大学》,意译为 become more prosperous day by day。
2. 我很高兴作为大家的代言人,送上我们衷心的祝贺:I am pleased to be their voice in presenting our heartfelt congratulations here. 将"作为……的代言人"译为 to be one's voice,非常形象,而且简练,比 to be the spokesman /mouthpiece of 更恰当。
3. 在 11 世纪,由于人类文明的发展,大学产生了:大学在今天是指综合性的提供教学和研究条件并授权颁发学位的高等教育机关。大学是一个不断发展的概念。在中世纪的西欧,已产生了大学的雏形。当时的大学是从教会办的师徒结合的行会性质学校发展起来的。在 11 世纪时,拉丁文"大学"一词和"行会"一词同样被用来形容行业公会,但是到了 13 世纪时,"大学"一词就被用来专指一种学生团体。11 世纪在意大利诞生的博洛尼亚大学,堪称西方世界第一所大学。
4. 伟大知识宝库中的真知灼见:结合上文,将"真知灼见"译为 the best of...。
5. 继续思考我们的生活,继续探究无涯的知识:此句是排比句,是演讲辞中常见的修辞方法,以增强语气。译成 to keep pondering over our life and exploring the endless knowledge。"无涯的知识"也用了典故,语出《庄子·养生主》:"吾生也有涯,而知也无涯。以有涯随无涯,殆已。"
6. 传统不易树立,也不可能在顷刻间树立:译为 A tradition is not built easily or quickly。用"or"可表示连续的否定。
7. 愿我们的友谊与日俱增:可译成 May our friendship flourish with the days! friendship 与 flourish 两词以同样辅音开头,修辞学上称之为押头韵(alliteration),使语言有回旋反复之感。

 **Developing Vocabulary and Expressions**

- 在世纪之交 at the turn of the century
- 值此……之际 on the occasion of...
- 纪念 in commemoration of; to commemorate; to observe
- 庆祝 in celebration of; to celebrate; to observe
- 司仪 MC (Master of Ceremonies)
- 回顾过去 look back on/in retrospect
- 展望未来 look ahead/look into the future
- 与时俱进 keep abreast of the times
- 结束过去,开辟未来 leave the past behind and open a new chapter for the future
- 承前启后,继往开来 view on the past and prepare for the future

# 第4单元 庆典致辞 Celebrative Speeches

- 开创新的历史纪元 to usher in a new era
- 远道而来的朋友 visiting friends coming from a distant land/friends coming from a distant land
- 来自太平洋彼岸的朋友 friends from the other side of the Pacific
- 各界人士 people of all circles; people from all walks of life; a cross-section of people; people from all strata of society
- 热情洋溢的欢迎辞 gracious speech of welcome
- 热情洋溢而又令人信服的讲话 very gracious and eloquent remarks
- 发表热情友好的讲话 make a warm and friendly speech
- 在热情友好的气氛中 in a cordial and friendly atmosphere
- 在认真坦率的气氛中 in an earnest and frank atmosphere
- 无与伦比的热情好客 the incomparable hospitality
- 作为贵国人民的友好使者 as an envoy of friendship of your people
- 怀着对贵国人民的深厚感情 with profound and amicable sentiments for your people
- 致以亲切的问候和良好祝愿 extend cordial greetings and best wishes
- 促进我们之间的友好合作关系 promote/facilitate/enhance/strengthen/advance our friendly cooperative relation
- 增进我们彼此之间的理解 increase/strengthen/promote/expand our mutual understanding and friendship
- 今天我们在这里集会隆重纪念……周年。We meet here today to solemnly commemorate/observe the... anniversary of...
- 我能参加这次……开幕式并发言,真是非常荣幸且高兴。It is really a great honor and pleasure for me to attend and speak at the opening ceremony of...
- 我提议,为母校的百年华诞举杯。I'd like to propose a toast to our Alma Mater on her centennial anniversary.
- 我提议为我们之间的友谊干杯! Allow me to raise the glass to our friendship!
- 我希望你在逗留期间惬意舒适。I hope you will have a very enjoyable stay.
- 在这临别的时刻我们都感到依依不舍。We all feel sorry at the moment of parting.
- 愿我们的友谊青春常在,绿水长流。May our friendship remain in perpetual youth and last for ever like an ever-flowing river.
- 有朋自远方来,不亦乐乎? Isn't it a delight that congenial minds come to seek you from afar? /It is such a delight that I have friends visiting from afar!
- 海内存知己,天涯若比邻。A bosom friend afar brings a distant land near.
- 但愿人长久,千里共婵娟。I wish you a long life and the joy of sharing the silvery moonlight even with a thousand miles' distance between us.

## 译操练 Interpreting Practice

### 1. 听译 ▶▶ Listening Interpreting

A. **Listen to the sentences and interpret them into English.**
   Sentences 1—10

B. **Listen to the paragraphs and interpret them into English.**
   Paragraphs 1—2

## 2. 视译 ▶▶▶ Sight Interpreting

**A. Interpret the following sentences into English：**

（1）在这个美丽无比、明月当空的夜晚，我谨代表总经理，以及公司的全体同仁，感谢各位光临我们的新千年联欢晚会。

（2）今天，我们聚会于此，庆祝 A 大学的宏大校庆。作为一名在这里学习、工作和生活了 50 年的教师，我感到非常激动和荣幸。

（3）我谨代表本大学所有院系的成员，向所有的领导和客人表达我们热烈的欢迎和由衷的敬意。

（4）今天能够来这里和大家一同庆祝 A 大学的百年校庆，我感到十分荣幸。在过去的 100 年里，A 大学曾为你们国家的发展发挥过重要的作用。

（5）感谢各位在百忙中参加我们的庆典宴会，与我们一起庆祝这家分支机构的成立。

（6）亲临 B 公司的揭幕典礼，我感到非常荣幸。贵公司的成立对世界知识经济和信息产业的发展有着十分重要的意义。

（7）我希望中美两国青年在建设各自国家、促进世界和平与发展的事业中，加深了解，互相学习，增进友谊，为创造美好的未来而努力奋斗。

（8）有幸参加这次精彩绝伦的聚会，我再次向你们表示衷心的感谢。

（9）我们真诚地希望我们继续密切合作，进一步加强我们的友好关系。

（10）我坚信，中国的明天会更加繁荣，世界的未来将会更加美好。

**B. Interpret the following paragraphs into English：**

（1）欢迎光临 YF 公司上海分公司的揭牌典礼。各位光临，在此与我们共度 YF 公司历史上的这一重要时刻，我感到万分荣幸。请允许我借此机会向各位简单介绍一下我公司的历史、公司的上海市场营销策略以及公司未来在这里运作的目标。

（2）我很荣幸参加为庆祝第三届香港国际玩具展开幕举办的这次酒会。祝愿各位在香港度过非常富有成果和愉快的时光。香港以被称作"世界玩具中心"为荣。香港现在已成为世界第二大玩具出口地。更重要的是，我们的玩具制造商坚定地致力于保证产品的高质量和安全性，并以创新性和可购性著称。

## 3. 情景练习 ▶▶▶ Situational Interpreting

Interpret based on the information given below. Add any information when necessary.

> **Roles**
> 高先生：中国 A 大学校长，美国 B 大学毕业生

在美国 B 大学的百年校庆上，高先生应邀参加庆典并代表中国校友致贺辞。他致辞的主要内容包括以下几方面：

- 代表全体中国校友对母校百岁华诞表示祝贺，向校方邀请他参加校庆并代表致词表示感谢，向母校的教职员工表示诚挚的感谢和敬意。
- 讲述了他在 B 大学的 3 年学习生活中几个意义非常的片断，以切身经历侧面讲述了 B 大学从创立以来一贯坚持的教学育人方法所取得的卓越成就。
- 回顾了中华文化中的"大学"精神和传统，并以中国 A 大学校长的身份表示友好的愿望：希望 A 和 B 两所大学能够在新世纪有更多的相互学习和合作。

- 再一次向母校表示祝贺和祝福,向所有参加庆典的老师和朋友表示良好的祝愿。

# 译常识与技巧  *Interpreting Tips and Skills*

**公共演讲 (Public Speaking in Interpreting)**

口译作为语言交际活动,需要译者在知识体系、语言能力、心理素质、道德意识、语言知识、社会知识、通用知识、专用知识、语言感知能力、辨析解意能力、转码处理能力、连贯表达能力、公众演讲能力、短时记忆素质、压力承受素质等诸多方面都能游刃有余,应对自如。而其中,公众演讲能力是口译人员必须具备的能力之一。无论是面对一个人还是面对几千人进行翻译,口译员都是在公众场合进行表达,因此演讲能力显得非常重要。

不过,大多数人都害怕在公众面前演讲。其实大可不必害怕或担心,因为公众演讲能力也并非先天得来,它和其他能力一样,都是可以通过后天训练,而逐步完善熟练的。演讲是实践性很强的活动,所以训练是最为关键的,其目的在于使自己具备应有的演讲知识和技能,并且逐步让自己表现得更好。学习者应争取一切机会练习,掌握公共演讲技能。

译员在公众演讲时,应注意以下几点:
1) 口译中应该吐字清晰,音量适中,声音自然,语调中肯。口译员开头译的几句话对赢得现场听众的信任有着特殊重要的作用,所以特别要说好。
2) 讲话时注意嘴巴与麦克风的位置和距离,根据声音效果适时进行调整。
3) 确保听众能跟上并听懂自己的讲话,注意观察听众的反应来调整自己的语速。译到专有名词和头衔时应稍微放慢速度,注意发音准确、清楚。
4) 讲话时适当保持与现场听众的目光交流。一个好的译员不应该只是埋头翻译或只盯着自己的笔记,也应该像一个演讲者一样,除了看笔记,还要偶尔抬头与听众进行目光交流。
5) 口译中一般使用第一人称,而无须转述,但在同时兼任会谈双方多人的翻译时,需要指明发言者身份。
6) 做口译时少用或不用手势,表情不要夸张。即使出现口误,也不要做鬼脸或皱眉头,偶尔被人纠正错误,口译者应该虚心接受。
7) 听众对讲话鼓掌或哄笑时,口译员应该适当停顿。

若要把握这些口译公众演讲能力技巧,译员在口译时应该做到:
8) 话一出口,必须说完。就是说,应养成习惯,开口说出的句子一定要想办法说完整,不可以半途而废,声音渐弱直至消失,也不应该回头重说或者不断回头修正。
9) 说得清楚,听得明白。就是说,发音要流畅,无赘音。口语表达应简洁、到位,遣词造句要让听众听得明白。若信息之间有逻辑上不能衔接的地方,或指涉不清楚者,要加以说明,使听者容易听懂意思。

要提高口译水平、提高自己的公众演讲能力,就要练好自己的口才,提高口语表达能力。口语的一些典型特征有用词通俗,生动、活泼,句式比书面语言自然灵活,以短句、散句、省略句、排比句等为主。要了解这些口语特点就必须通过各种途径不断分析和总结,比如经常分析别人的演讲稿、观摩别人的演讲、讲话活动等。扎实的基本功靠长时期一点一滴的学习和积累。练基本功是艰苦而乏味的,要静下心来,下苦功夫,只有基本功练扎实了,演讲能力才能达到更高的水平。

另外,提高口译公众演讲能力还要提高口译员的心理素质。译员经常会觉得翻译时"心发慌、嘴发紧",无法做到畅快表达,平时熟悉的内容也有可能会译得很糟糕,这主要是心理素质欠佳造成的。口译员要有良好的心理素质,把机智当成职业习惯,要能做到"处乱不惊、情绪稳定"。口译员要有较强的情绪控制能力,在任何情况下都要保持镇定。如果情绪不稳定,就会出现怯场现象,影响理解,影响翻译质量。要具备良好的心理素质,主要靠平时的打造,基础打扎实了,自信心自然就有了。有了自信心,心理状态也便容易调整,这样演讲效果就会更好。

　　公众演讲能力的提高就好像游泳,在岸上是练不出真功夫的,必须"下水"去多练。特别是要多在大庭广众之下练习,以锻炼自己的胆量和应变能力。如果有正式的演讲比赛、发言机会,那就更要积极参加,因为这是锻炼演讲与口头表达能力的最好机会,是提高演讲与口才的最佳途径。没有天生的绝佳口才,出色的演说家都是在许许多多讲演、讲话经历中不断吸取成功经验和失败教训而成长起来的。

# 第 5 单元 Unit 5

## 海外学习
## Overseas Educatiou

# 第5单元 海外学习 Overseas Education

# 第1部分 Section 1

## Vocabulary Work

| | | | |
|---|---|---|---|
| enroll | 入学,录取 | assess | 评估 |
| academic | 学术的 | extracurricular | 课外的,业余的 |
| ascertain | 确定 | threshold | 门槛 |
| mechanism | 机制 | architecture | 建筑 |
| criteria | 标准 | graduate program | 研究生课程 |

## Text Interpreting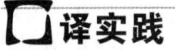

Interpret the following conversation into Chinese:

### An Interview with the President of Yale University

Journalist (J): What qualities does a university require when enrolling students?

President (P): That's a good question. Before students come into Yale, they have to show a high level of academic achievement with a series of tests to be taken. Then they're also expected to have very excellent grades in their high school education and also show some potential for leadership, which is very hard to assess. It's certain not to mean an assessment just from one's academic performance, so we look at—

J: You have face-to-face interview.

P: There are still those, but frankly those can be deceptive. I think we look more to the record of what students have done in their extracurricular activities. Have they done something unusual? Have they founded a new organization or led? Been active in volunteer service in their communities, or have they been excellent athletes and perhaps elected captain of their team and shown leadership skill in that way? So through a variety of mechanisms, we try to ascertain the potential for leadership. The other thing that's important is we actually expect to have students who've made enough of an impression on their teachers and other adults

· 57 ·

who would write letters of recommendation. And these letters don't just say that, "This is the brightest student I've had in five years," but actually say something of the character of the individual. And the most effective letters of recommendation are those that really do try to describe the person and give a sense that this is really someone who has great potential. It's all very forward looking you try to pick the people who will end up being leaders and you know, we've been fortunate to have a very good record.

J: As more and more young people want to get into Yale, do the criteria for enrollment become more and more critical?

P: Well, the criteria won't change, but the threshold, the level of achievement has gone up and it's remarkable today right now we have about seven or eight application for everyone we admit and already there are many who don't apply, because they know they don't have a chance to come, so we have a very strong pool of applicants, but at the same time, we're very eager to expand that pool internationally. One of the things that's most important to me is to make Yale a truly global institution and get the very best students from around the world.

J: Any comments on the Chinese students in Yale?

P: Oh, we have fabulous Chinese students. I mean these Chinese students have the kind of extreme creativity and imagination that we like to see in our students. In my department of economics, we've seen really excellent students in the graduate level. We have now over 300 students from China at Yale, most of them, now in graduate programs, mostly Ph.D. programs, but some of the other professions are law and music, especially, architecture. We would like to see more at the undergraduate level and but we're very pleased with the ones we have.

## 课文注释  Notes on the Text

1. What qualities does a university require when enrolling students? 在口译过程中，为了实现表达的顺畅，某些状语从句可以处理成定语从句的关系。例如在本句中，以"when..."引导的时间状语从句可以翻译为定语的逻辑关系，可译为："大学录取学生的要求是什么？"

2. The other thing that's important is we actually expect to have students who've made enough of an impression on their teachers and other adults who would write letters of recommendation. 该句较长，信息量较多。在口译时，为了使信息的表达及时到位，可以适当对句意进行切分，如前半句可译为"另一点也很重要，我们希望录用的学生曾给教师或别的成年人留下深刻的印象"，而后半句以 who 引导的定语从句可以独立出来，合并到之后的信息之中，可译为："他们写来推荐信……"

3. It's all very forward looking you try to pick the people who will end up being leaders and you know, we've been fortunate to have a very good record. forward looking 指的是"有远见的"，end up doing... 指的是"以……为结束/结果"，翻译时往往并不需要将"结束/结果"等字译出，have a very good record 指的是"做得很

好",record 一词也并不需要据实译出,行文的字里行间自然会带出这层含义。
4. As more and more young people want to get into Yale, does the criteria for enrollment become more and more critical? critical 一词词义众多,在这里指的是"苛刻的"。
5. a very strong pool of applicants:pool 指的是 an organization of people or resources that can be shared,即可译为"申请我校的学生"。

# 词语扩展 Developing Vocabulary and Expressions

- admission age                入学年龄
- admission qualification       入学资格
- admissions office            招生办公室
- advanced placement           跳级
- affidavit of sponsorship      担保书
- certificate for courses completed  结业证书
- certificate of attendance     肄业证书
- class attendance sheet       点名簿
- commencement               毕业典礼
- conduct of a student         操行
- cover letter                求学/求职信
- entrance requirement        入学标准
- graduation appraisal         毕业鉴定
- graduation oral examination   毕业答辩会
- letter of admission          入学通知书
- letter of application         申请书
- marital status              婚姻状况
- personal qualifications      个人条件
- promotion or holding back system  升留级制度
- registration fee             报名费
- retain one's status as a student  保留学籍
- roll call                   点名
- sundry expenses            杂费
- suspend one's schooling     休学

**国外部分名校：**
- Brown University            布朗大学
- Cambridge University        剑桥大学
- Carnegie Mellon University   卡内基•梅隆大学
- Columbia University         哥伦比亚大学
- Cornell University          康奈尔大学
- Harvard University          哈佛大学
- Imperial College of Science, Technology and Medicine  帝国理工学院
- Lancaster University        兰卡斯特大学
- London Business School     伦敦商学院
- Massachusetts Institute of Technology  麻省理工学院
- Oxford University          牛津大学

- Princeton University 普林斯顿大学
- Stanford University 斯坦福大学
- The University of London 伦敦大学
- The University of Michigan 密歇根大学
- The University of Nottingham 诺丁汉大学
- The University of Pennsylvania 宾州大学
- University of Chicago 芝加哥大学
- Washington University 华盛顿大学
- Yale University 耶鲁大学
- York University 约克大学

## 口译操练 Interpreting Practice

### 1. 听译 Listening Interpreting

**A. Listen to the sentences and interpret them into Chinese.**
Sentences 1—10

**B. Listen to the paragraphs and interpret them into Chinese.**
Paragraphs 1—2

### 2. 情景练习 Situational Interpreting

Interpret based on the information given. Add any information when necessary.

> **Roles**
> Mrs. Smith: an office clerk
> Jane: a student
> Raymond: an interpreter

Jane will graduate from high school within the next six months and she is interested in an MA program of an American university. Now she is in the Admission Office asking for information about the requirements, courses, accommodation, and social life.

- Requirements: your undergraduate transcripts, the GRE score, three letters of recommendation, statement of interest...
- Courses: first-class, friendly, flexible teaching and research, a range of compulsory and selective courses, lectures, seminars...
- Accommodation: inexpensive on-campus and off-campus residence, for single students and families...
- Life: great social life with various clubs and organizations, part-time jobs, a place well-placed for traveling and within reach of some of the most beautiful scenery in the world...

# 第5单元 海外学习 Overseas Education

# 第2部分 Section 2

 **Vocabulary Work**

| | | | |
|---|---|---|---|
| 目的陈述 | statement of purpose（SP） | 条件 | qualification |
| 招生人员 | recruiter | 头脑清晰 | clear-headed |
| 夸张 | exaggeration | 招生办 | admission committee |
| 专业目标 | professional goal | 晦涩难懂 | obscure |

 **Text Interpreting**

Interpret the following lecture into English:

怎么写"目的陈述"

各位,早上好!

今天,我们讲怎么写"目的陈述"。尽管求学申请的所有材料都在介绍自己,但"目的陈述"才是真正的自我介绍。它的目的就是描述自己的经历和目的,以说服招生委员会的委员们认可你。在写目的陈述的时候,所谈内容都是私人性的:你得说自己是谁,你懂什么,能干什么,还有你想干什么。目的陈述的总的写作方法是这样的:从自己的背景写起,介绍你的目的,再表明这两者有什么关系。也就是说,证明自己的学识有助于达到自己的目的。然后,表明这一目的是如何激励你来申请那所学校或专业。招生的人希望你能证明你、你的目的,以及申请学校这三者之间并不矛盾。表明你自身的条件和他们所要的东西之间相得益彰。记住,这是个如何阐述的问题:不要胡编乱造,恰到好处地说明自己的条件就行。当然,这就意味着申请对象不同,目的陈述也就应该相应有所不同。

撇开每所学校的具体要求不谈,一份目的陈述应该证明自己头脑是清晰的,有清晰的思维,不糊涂,是一个好学的、有上进心的人。动笔之前,先想一想自己,自己的目的以及自己的能力。在开头部分说明自己的目标。主体部分的结构应该跟上面我讲的逻辑一致。先介绍事实——你的学习经历,学的什么专业、在哪儿上的学、为什么学那个专业,以及所学在申请中有什么用处。如果你原来的专业和所申请的不同,讲出令人信服的理由来。换句话说,为什么要换专业。在主体部分的第二节写自己的专业目标,说明这些目标和所学之间的联系。说出你的长远打算,说明所申请的专业在哪些方面有助于你实现这些目标。最后就剩下文章的结尾了,讲了自己的经历和目标之后,再把这两者和你所申请的专业联系起来。讲清楚由于你的经历,所以你才申请这个专业;这个专业反过来有助于你实现你的长远目标。在这部分,你还要说明你为什么选择那个大学,课程设置、教师队伍、研究兴趣等都可能是原因。结尾时,应总结一下自己的主要观点,并阐述一下自己对该专业会有什么贡献。

目的陈述的结构并不复杂,一旦你领会了其内在的逻辑性,事实上是很容易掌握的。然而,要写出好的初稿也不那么容易。要花点时间修改。不要太看重你在其他材料中已经说过的东西,要在它们的基础上锦上添花。行文要清晰,有逻辑,而不要晦涩难懂——不要忘了,一同送到招生办的,除了你的目的陈述之外,还有数以百计其他人的。不要害怕修改;改上10遍,才能拿出一份像样的目的陈述,这一点也不夸张。一个办法是,改完一稿,放几天,然后再看,这样视角会更客观。

谢谢你们! 祝大家好运!

# 课文注释  *Notes on the Text*

1. ……才是真正的自我介绍。. . . is the very document about yourself. 该句中"真正的"不应翻译为 real 或者 true,因为这里"真正的"的含义是:和其他材料相比较,SP 更偏重于介绍自己,所以翻译为 very 更合适,更能突出并强调这一含义。

2. 目的陈述的总的写作方法是这样的。The overall philosophy of a statement of purpose goes like this. 通过上下文看,该句中的"总的写作方法"指的不是具体的写作方法(approach 或 method),而是写作的指导思想或原则,所以翻译为 the overall philosophy 更能体现这一含义。

3. 表明你自身的条件和他们所要的东西之间相得益彰。Show how what you have matches what they want. 这里说的"相得益彰"可以用 match 一词来表示。汉译英时往往需要做减法,减去中文中冗余重复的信息,使之符合英文表达习惯,此处用 match 一词不仅符合原句意义,而且具有一定的口语色彩。

4. 当然,这就意味着申请对象不同,你的 SP 就应该有所不同。整句可以译为:This means, of course, that you have to personalize your SP for each program you are applying to. 这里所用的 personalize 的意思是 make something suitable for someone's particular needs or desires,可以相对精简地表达出原句含义。又如:"向客户提供个性化服务"可译为 to personalize the service to customers。

5. 撇开每所学校的具体要求不同不谈,一份 SP 应该证明自己头脑是清晰的,有清晰的思维,不糊涂,是一个好学的、有上进心的人。注意这句话的意思是:尽管每所学校的具体要求不同,但所有的 SP 都要证明自己头脑清晰。因此,这里"撇开每所学校的具体要求不同不谈"可以译为 beyond the particular skills required by each school。而后半句中信息较多,翻译时要注意主从关系,可译为 an SP should depict you as a clear-headed person, capable of thinking clearly without confusion, and as a motivated, active learner。

6. 最后就剩下文章的结尾了,讲了自己的经历和目标之后,再把这两者和你所申请的专业联系起来。"最后就剩下文章的结尾了"是口语中的说法,如果翻译为 The last part is the conclusion,显然就是"大白话",因为谁都知道一篇文章的最后一部分就是文章的结尾。所以,不可以不假思索地直译,而是可以适当删减,避免信息的冗余与重复。

## 词语扩展 Developing Vocabulary and Expressions

- 毕业证书 graduation certificate; diploma
- 博士生 doctoral student
- 成绩单（成绩报告单，成绩通知单）record/academic report; school report/transcript
- 存款证明书 certificate of deposit
- 大学简章 catalogue; bulletin
- 非全日制学生 part-time student
- 非正式学生 non-matriculated student
- 公费留学生 state-funded student studying abroad
- 公证处 notary office
- 公证书 notarial certificate
- 归国留学生 returned student
- 海外留学生 overseas student
- 奖学金 scholarship
- 奖学金学生 student on scholarship; prize fellow
- 交换生 exchange student
- 课程安排 course arrangement
- 临时住址 temporary address
- 旁听生 guest student; auditor; non-matriculated
- 全日制学生 full-time student
- 荣誉生 honour student
- 膳宿 accommodation
- 失学学生 school dropout
- 实习生 intern; trainee
- 通讯地址 address for correspondence
- 委培生 student enrolled on contract with a certain unit; student on commission
- 学生服务中心 student service center
- 在职研究生 working graduate student
- 长期住址 permanent address
- 正规学生 full-time student
- 助学金 grant
- 住校生 boarder; resident student
- 住宿费 residential fee
- 转校学生 transfer student
- 自费生 self-supported student; commoner
- 自费走读生 self-supported nonresident student

## 译操练  Interpreting Practice

### 1. 听译 ▶▶▶ Listening Interpreting

A. Listen to the sentences and interpret them into English.
   Sentences 1—10

B. Listen to the paragraphs and interpret them into English.
   Paragraphs 1—2

### 2. 情景练习 ▶▶▶ Situational Interpreting

Interpret based on the information given below. Add any information when necessary.

> **Roles**
> 王先生：演讲人
> 陈小姐：翻译

王先生的演讲题目为：如何写作个人简历。
一份简历应该包括以下内容：
- 申请人的详细联系方式
- 申请人的教育背景
- 申请人的工作经历
- 申请人的业余爱好
- 咨询人的姓名及联系方式

## 译常识与技巧  Interpreting Tips and Skills

**听辨与理解（Identification and Comprehension）**

正确地理解原意是外语学习的基本要求。同样，听辨与理解是整个口译过程的第一步，也是关键而艰难的一步。如果不能完全理解说话者所要传递的意图、要旨和情绪，如果不能准确地接收并辨析源语信息，译员则无法完整、准确、清晰地进行语言转换和表达。口译的认知过程要求译者在很短的时间内实现工作内容的高效化与准确化，但译员的听力并不总是"万无一失"的，种种听力障碍与问题往往难以避免。因此，译员应该建立起有效的学习模式，消除口译过程中的障碍与困难，切实培养敏锐、强大的听辨能力。

译员在口译开始之前，就应该具备扎实的语言基本功和广博的知识面。译员必须在平时多留意英语的多种口音、方言和变体，注意总结各自特点和规律，熟悉和了解源语的词汇、语法、句型结构和各种习惯用法。其次，译员广博的知识面，尤其是口译现场所要求的专业知识也是必不可少的。因主题知识或百科知识的欠缺而出现无解或误解的现象屡见不鲜。再者，在步入会场之前，译员必须对该口译任务的性质、时间、地点、内容及相关背景知识等有充分的了解，在一切了然于胸的情况下进行口译，可以大大提高听觉感知的敏锐度、反应力、自信心和准确性。另外，口译的工作现场肃穆紧张，译员需做好充分心理准备，时时准备好承受现场的紧张气氛与压力。

在整个听辨理解过程中,译员具体可以做到:

(1) 抓住关键词

译员可根据语篇的内容信息和说话人的表述特征来进行分析、判断,以把握整个听解篇段的要旨,并做到承上启下、成竹在胸。例如:

The Irish tourism industry is now well accustomed to the vagaries of the international marketplace and it has proven very adept at responding to the challenges.

在这段话中,Irish tourism, international marketplace, challenges 是关键词语。抓住这几个关键词语,该段落的意思就一目了然。

再看一个段落:

As you all know, marketing is a risky business at the best of times. It requires the best information and intelligence available. It also needs the application of sound commercial judgment. The element of risk can be minimized but, as we all know, never eliminated.

在这段话中,marketing, risky, information, intelligence, sound commercial judgment, minimize, eliminate 的词性分别为名词、形容词和动词,这些实意词语构成了该小段中理解的主体信息,理解了这几个词,也就抓住了这段话语的精髓,该篇段的理解也就迎刃而解。

(2) 关注话语标记词

当译员理解一篇话语时,首先要识别各种观点,其次要分析这些观点之间的逻辑联系。而表现种种逻辑联系、能够使译员就此展开语篇推理的语词就是话语标记词,既包括诸如 moreover, so, for, because 等单个语词,也包括如 you know, you see, I mean 等语用表达式。例如:

The stock response in times like these, as we all know, would be for non-statutory services to be the first to suffer, the first for cuts and in line for savings. I'm sure that is a real pressure colleagues here are facing at the moment.

其中,as we all know 所暗示的就是大家都知晓的信息。选择这一标记词即强调或突出即将说出的内容,译员听到这个词,就对下文要听到的信息有所准备。

再以美国总统奥巴马在国会两院联席会议上演讲中的一句话为例:

I know that for many Americans watching right now, the state of our economy is a concern that rises above all others. And rightly so.

上例中的 and 一般被认为是上下句的连接词,但在此处,作为话语标记词,它则不仅仅是单纯的表连贯和衔接的连接词。and 一词一方面发挥了并列连词的语法作用,同时又肯定了前文信息,即前面说的 I know that for many Americans watching right now, the state of our economy is a concern that rises above all others.（我知道,对于现在正在看电视的许多美国人而言,没有什么比我们的经济状况更令人担心的了。）这一事实的肯定才引出了后文 And rightly so.（事实正是如此。）译员在听到 and 一词后,就会对后文的逻辑关系有所准备,即会预期说话人对前述内容表示肯定。

(3) 掌握话语预测能力

预测是一种有理有据的逻辑推理。该策略包括语言系预测和非语言系预测。语言系预测就是译员根据语言规律与规则,如短语搭配、句子之间表示逻辑关系的连接词等来预测说话人下一步所要表达的意思。比如在英语里,介词后面接代词或名词的概率很高,而接另一个介词或动词的概率则很低。非语言系预测主要指译员对讲话中要表达的思想的预测,而非准确无误地预测讲话人的具体措辞。非语言系预测既包括译员的译前预测,又包括在口译过程中所做的预测。口译活动是一种目的性很强的现场言语交际活动,其主题往往事先给定,会议内容、会议话语都与主题紧密联系,为译员提供了大量可帮助其预测下文的信息。例如,2009年5月21日英国驻华大使欧威廉爵士(Sir William Geoffrey Ehrman)访问中国政法大学,并对在座师生发表了讲话。发言人的身份为驻华大使,发言的对象群体是中国政法大学的学生,在这一特定的语境中,译员在大使讲话前就可预测到以下内容:法律在英国的重要性;中英双边关系;法律对于中英关系的意义;对中国学生的美好祝愿与期望。在口译过程中,译者仍然可以继续对语篇进行预测。

(4) 借助冗余信息

在口译的源语发言中,说话人把同一个意思用不同的方式说一遍以上,有时甚至多遍,这一现象为译员在听解过程中提供了不可多得的宝贵机会。有了冗余部分,译员也多了一些自由度,听解的过程会更为从容,译出的语言也会显得通顺流畅。

第六单元 教育论坛

Unit 6 **On Education**

## 第6单元 教育论坛 On Education

# 第1部分 Section 1

### Vocabulary Work

| | | | |
|---|---|---|---|
| address a conference | 在会议上发言 | functional illiteracy | 半文盲,无知 |
| predominantly | 占主导地位的 | election ballot | 选票 |
| income-tax return | 所得税申报表 | life-insurance form | 人寿保险表 |
| all told | 合计,总之 | decipher | 辨认出 |
| poignant | 惨痛的 | antidote | 解毒剂 |
| staggering | 令人惊讶的 | exploitation | 剥削 |
| juvenile offender | 少年犯 | wield | 掌握,运用 |

### 口译实践 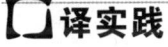 Text Interpreting

**Interpret the following talk into Chinese:**

### Illiterate America

I was once in Detroit to address a conference on the crisis in America's cities. I happened to learn that an astonishing 47 percent of Detroiters, nearly one out of two adults in this predominantly black city, are functionally illiterate. Functional illiteracy relates to the inability of an individual to use reading, writing and computational skills in everyday life: filling out a job application, reading traffic signs, figuring out an election ballot, reading a newspaper, understanding a bus schedule or a product label—or an address on a sheet or paper. In the richest country on earth, 23 percent of adult Americans—44 million men and women—cannot do these things.

If anything, the situation is worse than those statistics suggest, because 50 million more Americans cannot read or comprehend above an eighth-grade level. To appreciate what that means: you need ninth-grade comprehension to understand the instructions for an antidote on an ordinary can of cockroach poison in your kitchen, tenth-grade to follow a federal income-tax return, twelfth-grade comprehension to read a life-insurance form. All told, a staggering percentage of America's adults are in effect, unequipped for life in a modern society.

It's startling enough for foreigners to realize there is such a thing as American illiteracy. More poignant is that, unlike in the developing world, where illiteracy is predominantly a rural problem, in the United States it occurs overwhelmingly in the inner cities, with a heavy concentration among the poor and those dependent on welfare. Nearly half of Detroit's citizens between the ages of 16 and 60, I was told, are jobless and not seeking work. Why? It's a fair guess that most of them do not have the required literacy skills to apply for available jobs, or even to be trained for them.

Business losses attributable to literacy deficiencies cost the United States tens of billions of dollars every year in low productivity, industrial accidents, lawsuits and poor product quality.

What's worse, the standards and requirements for literacy have increased in recent years, as computerization has taken over the world. "You've got mail" may be the defining slogan of our age, but it excludes those who can't decipher their mail, electronic or otherwise. In a world where you can tell the rich from the poor by their Internet connections, the poverty line trips over the high-speed-digital line. The portal to the computer age is the keyboard—but too many Americans literally cannot read the keys.

The cost in terms of lost human potential is devastating. Consider crime. Sixty percent of all juvenile offenders have illiteracy problems; seven out of 10 adult prisoners have low literacy levels, and the current prison population of 2 million represents a dramatic concentration of illiterate Americans. As for those functionally illiterate young man in Detroit, they will always have to rely on others for vital information to lead their lives; they will always be vulnerable to abuse and exploitation by those who wield that one vital skill they don't have.

## 课文注释  Notes on the Text

1. eighth-grade level：包括后文中的 ninth-grade, tenth-grade 都是美国学制的具体年级。在美国学制中，一般说来，从小学到高中共 12 个年级，分别是小学 1—5 年级，初中 6—8 年级，高中 9—12 年级。

2. All told, a staggering percentage of America's adults are in effect, unequipped for life in a modern society. "staggering"在句中本作定语，但如果按原语序直译将使译文主语拖沓难懂，所以将其后置成补语：总之，美国成年人中无法适应现代社会生活的人口百分比实际高得惊人。

3. inner city：即"内城"，从 20 世纪 40 年代末开始，美国城市出现了"城市更新运动"，就是地方当局在联邦资金的帮助下，对城市进行改造，尤其是城市中心区或称为内城的贫民窟，常是黑人聚居的地区，居民收入都比较低。

4. It's a fair guess that most of them do not have the required literacy skills to apply for available jobs, or even to be trained for them. "It's a fair guess"在这里辖指全句，可以放置句末，并采用反译法译出，整句可以译为："他们大多数不具备申请眼下工作所要求的文化技能，甚至达不到接受岗前培训的基本文化要求。这种推测不无道理。"

5. "You've got mail"：美国电影，该片中文译名在香港地区译为《网上情缘》，台湾地区译为《E-mail 情人》，也有译为《电子情书》的。在这片文章中，被作者套用。

6. the poverty line trips over the high-speed-digital line：此处的 trip over 是"在……地方绊倒"的意思，全句可以译为："不通'高速数字'线路，就难免绊倒在贫困线上。"

# 第 6 单元 教育论坛 On Education

## 词语扩展 Developing Vocabulary and Expressions

| | |
|---|---|
| after-class instruction/coaching | 课外辅导 |
| auditor | 旁听生 |
| board of examiners | 考试团 |
| brain drain | 人才流失 |
| campus digitalization | 校园数字化 |
| case study teaching | 实例化教学 |
| heuristic education | 启发式教学 |
| competition for talented people | 人才战 |
| comprehensive quality | 综合素质 |
| short course | 短训班 |
| cultivate one's taste (temperament) | 陶冶情操 |
| education with record of formal schooling | 学历教育 |
| enrolment rate for children of school age | 适龄儿童入学率 |
| enrolment/dropout rate | 入/失学率 |
| GRE (Graduate Record Examination) | (美国)研究生资格考试 |
| hot spots of society | 社会热点问题 |
| illiterate or half illiterate | 文盲和半文盲 |
| intellectual support | 智力支持 |
| literacy class | 扫盲班 |
| on-the-job doctorate | 在职博士生 |
| on-the-job postgraduate | 在职研究生 |
| (thesis) oral defense | 论文答辩 |
| physique; physical constitution | 身体素质 |
| recruit / introduce (foreign) talents | 智力引进 |
| regular higher education | 普通高等教育 |
| technical school student | 中专生 |
| self-taught examination | 自学考试 |
| students' affairs division | 学生处 |
| talent highland | 人才高地 |
| talents exchange | 人才交流 |
| acquire a particular skill | 学到一技之长 |
| eliminate illiteracy | 扫盲 |
| wipe out/eliminate illiteracy among youth and adults | 扫除青壮年文盲 |
| part-work and part-study system; work-study program | 勤工俭学 |
| running of schools by non-governmental sectors | 社会力量办学 |

## 口译操练  Interpreting Practice

### 1. 听译 ▶▶ Listening Interpreting

**A.** Listen to the sentences and interpret them into Chinese.
Sentences 1—10

**B.** Listen to the paragraphs and interpret them into Chinese.
Paragraphs 1—2

### 2. 情景练习 ▶▶ Situational Interpreting

Interpret the following conversation alternatively into English and Chinese：

> **Roles**
> Jane：an American exchange student studying in China
> Miss Huang：a Chinese university student
> Miss Chen：an interpreter

Jane： Today I'm very glad to have this opportunity to talk with you on the worldwide problem of illiteracy elimination.

Huang：是啊,这是个比较严肃的话题。

Jane： Have you ever heard of "the United Nations Literacy Decade"? That is a program named "Education for All," launched at UN Headquarters on 13 February 2003. It is spearheaded by UNESCO, as the lead agency for the decade. "Literacy as Freedom" is the theme of the decade.

Huang：听说过。可见扫盲任务之重大。但我认为扫盲的内容不只是包括读和写——它还关系到我们如何在社会中进行交流,涉及社会活动、社会关系、知识、语言和文化。在我们的生活中,识字教育,或者说用书面交流,与其他交流方式一样重要。

Jane： Yes. Literacy takes many forms：in reading a paper, typing, or seeing a movie, etc. Those who use literacy take it for granted, but those who cannot use it are excluded from the information exchanges in today's world.

Huang：确实,仅仅识字本身,形式多样,在当今社会中,识字的人交流当然没什么障碍,而对那些文盲则不然,正是这些被排除在外的人才能深切体会到"识字即自由"的真正含义。

Jane： But as far as I know, the definition of "illiteracy" seems to have changed, or extended a lot. Illiteracy means not only being unable to read or write, but the inability to learn in this information era and knowledge-based economy.

Huang：我很同意你的看法,而且我认为,扫盲也绝不仅是一两个国际机构或政府部门的任务,它需要所有人的关心和支持。我们大学生更是责无旁贷。

Jane： Yes. Anyway, I believe the problem will be and can be solved as long as all the efforts from UNESCO's to ours are combined.

# 第6单元 教育论坛 On Education

# 第2部分 Section 2

## 词汇预习  Vocabulary Work

| | | | |
|---|---|---|---|
| 人格发展 | development of personality | 屡见于…… | make frequent appearances in |
| 热潮 | surge of enthusiasm | | |
| 双语教育 | bilingual education | 排斥 | feel repulsion (toward) |
| 国耻 | national disgrace | 主导地位 | dominant place |
| 霸权 | hegemony | 远程教育 | distance education |
| 市场调研公司 | market research company | 语言群体 | linguistic community |
| 分化成 | fragment into... | 民族认同感 | national identity |
| 方言 | vernacular tongue | 人口发展趋势 | demographic trends |
| 洋泾浜英语 | pidgin English | | |

## 口译实践  Text Interpreting

Interpret the following conversation alternatively into English and Chinese:

### 关于学习英语的讨论

A: 我最近听说国家教育部门表示,幼儿园不能全英语进行教学,也不能将英语列为科目教学,引用某些人的话就是,"以免对幼儿的人格发展带来负面影响"。

B: Is that true?

A: 是的,至少媒体是这样报道的。但是,以我的观察,现在在中国甚至是全世界,许多地区和国家都掀起了学习外语,尤其是学习英语的热潮,"双语教育"的字眼也屡屡见于报端。

B: You do have sharp eyes! And that's part of the reasons why I have come from the United States to Shanghai here. You know, I have been working here as an English teacher for about two years.

A: 说到学习英语,教育界许多人士认为,语言学习最好由近到远,先学好母语再学英语。幼儿越早学习英文,也越早有挫折感,反而提早排斥英文。而且,儿童在幼儿园有很多东西要学,幼儿情绪的发展、观察能力的培养比英语更重要,如果用英语阻碍了其他能力的发展,对孩子的一生很不利。

B: That's absolutely true. Though I am myself an English teacher, I think anyone who learns English, whether he is from China or from any other country, should adopt a reasonable, or wise attitude. I have learned that Mr. Gao Zhendong, a well-known principal in Taiwan once remarked that learning English is a national disgrace for all the Chinese. I'm afraid his reaction is somewhat irrational, but I do appreciate his pride in his native tongue.

A: 是的,掌握好母语的确十分重要,是学习其他语言和文化的基础。您作为一位美国人,您对英语如今在世界日趋于主导的地位如何看呢?

B: An estimated 335 million people speak English as mother tongue—fewer than those who speak Spanish or Mandarin—and demographic trends indicate that native English speakers will decline as a proportion of the world's population. Probably more than 1 billion people speak English with varying degrees of proficiency as a second language. But has English become the global language of communication and education? The question might seem obvious, but the answer is not so simple.

A: 不错,英语是商贸和科技的国际性语言,而且它的使用范围也扩大了,因为迄今为止它还是推动互联网发展的首要语言。但是这种情况在开始改变,而且速度很快。我们越来越多地注意到其他语言开始在因特网上盛行起来。像俄语、德语、西班牙语、汉语这些语言的使用频率在因特网上正迅猛增加。其他语言也开始挑战英语在远程教育领域的霸权地位。我还听说一家市场调研公司的调查结果显示,目前因特网使用者中以英语为母语的人不足五成,而这个比例还一直在下降。

B: Yes, indeed. English, like Latin before it, has become a language that is no longer the property of its native speakers, and like Latin, it too may give way to a variety of vernacular tongues. English is so important in some countries that people use it in part to create their own social and even national identity. When that happens, the language starts going its own way. The very reason for the rise of English, that is, its function as a guarantee of mutual understanding among people of different cultures might dissolve if the language continues to fragment into a variety of "Englishes."

A: 照你这么说,虽然英语仍然是世界交际性语言,但是将来人们将说着各自的洋泾浜英语走到一起来。这就是说,也许有一天会有一场保卫纯正英语的运动了!

## 课文注释  Notes on the Text

1. 现在在中国甚至是全世界,许多地区和国家都掀起了学习外语,尤其是学习英语的热潮。这句话译为较为客观的存在句为宜,可以选用 there be 的结构,全句可译为: There has been a surge of enthusiasm of learning foreign languages, especially English, in both China and other regions and countries of the world.

2. 语言学习最好由近到远,先学好母语再学英语。"由近到远"实质就是"循序渐进",因此可译为 step by step 或 gradually.

3. 幼儿越早学习英文,也越早有挫折感,反而提早排斥英文。此句翻译较难,要把握好主要结构,分清主次,全句可译为: The sooner a child learns English, the more probable he or she might be frustrated in the process, which might in turn make the child feel repulsion toward the foreign language from the beginning.

4. I'm afraid his reaction is somewhat irrational, but I do appreciate his pride in his

native tongue. irrational 本意指不理智的,结合 reaction 译为"过于激烈了",后半句原文很精练,译为"但我很欣赏他为自己的母语自豪的心情"。

5. and like Latin, it too may give way to a variety of vernacular tongues. give way to 指的是"让位于,为……所替代",此句可以译为:"像拉丁语一样,英语也可能分裂为一些不同的地方性语言。"

## 词语扩展  *Developing Vocabulary and Expressions*

- 保证学生身心健康成长 ensure the healthy physical and mental growth of students
- 成为有理想,有道德,有文化,守纪律的劳动者 become working people with lofty ideals, moral integrity, education and a sense of discipline
- 创新精神 be innovation-minded; have a creative mind
- 辍/失学青少年 school dropout/leaver
- 德才兼备 combine ability with character; equal stress on integrity and ability
- 德智体全面发展 well developed morally, intellectually and physically
- 定向招生 admit students to be trained for pre-determined employers
- 发挥学生主动性、创造性 to give scope to the students' initiative and creativeness
- 高度重视精神文明建设 pay close attention to cultural and ethical progress
- 弘扬民族优秀文化 advance and enrich the fine cultural heritage of the nation
- 积极发展民办教育 make efforts to develop schools operated by non-government education departments
- 基本普及九年制义务教育 accomplish general outreach of 9-year compulsory education
- 基本扫除青壮年文盲 general elimination of illiteracy among the young and middle-aged
- 教学、科研、生产的三结合 integration of teaching, research and production
- 具有中国特色的社会主义教育体系 an education system with distinct Chinese characteristics
- 科教兴国 rejuvenate the country through science and education
- 面向现代化、面向世界、面向未来 gear education to the needs of modernization, the world and the future
- 培养创新精神和实践能力 help students develop practical abilities and a spirit of innovation
- 培养独立分析问题和解决问题的能力 cultivate the ability to analyze and solve concrete problems independently
- 培养复合型人才 produce students with interdisciplinary knowledge and well-rounded abilities
- 培养学生自学能力 foster the students' ability to study on their own
- 片面追求升学率 place undue emphasis on the proportion of students entering schools of a higher level
- 启发学生独立思考的能力 help develop the ability of the students to think independently
- 切实减轻中小学生过重的课业负担 effectively reduce too heavy homework assignments for primary and secondary school students
- 全面推进素质教育 provide an education with all-round development in all schools

and institutions of higher-learning
- 人才枯竭 exhaustion of human resources
- 实现高等教育大众化 strive for providing higher education to the majority of people
- 树立正确的世界观、人生观、价值观 instill/foster a sound outlook on the world, life and values
- 填鸭式教学法 cramming/forced-feeding method of teaching
- 推进素质教育 push ahead quality education for all-round development
- 优化教师队伍 optimize the teaching staff
- 增强综合国力 enhance the overall strength of the country
- 争取实现高等教育大众化 work to make regular higher education accessible to the majority of the young people

## 口译操练 Interpreting Practice

### 1. 听译 Listening Interpreting

A. Listen to the sentences and interpret them into English.
Sentences 1—10

B. Listen to the paragraphs and interpret them into English.
Paragraphs 1—2

### 2. 情景练习 Situational Interpreting

Interpret based on the information given. Add any information when necessary.

Roles
黄老师：某大学留学生处主任
严小姐：翻译

黄老师在新学期开始时对刚入学的英语国家留学生做了一次关于汉语学习的报告。他报告的主要内容有：

- 学习第二语言的重要性。在21世纪，人类生产力高度发展，科学技术的发展既打破国界又打破学科界限。从社会方面而言，不同民族、国家的人相互接触和交往的首要条件是语言相通；从个人方面而言，学习第二语言，熟悉不同种文化将促使人的智力的性质和结构发生变化。
- 学习好汉语对留学生的意义。在英语之外，汉语不但是使用人数最多的语言，而且是四大文明古国中唯一得以延续至今的中华文明的文化载体。汉字的象形特点时时刻刻把我们的想象拉近现实世界，使我们心中浑然不觉地产生物我交流的境界。学习汉语有利于打破东西方文明的樊篱，加强东西方文化交流。
- 留学生学习汉语对汉语本身的意义。苏轼有名句道："不识庐山真面目，只缘身在此山中。"我们往往对第二语言具备对母语所没有的新鲜感和好奇心。留学生学汉语往往会从某种全新的角度加深对汉语的理解，丰富汉语的内涵和表达法。
- 黄老师给留学生提供了一些具体的学习汉语的经验和方法。

## 第6单元 教育论坛 On Education

### 口译常识与技巧  *Interpreting Tips and Skills*

**口译的笔记(Taking Quick Notes)(1)**

　　口译的理解始于听觉感知,听觉感知接收语音符码,进入理解阶段。记忆几乎和理解同时发生,记忆可以使信息在理解转码过程中不至于丢失,理解是记忆的基础。口译成功与否在很大程度上取决于译员的记忆力,确切地说是取决于译员的短时记忆能力。而短时记忆是有其自身规律的,口译的时候必须要遵循并利用短时记忆的规律。短时记忆是指信息保持在一分钟以内的记忆,若不设法保持,信息就会从短时记忆中消失,因此口译中,尤其是大段口译中,笔记是必要的。虽然因为个人习惯等差异,每个人的笔记方式不尽相同,但是人们一致认为口译中笔记是一大关键和难题,一个好的笔记往往是口译成功的关键。好的笔记要基本做到两点:第一,必须掌握主要思想;第二,要做到在有限的时间里尽可能多地记下所听到的细节。具体地说就是在听的时候,不能拘泥于个别字词的理解,而是要整体把握句子的大意,这是正确口译的前提。

　　口译中时间是非常短暂的,在短暂的时间内,要把整个句子记下来,几乎是不可能的,因此口译笔记应该简短、清晰、易辨,寥寥几个关键词,能为理解后的表达起到很好的提示作用。笔记时应该记下的是数字、机构等关键词,而对那些英汉语句子构成中不可避免的一些连接词、功能词,省略不记录对句子的翻译不会产生太大影响。关键词,再加上符号、缩写、简写等笔记方法一起使用,才是科学的笔记方法。以下列举一部分符号,供大家参考使用:

| 信息意义 | 速记符号 |
|---|---|
| 出口、输出、向前、到达 <br> 前往、派遣、交给、导致 <br> 屈服于、打入、造成 | → |
| 来自、源于、进口、收到 <br> 回归、回顾、是……的结果 | ← |
| 增长、扩大、提高、上升 <br> 发展、提拔、起飞、发射 | ↑ |
| 减少、下降、向下、下调 <br> 降职、削减、恶化、裁减 | ↓ |
| 渐渐好转;上扬;越来越好 | ↗ |
| 不断亏损;下挫 | ↘ |
| 双向交流 | ⇄ |
| 交换 | ↻ |
| 加上、此外 | + |
| 减去、缺乏、删除 | — |
| 对的、正确、好的 | √ |
| 不对、错的、不好的 | × |
| 问题、疑问、问 | ? |
| 因为 | ∵ |
| 所以 | ∴ |
| 包括,在……之内 | ( ) |
| 会议,研讨会 | ⊙ |
| 国家 | 囗 |
| 国与国 | 囗/囗 |

|  |  |
|---|---|
| 对立、冲突 | ><  |
| 替换为 | S |
| 最佳的、杰出的 | ☆ |
| 分歧 | ⊥ |
| 属于 | ∈ |
| 胜利 | V |
| 结论是 | ⇨ |
| 一方面 | ./ |
| 另一方面 | /. |
| 关系 | ./. |
| 和……一道 | & |
| 接触、交往 | ∞ |
| 停顿、中止 | // |
| 代表 | △ |
| 去年 | .y |
| 前年 | ..y |
| 明年 | y. |
| 后年 | y.. |
| 总和 | Σ |

举例1：

首先，请允许我代表我们公司及全体成员，并以我个人的名义，对董事长先生和美国的同行们，表示衷心的感谢。

Notes： 1st
△ 公司
成员
个人
→ Chair.
US 同行
TKS//

举例2：

We know that there is a big deficit between France and England and between France and Canada. Would you explain whether there is difference between the two kinds of trade deficits, and what France policies towards the two different kinds of trade deficits are? We think you are adopting double standards.

Notes： 赤 F & UK
F & CAN ? 区
? F pol
双标//

# 第 7 单元 人物访谈

## Unit 7 Interviews

# 第7单元 人物访谈 Interviews

# 第1部分 Section 1

##  Vocabulary Work

| | | | |
|---|---|---|---|
| debut | 首张（唱片） | vocalist | 歌手 |
| icing | 糖衣 | play pool | 打桌球 |
| a cappella constructively | 积极地 | gigs | 演奏会 |
| a cappella | 无伴奏演唱 | aspiring | 有抱负的 |

##  Text Interpreting

Interpret the following interview alternatively into English and Chinese:

### An Interview with a Songwriter

*Mary Smith (S), songwriter, recently spoke to a journalist (J) about her debut album, "One Moment More," and her writing method.*

J：对媒体，你有什么忌讳吗？

S：No, inquiries are fine, because as long as people are asking questions, I'm doing okay.

J：你把你的专辑献给你的母亲。请问她对你的人生道路有着什么样的影响？

S：She was a vocalist and one of my best friends. I adored her. She was a tremendous individual on so many levels：spiritual and musical.

J：在创作方面，你有没有不同寻常的写作方式？

S：Well, I start with the music. I try to be melodic first and then I go ahead and see if the words will come. Generally, if the music isn't happening, nine out of ten times the words aren't happening.

J：你的专辑有没有一个主题？

S：I don't know if there is a message. I think it's just honesty. It's just the way I've experienced it. I'm just expressing myself. Songwriting is like looking at a painting. It is an expression of my personal experiences, and if people find that interesting, then that's the icing on the cake.

J：歌曲创作有助于你从个人经历中解脱出来吗？

S：I think any creative avenue, any creative outlet, is a way to sort out your issues or emotional distress. A lot of people are encouraged to do that, and I definitely encourage that. Be it art, music, poetry, or journalism. Creativity is important. People who lack that gift appreciate others' ability. People say to me:"Thank you, I didn't know how to put that in words or how to get that image on paper." That's been my experience; people are very kind to me. Creativity is definitely a great element in coping with life.

J: 你有什么业余爱好?

S: I enjoy catching up with my friends, 'cause I'm rarely at home. With that said, my favorite recreational activity is playing pool. I also like to see my friends' bands play. I also enjoy painting or drawing, when I get around to it.

J: 你还记得你参加的第一次演奏会吗?

S: I was in a band for a short time when I lived in a small town and we did a show. The band broke up two weeks later. We didn't have a name, but it was fun. When I got to New York, I started playing at a place in an area known as the Old City. Those were really my first gigs, and I didn't even play guitar then, I just sang a cappella. I didn't know how to play the guitar until I was 24.

J: 用三个词来总结一下自己。

S: I'm complex, a free spirit, and I just love making music. Three words: complex, free-spirited, musician. How's that?

J: 很好呀!

S: It's good because I don't make any sense.

J: 你对希望当歌手或者词曲作家的人有什么建议?

S: Take criticism constructively. It's not fun when you get criticized, but it does help you with endurance. If you learn early that not everyone is going to love what you do, it's easier to cope. Nine times out of ten, if one person gets it, everyone else wants to get it. You should just stick with it if you're driven. I would suggest keeping writing and making your own music. When it works out, it is incredibly rewarding to use your own material, which sometimes takes a while. For me it took ten years, for some people it takes significantly less, and for others it never happens. Maintain your love for music. That will carry you through. Don't make it about money and don't make it about fame. I think that will make it a lot easier.

## 课文注释  Notes on the Text

1. that's the icing on the cake:"the icing on the cake"的字面意思是"蛋糕上的糖衣",其真正的含义是"锦上添花"或者"好上加好",此处可译为:"那就再好不过了。"例如,"It was a great party, but meeting you here was just the icing on the cake."意思是:"这个晚会不错,又在这里遇见你,真是锦上添花。"

2. I also enjoy painting or drawing, when I get around to it:get around to (doing) sth. 的意思是"终于找到时间做一直想做的事情"。此句可以译为:"如果真有时间,我还喜欢画油画或者素描。"例如:"I'll get around decorating the house one of these days."意思是:"这几天我要找时间把房子布置一下。"

3. The band broke up two weeks later. break up 的意思是"解散"或"散伙",此句的意思是:"两周后那个乐队就解散了。"例如:The marriage broke up just a few years later. 意思是:"仅仅几年后婚姻就破裂了。"

4. I'm complex, a free spirit, and I just love making music. free spirit 指的是 a person who lives life the way he/she wants to and does not care about rules and customs, 也就是"无拘无束的人"。此句意思是:"我很复杂,无拘无束,热爱音乐制作。"
5. When it works out, it is incredibly rewarding to use your own material: work out 是"带来好结果"或"有预期的结果"之义,整句可译为:"如果成功的话,使用自己的材料会有意想不到的丰厚回报。"再如: If it doesn't work out, you can always come back here. 可译为:"如果不行,你随时可以回到这儿来。"

## 词语扩展 *Developing Vocabulary and Expressions*

| | |
|---|---|
| ❖ Album of the Year | 年度专辑奖(年度最佳专辑) |
| ❖ aria | 咏叹调 |
| ❖ chorus troupe | 合唱团 |
| ❖ Christmas carol | 圣诞颂歌 |
| ❖ composers alliance | 作曲家联盟 |
| ❖ concord | 和声 |
| ❖ curtain time | 音乐会开演时间 |
| ❖ elegy | 挽歌 |
| ❖ ethnic music | 民族音乐 |
| ❖ finale | 尾曲(终曲) |
| ❖ folk music association | 民间音乐协会 |
| ❖ impromptu concert | 即席音乐会 |
| ❖ instrumental music | 器乐 |
| ❖ meditation | 冥想曲 |
| ❖ orchestral performance | 弦乐队演出 |
| ❖ pastoral song | 牧歌 |
| ❖ percussion group | 打击乐队 |
| ❖ prelude | 前奏曲 |
| ❖ repertoire | 演唱曲目 |
| ❖ rhapsody | 狂想曲 |
| ❖ rhythm and blues | 节奏与蓝调音乐 |
| ❖ serenade | 小夜曲 |
| ❖ solo concert | 独奏音乐会(独唱音乐会) |
| ❖ sonata | 奏鸣曲 |
| ❖ Song of the Year | 年度最佳单曲 |
| ❖ soul Gospel music | 灵魂音乐 |
| ❖ staff | 五线谱 |
| ❖ string quartet | 弦乐四重奏 |
| ❖ symphony orchestra | 交响乐团 |
| ❖ the Grammy Awards | 格莱美奖 |
| ❖ traditional instrumental band | 民乐队(传统乐器乐队) |
| ❖ tuning | 演出前调弦 |
| ❖ violin concerto | 小提琴协奏曲 |
| ❖ vocal accompanist | 伴唱人员 |
| ❖ world tour | 世界巡回演出 |

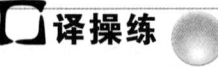 **Interpreting Practice**

### 1. 听译 ▶▶ Listening Interpreting

A. Listen to the sentences and interpret them into Chinese.
   Sentences 1—10

B. Listen to the paragraphs and interpret them into Chinese.
   Paragraphs 1—2

### 2. 情景练习 ▶▶ Situational Interpreting

Interpret based on the information given. Add any information when necessary.

> **Roles**
> Mr. Wong: Editor of *Arts Magazine*
> Edward Smith: an American Actor
> Miss Chen: an interpreter

Mr. Wong is having a conversation with Edward Smith about his education, experience, hobbies, and future plans. The following information may be useful:

- Edward Smith switched from teaching to acting when he was thirty-one years old.
- He has been awarded several national and international prizes since then.
- His recent film was *When I Was Younger*, which secured him the Best Actor prize in a French festival.
- Edward Smith likes golf, chess, and mountaineering.
- He has contributed a lot to an international charity organization for the disabled.

# 第7单元 人物访谈 Interviews

# 第2部分 Section 2

## 词汇预习  Vocabulary Work

| | | | |
|---|---|---|---|
| 冰球 | hockey | 精准优美 | concision and elegance |
| 载体 | carrier | 中国人智慧的结晶 | the legacy of Chinese wisdom |
| 仁爱民本 | benevolence and love of people | 和而不同 | pursuit of harmony without uniformity |
| 枫糖 | maple syrup | | |
| 斯坦利杯（冰球联赛） | Stanley Cup Playoffs | | |

## 口译实践  Text Interpreting

Interpret the following interview alternatively into English and Chinese：

### 一场有关学习汉语的对话

中华文化促进会主席（P）和对汉语学习感兴趣的加拿大学生（S）展开对话。

S：Mr. President, it's a real honor for us to have a dialogue with you about China and Chinese language. Every student present today is very interested in Chinese and the Chinese culture.

P：和大家谈话，我也很高兴。我来加拿大已有一个星期，走了许多地方，接触到许多人，令我吃惊，后来又习惯的是，许多加拿大人，年龄比你们大，都喜欢用汉语同我交谈，让我又兴奋，又失落。兴奋的是有越来越多的加拿大人了解中国或正在了解中国。失落的是今后我在这里用英语的场合就比较少了，这对我提高我的英语水平可不是个好消息。

S：Would you please give us students some suggestions on learning Chinese?

P：当然可以。对你们当中那些学汉语轻而易举的人，我想借现在中国年轻人中最流行的形容词夸一句：你们真"给力"。对你们当中那些曾为学汉语伤脑筋的人，我想说：别担心，我们当年学外语也是这么过来的。就我个人经历来看，无论是学汉语、英语还是法语，都跟打冰球一样，要做到三件事，就是练习，练习，再练习。当你决定修这门说话像唱歌，写字像画画，同音不同字，同字不同音的语言时，很难有捷径可走。所以有人感叹道，汉语能学好，什么事都难不倒。正如冰球对你们来说不只是一项运动一样，汉语也不仅仅是一个交流的工具。它是中华文化的载体、中国人智慧的结晶,更是一种独特的生活与思维方式。

S: I find, in my course of study, I learn not only the tones but also China's 5000 years of history and culture.

P: 是的。你们对汉语的学习,学到的远不止汉字的精准优美,还有中国人主张的仁爱民本、和而不同等哲学理念。你们对汉语的运用,用到的将不只是成语典故,还有中国看自己、看世界的角度和思路。这就是为什么从伦敦到新德里再到渥太华超百万你们的同龄人将汉语作为优先选修的外语。这就是为什么越来越多的青年人选择到中国留学。这也是为什么全球有超过一亿来自不同国家、不同行业的人在学习和使用汉语,刮起一股"汉语热"。

S: Do you agree with the saying that there's no better time to learn Chinese here than now?

P: 是的。近年来,中加两国在经贸、旅游、文化、教育和民间交往等方面合作愈加紧密。越来越多的加拿大企业到中国做生意,中国企业也纷纷将目光投向加拿大。去年6月以来,有超过50万中国游客来加拿大赏湖光山色,品冰酒枫糖,看斯坦利杯。目前,超过12万名中国留学生在加深造,你们或许已经结识了不少来自中国的伙伴。中加伙伴关系的延续与深化需要你们这样既能讲英语、法语,又懂汉语、熟悉两国情况的人才。

S: But I think the best place to learn Chinese is still China.

P: 这是毫无疑问的。中国政府为加拿大学生设立了赴华奖学金,鼓励你们和你们的同学去中国攻读学位或短期交流,多走走,多看看,亲身感受当地的发展变化、风土人情,跟中国大学生们交流与互动。同时,中国的年轻人们也在努力学习英语、法语。他们也期待着同你们一起探讨感兴趣的话题,了解加拿大的现在和过去。我相信你们将为中加友谊、中加合作添砖加瓦。最后,祝大家学习进步、美梦成真。

## 课文注释  Notes on the Text

1. 对你们当中那些学汉语轻而易举的人,我想借现在中国年轻人中最流行的形容词夸一句:你们真"给力"。这句"你们真给力"是说话人刻意突出的流行语,所以可选择将汉语照搬,同时为了减少理解的困惑,应在之后再加上适当的解释 meaning You Rock。You Rock 在英语口语中,用来表示"太棒了!"也就是"给力"的意思。

2. 当你决定修这门说话像唱歌,写字像画画,同音不同字,同字不同音的语言时,很难有捷径可走。"这门说话像唱歌,写字像画画,同音不同字,同字不同音的语言"这一宾语很长,翻译的时候不能慌乱,要先找到中心词,即"语言",再定位逻辑关系,选定关系代词之后,在从句中补充主语"人们",依次逐层处理,可译为 a language where people talk like singing, write like sketching, different characters sound the same, same character reads differently.

3. 全球有超过4000万来自不同国家、不同行业的人在学习汉语,刮起一股"汉语热"。这句话是典型的汉语表达,句意连贯,句式松散,在翻译时可以进行适当的整合。全句可以用 Chinese 来做主语,可以译为: Chinese is riding a wave of popularity with more than 40 million learners around the world.

4. 品冰酒枫糖,看斯坦利杯。这三者都是加拿大的著名象征,其中斯坦利杯指的是加拿大人特别热衷的冰球联赛,可译为 ice wine, maple syrup and their favorite teams in the Stanley Cup Playoffs.

5. 期待你们为中加友谊、中加合作添砖加瓦。汉语往往多具体表达,而英语则多抽象表达,因此如"添砖加瓦"之类的词语可以去除那些具体的意象,在此句中可用 contribute a unique share to 这样的习惯表达。

## 词语扩展  Developing Vocabulary and Expressions

- 笔力　　　　　　　　vigor of strokes
- 笔顺　　　　　　　　order of strokes
- 繁体字　　　　　　　traditional character
- 工作语言　　　　　　working language
- 古体诗　　　　　　　classical style poetry
- 官方语言　　　　　　official language
- 国际化　　　　　　　internationalization/globalization
- 汉字体系　　　　　　Chinese character system
- 横批(横轴)　　　　　horizontal scroll
- 计算机辅助教学　　　computer-assisted instruction
- 简化字　　　　　　　Chinese mainland simplified character
- 近体诗　　　　　　　modern style poetry
- 卷轴题词　　　　　　inscrolling
- 科技英语　　　　　　English for science and technology
- 描红　　　　　　　　trace in black ink over character printed in red
- 铭文　　　　　　　　epigraph, inscription
- 墨宝　　　　　　　　treasured scroll of calligraphy
- 目标语　　　　　　　target language
- 普通英语　　　　　　general English
- 商贸英语　　　　　　business English
- 少数民族语言　　　　minority language
- 书法　　　　　　　　Chinese calligraphy
- 水平考试　　　　　　proficiency test
- 特殊用途英语　　　　English for special purposes
- 题词　　　　　　　　autograph; dedicatory script
- 习字帖　　　　　　　copybook, calligraphy model
- 语法结构　　　　　　grammatical structure
- 语言行为　　　　　　linguistic behavior/performance
- 语言环境　　　　　　language environment
- 语言能力　　　　　　linguistic competence
- 语言习得　　　　　　language acquisition
- 语言知识　　　　　　linguistic knowledge
- 源语　　　　　　　　source language
- 职业英语　　　　　　vocational English
- 字根　　　　　　　　radical

**Interpreting Practice**

### 1. 听译　Listening Interpreting

A. Listen to the sentences and interpret them into English.
   Sentences 1—10

B. Listen to the paragraphs and interpret them into English.
   Paragraphs 1—2

### 2. 情景练习　Situational Interpreting

Interpret based on the information given. Add any information when necessary.

> **Roles**
> 张教授：大学英语系教授
> Edward Smith：美国记者
> 陈小姐：翻译

Edward Smith 在采访张教授。谈话中涉及下列内容：
- 英语的普及情况：所有中小学和大学都开设英语课程；在求职的时候，很多用人单位都要求一定英语水平；不少学生到美国等英语国家深造，事先也要参加托福（TOEFL）和雅思（IELTS）等国际考试。
- 学校英语的教育现状：学生在学校主要学习语法和阅读，不大重视口语交际能力的培养，书面表达能力也在很大程度上被忽视了。
- 对英语的看法：大部分人认为英语目前已经发展成为一门很重要的国际语言（international English），英语已经成为个人事业发展的必需工具。但是，也有不少教育家认为不应盲目强调英语的重要性，应该保持并弘扬自己的传统、语言和文化。还有人认为，汉语的地位不断提升，总有一日会和英语平分秋色。
- 英语国际化对英语教育的影响：在重视英语教育的同时，应该采取措施加强汉语能力的培训。

 **Interpreting Tips and Skills**

#### 口译的笔记（Taking Quick Notes）（2）

笔记是高级口译的关键。使用笔记，是为了补充大脑短期记忆和耐久力的不足，以保证译文的精确度，并保证其不受讲话人持续时间的影响。记笔记并不是把讲话者的原话一字不落地全部记下来，而是将听到的话按意思记下来。除了使用符号，简写和缩写也是节约时间的笔记方法之一。笔记中常用的简写很多，例如：

| | |
|---|---|
| cf | compared with |
| e.g. | for example |
| ibid | in the same place of a book or article |
| i.e. | that is |

| | |
|---|---|
| viz | namely |
| coo | cooperation |
| corp | corporation |
| eco | economy; economic |
| sicio | society; social |
| stab | stability; stable |
| poli | political; politics |
| cul | cultural; culture |
| bene | benefit; beneficial |
| pro | promote; promotion |
| C | China; Chinese |

简写不一定是约定俗成的,也可以根据自己的习惯将之简写,如:China Travel Service 就可以简写为 C tra serv,也可以简写为 C travel S 等。

缩写词不仅以文字形式广泛出现在报纸杂志上,在有声形式的口译中也频频出现。缩写词的广泛应用一方面对口译员在有限时间里完整地翻译出其意义提出了更高的要求,口译人员需要熟记诸多常用的缩写词,才能在口译时准确地翻译出所听到的缩写词的意思。口译中对组织机构名称的正确翻译是非常重要的,然而它们往往很长,缩写不失为记录组织机构名称的简便方法。例如,如果听到 International Monetary Fund,笔记上就可以直接写成 IMF。常用的缩写组织机构名称很多,例如:

| | |
|---|---|
| APEC | 亚太经合组织(Asia-Pacific Economic Cooperation) |
| MFA | 外交部(Ministry of Foreign Affairs) |
| GDP | 国内生产总值(Gross Domestic Production) |
| GNP | 国民生产总值(Gross National Production) |
| ADB | 亚洲开发银行(Asian Development Bank) |
| ASEAN | 东南亚国家联盟(Association of Southeast Asian Nations) |
| CEEC | 欧洲经济合作委员会(Committee for European Economic Cooperation) |
| CTC | 贸易合作委员会(Committee on Trade Cooperation) |
| EU | 欧盟(European Union) |
| EEC | 欧洲经济共同体(European Economic Community) |
| EMU | 欧洲货币联盟(European Monetary Union) |
| IAEA | 国际原子能机构(International Atomic Energy Agency) |
| IMF | 国际货币基金组织(International Monetary Fund) |
| NATO | 北大西洋公约组织(North Atlantic Treaty Organization) |
| UN | 联合国(United Nations) |
| UNFAO | 联合国粮农组织(United Nations Food and Agricultural Organization) |
| ILO | 国际劳工组织(International Labor Organization) |
| UNICEF | 联合国儿童基金会(United Nations Children's Fund) |
| UNDP | 联合国国际开发署(United Nations Development Program) |
| UNESCO | 联合国教科文组织(United Nations Educational, Scientific and Cultural Organization) |
| WHO | 世界卫生组织(World Health Organization) |
| WTO | 世界贸易组织(World Trade Organization) |

值得一提的是,在使用缩写语口译的时候也要根据具体情况做不同处理,不能随

意,如 EPT(English Proficiency Test)是中国教育部为出国人员组织的"英语水平测试"。如果给英国人翻译时就不要翻译为 EPT,而要将全文翻译出去,否则,英国人可能将之误认为是他们的 EPT,即 Early Pregnancy Test(早孕测试)。

简写和缩写的方式很多,每个人都应该形成自己熟练而又独特的简写和缩写方式,简写和缩写可以节约更多的时间,使口译人员更好、更准确地翻译。

## 技巧练习 Exercises for Skills

**Do the note-taking for the following information. You may use some of your own symbols.**

(1) 美国是中国第二大贸易伙伴,中国是美国第四大贸易伙伴。中国是美国汽车的第一大买主。到目前为止,总计购买了 240,980 辆,这个月又签订了购买 500 辆的合同和 300 辆的意向合同。中国还是美国小麦的第二大买主。随着经济的不断发展,中国将进一步扩大美国产品的进口。

(2) In 1980, there were no McDonalds' in China. Last year there were over 500. In 1980, there were no Chinese restaurants in the United States; last year there were over 150. In 1980, there were no exchange students between the universities from US and China; last year, there were over 2000.

# 第 8 单元 文化交流

## Unit 8 Cultural Exchange

# 第8单元 文化交流 Cultural Exchange

# 第1部分 Section 1

## 词汇预习 Vocabulary Work

| | | | |
|---|---|---|---|
| Little Mermaid | 小美人鱼 | pretentious | 自命不凡的 |
| bronze sculpture | 青铜雕塑 | graffiti | 涂鸦 |
| vandal | 破坏文化遗产的人 | crane | 吊车 |
| manual | 指导手册 | Langelinie | 长堤公园 |

## 口译实践 Text Interpreting

**Interpret the following dialogue alternatively into English and Chinese:**

The famous Danish stonecutter 46-year-old Flemming Brian Nielsen is going to make sure that the famous Little Mermaid is seen off from her spot in Copenhagen and arrives safely in Shanghai. He has worked as a stonecutter for 30 years and during his career, he has created new sculptures for artists, renovated old ones and moved them from one spot to another. The following is a dialogue between Flemming(F) and a journalist(J) on the Little Mermaid's trip to China.

J: 为什么您会被邀请搬移小美人鱼？

F: There is a very small market for this kind of business and, though it might sound pretentious, I am the most experienced in this field. It is impossible for me to keep track on how many statues and works of art I have moved but it must be several thousands.

J: 您以前有参与过涉及小美人鱼的工作吗？

F: Not really, because she is made out of bronze and I work with stone. But I did remove some graffiti from her once in the early 80s after she had been targeted by vandals.

J: 您将怎样搬移小美人鱼？

F: First I will measure up exactly how she sits on her rock at Langelinie so that she is placed in the same way in China. I will separate her from the rock underneath her, and later she will be lifted away by a crane to be taken by plane to Shanghai. When she arrives, I will place her in the Harbour Pool specially designed for her. I will bring my own tools to Shanghai to make sure that everything goes according to plan.

J: 小美人鱼雕像于1913年完成,这样算来她是一位老太太了。如此让她长途跋涉合适吗?

F: She is very fit. She is almost new compared to some of the older statues you can find in Copenhagen. You can also say that bronze sculptures like her, generally speaking, stay fit for a long time.

J: 你认为小美人鱼前往上海途中及在上海期间是否安全?

F: I think she will be very safe. I don't think that anyone will try to steal the Little Mermaid because she is too famous. I mean, what would they do with her? No one would buy her knowing that it was the real Little Mermaid.

J: 您长期从事石头雕刻。您是否认为此次任务将是您的主要挑战之一?

F: I would not say that this is one of my most difficult assignments. The modern or postmodern sculptures are much more complicated to work on. But she is by far the most famous. I cannot recall any other statue that has such a great history as the Little Mermaid. She is an essential part of Denmark and when I meet Chinese people, they often don't know Denmark but they have all heard about the Mermaid, Hans Christian Andersen and Copenhagen.

J: 您将前往中国,以确保小美人鱼安全抵达上海,但您自身和中国渊源颇深,可以和我们讲讲吗?

F: I started doing business in China eight years ago and now the basic work on many of my sculptures is done in China in Fujian Province. I give the Chinese workers a step-by-step manual on how to make the sculptures and then I come to China around five times a year to supervise the work.

## 课文注释  Notes on the Text

1. It is impossible for me to keep track on how many statues and works of art I have moved but it must be several thousands. keep track on 本意是"跟踪,追踪",根据这里的语境,可以翻译为"统计"。

2. Langelinie:这是位于哥本哈根市中心东北部的长堤公园。小美人鱼铜像自从1913年在长堤公园落成至今,已有近100年的历史。

3. You have had a long career as a stone cutter. 英语中常用"-er"等后缀构成的词语,往往表示一个人的职业或是一种较为稳定的特征,在翻译时往往不必翻译成名词,而是根据句意,翻译成相应的动词,此句可以译为:"您长期从事石头雕刻。"再如,He is a chain smoker. 可以翻译为:"他一根接着一根抽烟。"She is a good horse rider. 可以译为:"她马骑得很好。"

4. I cannot recall any other statue that has such a great history as the Little Mermaid. 在口译中,往往要求译文尽量精简到位。在这个用否定式的比较级来表达最高级的句子中,译者尤其要注意用词避免拖沓,可以译为:"我想小美人鱼的伟大历史是其他雕塑无法比拟的。"

5. Hans Christian Andersen:汉斯·克里斯蒂安·安徒生,丹麦作家,诗人,因创作童话故事而世界闻名。他最著名的童话故事有《海的女儿》《拇指姑娘》《卖火柴的小女孩》《丑小鸭》《皇帝的新装》等。

6. 您自身和中国渊源颇深,可以和我们讲讲吗? 这句话的表述是十分典型的汉语口语体,句式较为松散,在口译中可以将结构进行适当的整合,翻译为 Could you

share with us your close connection with China? 或者也可断为两句，使之更符合口语体的表达，可译为 You actually have a close connection with China. How is that?

# 词语扩展 *Developing Vocabulary and Expressions*

- 12 earthly branches 十二生肖
- a fictitious land of peace away from the turmoil of the world 世外桃源
- assimilate the achievements of civilizations the world over 吸取世界文明成果
- Chinese knot 中国结
- Chinese quarter/China Town 唐人街
- Chinese tunic suit 中山装
- clapper talk 快板
- contribute to the flourishing of culture of mankind 促进人类文化的繁荣
- crosstalk 相声
- cultural deposits 文化底蕴
- cultural establishments/infrastructure 文化基础设施
- culture-oriented travel 文化旅游
- dual nationality 双重国籍
- embroidery 刺绣制品
- enrich one's cultural life 丰富文化生活
- ethnocentrism 民族优越感
- exclusivism 排外主义
- handicraft art 手工艺
- intercultural/cross-cultural exchanges/communication 跨文化交流
- ivory carvings 象牙雕刻品
- meet the people's diversified needs at different levels 满足人民多层次多样化的需求
- monologue story-telling in Beijing dialect with drum accompaniment 京韵大鼓
- multiculturalism 文化多元主义
- puppet show/play 木偶戏
- Quyi balladry 曲艺
- seal cutting and paper cutting 篆刻与剪纸
- shadow play/ leather silhouette show 皮影戏
- six classical arts: rites, music, archery, riding, writing, arithmetics 六艺：礼、乐、射、御、书、数
- social effect and economic results 社会效益和经济效益
- styles and schools of art 艺术风格和流派
- the concept of individual moral autonomy 个人道德自治观念
- The Four Books (*The Great Learning*, *The Doctrine of the Mean*, *The Analects of Confucius*, *The Mencius*) 四书（《大学》《中庸》《论语》《孟子》）
- the Silk Road 丝绸之路
- water without a source, and a tree without roots 无源之水，无本之木
- weaving/knitting craft 编织工艺

## 口译操练 Interpreting Practice

### 1. 听译 ▶▶ Listening Interpreting

A. Listen to the sentences and interpret them into Chinese.
   Sentences 1—10

B. Listen to the paragraphs and interpret them into Chinese.
   Paragraphs 1—2

### 2. 情景练习 ▶▶ Situational Interpreting

**Interpret the following conversation alternatively into English and Chinese：**

> Roles
> 李华：a hostess
> Alice：an American Professor who is teaching in Beijing now
> Miss Chen：an interpreter

李华： 各位观众,晚上好,今天我们非常荣幸地邀请到北京大学的教授爱丽思女士参加我们关于文化差异与文化交流的节目。让我们掌声有请爱丽思女士。您好,爱丽思。

Alice： Good evening, Miss Li and everybody.

李华： 据我们所知,您一直从事东西方文化的比较研究,今天您能给我们谈谈文化差异吗?

Alice： It's my pleasure to have this chance to have a discussion with you all about such a meaningful topic.

李华： 那就让我们从文化的定义谈起吧,您认为文化应该如何定义呢?

Alice： Culture refers to the total way of life of a people, that is, their customs, traditions, social habits, values, beliefs, language, ways of thinking and daily activities.

李华： 据我所知,文化包括文学、戏剧、电影、音乐、绘画、哲学、历史等。

Alice： Yes.

李华： 我们都知道,不同的文化因为地域和历史的原因存在着种种差异,那么文化差异意味着什么?

Alice： Cultural difference calls for the cultural exchange. It blesses us with a colorful world and a rich life. It attracts us closer and draws the world nearer. The cultural differences existing among different nations are natural. Discussion of this matter is both interesting and significant.

李华： 是这样的。

Alice： And differences result in exchanges. Differences cause exchange. In this sense, cultural differences means cultural exchange.

李华： 但情况往往是,文化交流中常常出现这样或那样的冲突,那您觉得我们对待文化冲突的正确态度是什么?

Alice： When two cultures meet there may be things in one culture which do not fit into the tradition of the other. We don't necessarily have to agree

## 第 8 单元 文化交流 Cultural Exchange

with each other. It needs time. But keep one thing in mind: The understanding of our differences and the respect for our individualities are crucial. In the realm of existence, the most beautiful state is difference; in the realm of difference, the most beautiful state is understanding; in the realm of understanding, the most beautiful state is fusion.

李华: 下面是广告时间,让我们休息一下,广告之后我们再见。

# 第 2 部分 Section 2

## Vocabulary Work

| | | | |
|---|---|---|---|
| 任期 | tenure | 老派的 | stereotype |
| 文化部长 | Cultural Minister | 文学家的故居 | home museums of the great writers |
| 抽时间 | sneak out | 解说员 | curator |
| 宣传册 | brochure | 莎士比亚生日游行纪念活动 | birthday parades for Shakespeare |
| 保护主义 | protectionism | 儒家精神 | Confucianism |

## Text Interpreting

**Interpret the following conversation alternatively into English and Chinese：**

以下是《金融时报》记者 Lionel Barber（B）采访中国驻英大使（A）的对话：

B： Would you please share with us your impression about Britain?

A： 感谢你选择这家餐馆，我看了背景材料，这里很有英国特色。每次回国有人问我什么是典型的英国菜时，我总说是鱼、薯条和布丁，也许今后我可以推荐更多的英国菜。

B： Yes, this restaurant is very British. Well, You have been very helpful and kind during your tenure here. I have talked with many people about you and they are very positive about you. They said you are the first Ambassador to use wit and charm as a weapon. And you do have a sense of humour and you are quite different from the sort of stereotype Chinese diplomat.

A： 我认为外界对中国有不少陈旧观念。很多中国人都是机智、幽默的。中西方之间似乎有一些隔阂，我在英国留学的时候，对英式幽默也不能完全体会。但是有了在英国留学一年的经历，又在澳大利亚待过，因此能感受到这种隔阂，并思考个中原因。

B： Let's get back to this barrier a little bit later. Well, you are leaving at somewhat short notice, will you miss this country?

A： 当然，我会非常怀念英国。对于任何一个大使来说，告别总是不舍的。履新时需要时间适应，但相对容易，告别时，所有美好的记忆都会涌上心头。我将在公园里最后一次慢跑，在酒吧里最后一次品尝啤酒，在牛津街最后一次散步。意识到

# 第 8 单元 文化交流 Cultural Exchange

这是最后一次令我很不舍,我会带着对这个国家的美好记忆离开。
你知道著名中国作家王蒙吗?他曾经担任文化部长。他描述了很多自己到过的地方,我喜欢他的文字,非常流畅,就像在炎热的夏天喝一杯凉水。正如他所描述的:来到伦敦如同进入一幅早已熟悉的油画。我对此深有同感,不仅是伦敦,其他城市也给人这样的感受,好像通过文字或图像早已熟知,似曾相识的感觉。

B: What did you like most about your time in Britain?
A: 我喜欢参观文学家的故居,像简·奥斯汀和博朗特姐妹的故居。我不管去哪儿,总是尽量抽时间去看看名人故居。
B: I see. Yeah. It is because you are a great reader of western classics.
A: 中国人对英国文学巨匠耳熟能详。举个例子,参观简·奥斯汀故居时,我在为自己司机翻译解说员的介绍,那位解说员就问我能否帮忙翻译博物馆的宣传册?他说有许多中国人去参观,他不懂中文很难讲解。我欣然答应,一周后即把译文寄给了他。想不到会有这么多中国人参观简·奥斯汀故居吧,在中国有很多人知道她。
B: So you have been to Dickens' home?
A: 是的。我也多次去过莎士比亚故居。我在英国三年,曾两次参加莎士比亚生日游行纪念活动。
B: If you have to list two or three things that you found less appealing about our country?
A: 我们中国人有个"阴阳"的概念,就是每个事物都有两面性,都有积极面和消极面,不一定是不好的,也就是另外一面。
B: I heard of a great story that you came up with. It was in London where there were some comments about the protectionism. You looked around the room and said with a sweet smile: Yeah, you should be a little bit careful, because you know, if you start restricting China's export, look around at your clothes, you will be naked.
A: 我这样说过吗?
B: Yes, you did. It is very good, that is what I meant using humour to make an important point.
A: 我希望英国人多想想事物都有另外一面。比如,我参加一个关于热带雨林的论坛,这个论坛很不错,我完全赞同演讲者的观点,这应该是全球共同应对的重要问题。问题是,论坛在一个装饰精美的大厅举办,四周是用大量的木质墙围装饰的。参加论坛的其他发展中国家大使与我有同感,我们无法理解为什么演讲者意识不到问题还有另外一面:市场、木材的需求和消费者。
一些人总是告诉别人按照自己的标准来做事,总以为自己的生活准则、背景和价值观都是最好的,并以此衡量别人,要求他们仿效。这种感觉我经常会有,无论是听演讲还是在餐桌上。孔子说:三人行,必有我师。儒家精神几乎已经融入我们的血液,深植于中国文化。中国人一向谦虚谨慎,考虑方方面面的因素才做判断。我们有一个关于英国人的笑话,当然指的是部分英国人而不是全部英国人,对他们来说,"三人行,我必为师。"
B: Right. I see.

# 课文注释 Notes on the Text

1. Well, you are leaving at somewhat short notice, will you miss this country? at

short notice 是英语中的惯用习语,意思是 in a brief time,promptly,即"马上就",另外它也有 without much warning time for preparation 即"没有准备时间"的意思,如:He had to make the speech at very short notice when his boss suddenly fell ill. 可以译为:"老板突然病倒了,他不得不马上(替他)做个演讲。"

2. 简·奥斯汀、博朗特姐妹、狄更斯、莎士比亚:Jane Austin, the Bronte sisters, Dickens and Shakespeare,这些都是英国文坛上著名的文学家。

3. 阴阳:中国古代关于两种对立的基本力量的思想,始于汉朝的儒家哲学。与阳的范畴相联系的有雄性、热、光、天等,与阴的范畴相联系的有雌性、寒、暗、地等。阴阳二力被认为存在于多数事物之中,并使事物有周期地发生变化。

4. If you have to list two or three things that you found less appealing about our country? 英国记者问的这个问题中,特意用了 less appealing 这个词,其中运用了相当委婉的表达,来表示英国不太好的、不太令人欣赏的地方。

5. 三人行,必有我师。这一句以及下一句的"三人行,我必为师"。在遇到这类文言句式翻译时,首先需要读懂原意,将原句中的文言表达改写成白话,进行适当的增添,再依此翻译成英文,可分别译为 Where there are three men walking together, one of them must be qualified to be my teacher. 和 Where there are three men walking together, you must be qualified to be their teacher.

## 词语扩展  Developing Vocabulary and Expressions

- 边缘文化　　　　　marginal culture
- 表意文化　　　　　expressive culture
- 崇洋媚外　　　　　worship things foreign and fawn on foreign countries
- 大众文化　　　　　public culture
- 当代文化　　　　　contemporary culture
- 道德文化　　　　　ethical culture
- 东方文化　　　　　oriental culture
- 多元文化　　　　　diversified culture; multi-culture
- 古迹文化　　　　　relic culture
- 文化本源　　　　　cultural origin
- 文化标准　　　　　cultural norm
- 文化部　　　　　　ministry of culture
- 文化昌盛　　　　　culture flourishing
- 文化冲击　　　　　cultural shock
- 文化冲突　　　　　cultural conflict
- 文化多元主义　　　culture pluralism
- 文化国际化　　　　cultural internationalization
- 文化结丛　　　　　culture complex
- 文化界　　　　　　cultural circles; culture sphere
- 文化经纪人　　　　cultural broker
- 文化狂热分子　　　culture vulture
- 文化落后　　　　　cultural lag
- 文化内涵　　　　　cultural connotation
- 文化侵略　　　　　cultural aggression
- 文化热　　　　　　culture craze

## 第 8 单元  文化交流 Cultural Exchange

- 文化沙漠　　　　　　cultural desert
- 文化渗透　　　　　　cultural penetration
- 文化事业　　　　　　cultural establishments/undertakings
- 文化特质　　　　　　culture trait
- 文化消费　　　　　　cultural consumption
- 文化摇篮　　　　　　cradle of culture
- 文化遗产　　　　　　cultural heritage/legacy
- 文化遗址　　　　　　remains of an ancient culture; site of ancient cultural remains
- 文化意识　　　　　　cultural consciousness
- 原始文化　　　　　　primitive/primary culture

## 译操练 *Interpreting Practice*

### 1. 听译 ▶▶ Listening Interpreting

**A.** Listen to the sentences and interpret them into English.
Sentences 1—10

**B.** Listen to the paragraphs and interpret them into English.
Paragraphs 1—2

### 2. 情景练习 ▶▶ Situational Interpreting

Interpret based on the information given. Add any information when necessary.

> **Roles**
> Mr. Thomas：美国 ABC 公司董事长
> 唐先生：ABC 公司中国分公司总经理
> 岑小姐：翻译

据美国管理学会最近的一项调查表明，美国所有的企业中一般已经正式推行了旨在促动与管理多元文化的计划。

由于 ABC 中国分公司的员工组成比较复杂，存在着不同民族和不同种族的人员，Mr. Thomas 会见唐先生，并和唐经理讨论如何以更为宽广的文化价值观去领导和激励员工，使员工的多元化成为竞争优势。

Mr. Thomas 认为多元化的员工对未来意味着更广阔的思路和更多的好点子，能够促进企业的创造与革新。唐先生对这一做法表示赞同，并且提出一些具体做法，包括：大胆的招贤行动、多元人才培训、传帮带活动以及对各部门经理们促进多元文化进行奖励的鼓励性报酬项目。

译常识与技巧　　Interpreting Tips and Skills

**数字翻译（Interpreting Numbers）（1）**

（1）基数词（Cardinal Numbers）

数字的翻译是口译中的一大难关,特别是五位数以上的数字,给口译人员带来了很多困难。要提高数字口译的准确性和速度,译员首先必须掌握英汉数字不同的表达方式;其次,在翻译过程中,尽可能将原语中的数字用笔记录下来,遇到大数字时,可先标上段位记号,再将数字传译给另一方。最后,译员可以在平时经常进行数字互译练习。

首先,我们将英汉数字对照排列起来,了解它们的区别：

| 阿拉伯数字 | 英语 | 汉语 |
|---|---|---|
| 1 | one | 一 |
| 10 | ten | 十 |
| 100 | one hundred | 一百 |
| 1,000 | one thousand | 一千 |
| 10,000 | ten thousand | 一万 |
| 100,000 | one hundred thousand | 十万 |
| 1,000,000 | one million | 一百万 |
| 10,000,000 | ten million | 一千万 |
| 100,000,000 | one hundred million | 一亿 |
| 1,000,000,000 | one billion | 十亿 |
| 10,000,000,000 | ten billion | 一百亿 |
| 100,000,000,000 | one hundred billion | 一千亿 |
| 1,000,000,000,000 | one trillion | 一兆（万亿） |

用横向方式表示为：

```
                b.        m.       th.
万 千 百 十   千 百 十
亿,亿 万 万,万 万 千,百 十 个
 2, 8 6 3, 5 8 9, 4 0 0
```

汉语读作：二十八亿六千三百五十八万九千四百

英语读作：two billion, eight hundred sixty-three million, five hundred eighty-nine thousand and four hundred

 技巧练习　　Exercises for Skills

**A. Read aloud the following figures in Chinese numerical characters and in English.**

| 3,899 | 3,908 | 7,009 | 879 |
| 30,009 | 90,591 | 79,301 | 67,900 |
| 780,120 | 504,781 | 312,685 | 329,890 |
| 2,345,410 | 1,129,105 | 1,001,453 | 1,900,204 |
| 31,289,098 | 10,209,013 | 24,155,876 | 36,080,373 |
| 160,890,232 | 101,870,171 | 278,067,991 | 174,389,109 |
| 1,898,220,000 | 1,029,991,124 | 90,892,134,783 | 13,481,901,270 |
| 672,009,719,229 | 8,890,234,891,889 | | |

## 第8单元 文化交流 Cultural Exchange

**B.** Read aloud the following Chinese numerical characters in English, and also write down the figures in Arabic figures, marking them off with the digits ",", for thousand, one hundred thousand, million and billion.

六万　　　　　　　五十七万　　　　　　四百七十六万
九百六十一万　　　五千九百三十三万　　　七百五十亿
十一亿七千五百万　三千五百三十八万五千　九亿三千六百七十七万七千

**C.** Interpret the following paragraph into English.

中国的劳动力有7亿4000万，而欧美所有发达国家的劳动力只有4亿3000万。中国每年新增劳动力1000万；下岗和失业人口大约1400万；进城的农民工一般保持在1亿2000万。中国面临巨大的就业压力。中国13亿人口有9亿农民，目前没有摆脱贫困的有3000万左右，这是按每年人均收入625元的标准计算的。

**D.** Interpret the following sentences into Chinese.

(1) The population of this city in 2004 was 78,872,890.
(2) The natural reserve takes up an area of 123,880,000 square kilometers.
(3) The coastal line of this country is 7,723,605 meters.
(4) The number of college graduates will climb to a record high of 3,28 million this summer, an increase of 540,000, or 34％, over the year 2000.
(5) Australia, with its landmass of 7,686,850 square kilometers, or 2,967,893 square miles, has a population of 18,742,000.

# 第 9 单元 饮食文化

## Unit 9 Culinary Culture

# 第9单元 饮食文化 Culinary Culture

# 第1部分 Section 1

## 词汇预习 Vocabulary Work

| | | | |
|---|---|---|---|
| damask cloth | 锦缎台布 | butler | 司膳总管 |
| fowl | 家禽 | sherry | 雪利酒 |
| platter | 盘子 | garnish | 擦得发亮 |
| seating logistics | 座席安排 | alphabetize | 按字母顺序编排 |
| en route | 在路上 | table chart | 座位平面图 |
| cocktail hour | 鸡尾酒时间 | national anthem | 国歌 |

## 口译实践 Text Interpreting

Interpret the following talk into Chinese:

### A Talk about the Formal Dinner in the USA

Good evening, everyone!

It's my great pleasure to give you a talk about American culture. My topic tonight is about the formal dinner in the United States.

For a "truly formal dinner," we used to have all guests sit at one long U-shaped table covered with a white damask cloth. You know, this arrangement made conversation difficult and required a very lengthy dining room. Now people begin to use round tables for eight or ten. And as for the centerpiece decoration on the table, the hostess' own imagination should come into full play. A pretty setting of the table for guests helps make the food better and taste better. It makes the guests feel that an effort has been made on their behalf.

However, there are two elements of the formal dinner that have not changed over the years. One is the use of a butler and waiters for serving, and the other is the necessity for a chef who can produce a fabulous meal of five courses—usually a soup, fish, meat or fowl, salad and cheese, and dessert. At a formal dinner, we usually have a white wine, red wine, and champagne served with the meal (sometimes sherry first, too). The way the food served is extremely important at a formal dinner. The platters must all be garnished beautifully, so that the guests will admire each one as a work of art, not just the serving of a dish. For example, the butter might be rolled into balls or carved into flowers. The vegetables and desserts are served in imaginative ways. I notice that in China, you, too, have many beautifully-carved figures out of carrots or turnips.

If you are invited to a formal dinner, make sure that you do not sit at a wrong table. There are two ways of handling the seating logistics at a formal dinner. In one, after each man has given his coat to the butler or maid, he receives a small envelope with his name on it. Inside is a card bearing the name of his dinner partner. These envelopes with cards are kept on a tray in the front hall, alphabetized for easy finding. Now that we have round tables more often, the more popular way is for there to be an envelope for each guest, placed on the hall table in alphabetical order. As each guest arrives, he or she takes the envelope and finds inside a card with the proper table number written on it. There is no need to find one's dinner partner.

At a large formal dinner there should be a table chart shown to each guest as he arrives. The butler either holds the chart in his hand, or, if there are several round tables, the guests look at all the table charts on the hall table. When the party begins, the host and hostess should be near the entrance to the living room, so that they will be able to greet each arriving guest. They should see to it that newcomers are introduced to everyone through the cocktail hour.

Finally, I would say something about leaving. First, how to leave the table before the eating is finished. If you suddenly feel ill, or have an urgent need to go to the bathroom, no apologies are necessary. You may just say to the hostess, "Please excuse me for a moment," and depart. You need to make no explanations when you return. Secondly, how to leave the formal dinner. Except for some very good reason discussed previously with the hostess, no guest should leave after a formal dinner in a private home until the guest or guests of honor have departed. At formal public dinners guests who must leave early go quietly either before the speeches begin or between them, never while a guest of honor is speaking or while a national anthem is being played. Those who must leave, leave by the nearest exit without stopping to talk or bid farewell to guests encountered en route, except to bow briefly.

Well, I can't tell you all about the formal dinner within such a short time. Anyhow, if there is any chance of being invited, just ask people beforehand and be observant at the dinner, you won't be very wrong.

Thanks for your attention.

## 课文注释  Notes on the Text

1. Now people begin to use round tables for eight or ten: 句中 for eight or ten 译为"八至十人的圆桌",而且增加了"能坐"二字。在翻译时往往要根据语言习惯适当增译或减译。

2. At a formal dinner, we usually have a white wine, red wine...: 句中 white wine, red wine 译为"白/红葡萄酒"。中国的白酒度数很高,一般都在 35 度以上,英语中把酒精含量在 14% 以上的称为烈酒,英文是 spirits or liquor,如威士忌、杜松子酒、雪利酒、白兰地等。

3. The vegetables and desserts are served in imaginative ways: 译为"蔬菜和点心可做得别出心裁",imaginative 意为"充满想象力的",译为"别出心裁",恰到好处。

4. make sure that you do not sit at a wrong table：译为"切忌坐错席位"，简单明了。
5. They should see to it that newcomers are introduced to everyone through the cocktail hour：并且确保在喝开胃酒这段时间内把每一位新来的客人介绍给大家。原文中的被动语句 newcomers are introduced to everyone 用汉语常用的"把……"字句译出来，朗朗上口。see to it that，意为"确保"。
6. how to leave the table before the eating is finished：按原文译成"在吃完之前"，不如译为"在用餐过程中"。由于全文介绍的是正式宴会，译文也用较正式的用语，如"用餐""餐桌"。在翻译过程中译者要注重各种场合所使用的文体。
7. Those who must leave, leave by the nearest exit：译文中，没有将前面部分"那些一定要离开的人"译出，因为上下文已经很清楚，译出来就多余了。
8. I can't tell you all about the formal dinner：all 原意为"所有的东西"，译为"方方面面"，很适合汉语的语言习惯。

## 词语扩展 Developing Vocabulary and Expressions

常见的外国名酒
（1）Beer
- draught beer                生啤酒
- dark beer                   黑啤酒
- ale                         淡啤酒

（2）Wine 葡萄酒（大致分红、白、粉三种颜色）
- Burgundy Red                法国勃艮弟红酒
- Bordeaux                    法国波尔多葡萄酒
- Graves                      加来富白葡萄酒
- Malaga                      马拉加白葡萄酒
- Hock                        德国白葡萄酒
- Rhine Wine                  莱茵白葡萄酒

（3）Brandy 白兰地（经过蒸馏的葡萄酒，再加上其他果汁发酵制成，酒精含量 45%～50%）
- Cognac                      法国科涅白兰地
- Hennessy Napoleon           轩尼诗拿破仑
- Louis D'or Napoleon         金路易拿破仑
- Hine V. S. O. P.            御鹿 20 年陈白兰地
- Martell X. O.               马爹利
- Beehive                     蜂窝白兰地
- Remy Martin Three Stars     三星人头马
- Cordon Bleu                 蓝带
- Ginger Brandy               浆汁白兰地

（4）Whisky 威士忌（以玉米为主料，加入其他谷物酿成，酒精含量 45%～50%。威士忌需要储藏三年以上才能饮用）
- 100 Pipers Whisky           风迪 100
- Britania                    女神威士忌
- Scotch Whisky               苏格兰威士忌
- Bourbon Whisky              美国波旁威士忌
- Highball                    苏达威士忌

- Crown Royal 皇冠威士忌
- White Horse 白马威士忌
- Queen Anne 安妮皇冠
- Seven Crown 七皇冠
- Glen Grant 格莲格兰特
- Johnnie Walker Red/Black Label 红/黑牌威士忌

（5）Cocktail 鸡尾酒（一种混合饮料[Fancy/Mixed Drink]，它是以各种蒸馏酒如白兰地、威士忌、杜松子酒、朗姆酒等为主，加入香料和其他饮料调制而成。）
- Alexander 亚历山大
- Americano 阿美里卡诺
- Martini Cocktail 马提尼
- Gin Sling Cocktail 司令
- Snow Ball Cocktail 雪球
- Old Fashioned Cocktail 古式
- Egg Nogg Cocktail 爱诺格
- Pink Lady Cocktail 粉色佳丽
- Rob Roy Cocktail 罗布罗依
- Bloody Mary Cocktail 血红玛丽
- White Lady 白雪公主
- Manhattan 曼哈顿
- Rose 玫瑰

（6）Others 其他
- rum 朗姆酒
- gin 杜松子酒
- vodka 伏特加酒
- champagne 香槟酒
- sherry 雪利酒
- vermouth 味美思酒

## 口译操练  Interpreting Practice

### 1. 听译 ▶▶▶ Listening Interpreting

A. Listen to the sentences and interpret them into Chinese.
   Sentences 1—10

B. Listen to the paragraphs and interpret them into Chinese.
   Paragraphs 1—2

### 2. 视译 ▶▶▶ Sight Interpreting

A. Interpret the following sentences into Chinese：
   （1）Food is human's basic need, yet it differs from culture to culture.
   （2）All of man's history has been shaped by his search for food.
   （3）The United States is a country of immigrants, so there is an immense variety in its catering culture.

## 第 9 单元 饮食文化 Culinary Culture

(4) Our methods of cooking have not changed very much in the last century, but we do have better equipment that makes cooking easier and more convenient.

(5) Health food gained popularity when people began to think more seriously about their physical well-being.

(6) The need for better quality protein in the daily diet occurs mostly in the developing countries.

(7) The United States has shown a steady downward trend in per capita consumption of cereal-based food for many years.

(8) Health food includes natural food with minimal processing, that is, there are no preservatives to help it last longer or other chemicals to make it taste or look better.

(9) In the United States, fast food restaurants and cafeterias don't serve alcoholic beverages.

(10) Coffee shops are usually less expensive and less dressy than fine restaurants, and so are pizza places, pancake houses, sandwich shops and family restaurants.

**B. Interpret the following paragraphs into Chinese:**

(1) Many changes are taking place in Americans' food styles. The United States is traditionally famous for its very solid and unchanging diet of meat and potatoes. Now we have many different alternatives to choose from: various ethnic foods, nutrition-balanced health food, and convenient and delicious fast food, in addition to the traditional home-cooked meal.

(2) Americans' attitude toward food is changing, too. The traditional big breakfast is losing popularity. People are rediscovering the social importance of food. Dinner with family or friends is again becoming a very special way of enjoying and sharing. Like so many people in other countries, many Americans are taking time to relax and enjoy the finer tastes at dinner, even if they still rush through lunch at a hamburger stand.

## 3. 情景练习 ▶▶ Situational Interpreting

Interpret based on the information given. Add any information when necessary.

> **Roles**
> Mr. Green: a speaker
> Miss Chen: an interpreter

- Nothing should ever be spat into a napkin—not even a bad clam, and certainly not a piece of unchewable meat gristle or chicken bone. One should roll the offending morsel of food with his tongue onto his fork or spoon, and then place it on the plate.

- If you feel a sneeze coming at the table, and you have no time to reach for your handkerchief, you should cover your nose and mouth area with your napkin, but never blow into it.

- Don't speak with your mouth full. It is possible to speak with a bit of food in the mouth and still not be offensive. When you want to put a question to others at the table, you should also be considerate.
- If food gets stuck in your teeth and you can't dislodge it with your tongue, you should not sit there in front of people and get it out with a toothpick or your fingernail. You had better leave the table and retire to the rest-room or bathroom mirror.
- If you are a smoker, you may do it after everyone has finished dessert. Smoking in between courses is rude to the hostess, because it cuts down on the enjoyment of everyone's food.

# 第2部分 Section 2

## 词汇预习 Vocabulary Work

| | | | |
|---|---|---|---|
| 饮食习惯 | dietary habits | 热溶干酪 | fondue |
| 菜单 | bill of fare | 墨鱼 | cuttlefish |
| 鱿鱼 | squid | 供应便餐的小餐馆 | eatery |
| 咸豆糊（味噌） | miso | 刺身（生鱼） | sashimi |
| 名副其实的 | veritable | 美食家 | gourmet |
| 芹菜 | parsley | 形式简单 | simple in format |
| 有名的 | established | 葱花 | chopped green onion |

## 口译实践 Text Interpreting

Interpret the following conversation alternatively into Chinese and English：

### 上海饮食文化

Guide： We are so lucky to have Mr. Wang Heming with us today. He is both a great chef and quite a scholar on the culinary culture of Shanghai. Mr. Wang，we are tourists from USA. We hope to get some ideas about Shanghai foods and dietary habits. Would you tell us something about it?

王： 非常高兴有机会跟你们谈我们上海的饮食文化。上海食物，从本质上来说简单，具有乡土味，充分利用了丰富的自然原料。上海烹饪讲究清淡、自然和新鲜。上海的饮食文化基本上受两大因素的影响：上海的地理环境和外来影响。

Guide： What kind of influence has the unique geography brought upon Shanghai cuisine?

王： 你们知道，上海的自然资源很有限。因此，上海人靠大海提供基本蛋白质。如今的菜单上鱼和其他海鲜仍然占据主要地位。墨鱼和鱿鱼最受青睐，可用很多方式来做，可烤、可炒，还可清炖。排在海鲜后第二位的当数猪肉了。在上海，人们也吃鸡肉、牛肉和羊肉，但不像吃鱼或吃猪肉那么频繁，量也没有那么大。

Guide： Then what are the international influences?

王： 上海有日本的味噌——一种作为营养作料的发过酵的咸豆糊，和刺身。在上海也可以看到世界各地的食物。到处都有经营美国汉堡包、意大利比萨饼、日本的刺身、瑞士的干酪的餐馆,应有尽有。所有这些让上海成为名副其实的美食家乐园。

Guide: We toured around China before we are here and we had foods of a lot of different culinary styles like Sichuan and Cantonese flavours. So comparing with that of the whole nation, what is the feature of Shanghai cuisine?

王: 上海菜肴据说源自中国南方各省,但是上海菜肴又有别于其他各省。它没有西部的四川菜那么辛辣,也没有北方的菜那么味重。上海菜常用酱油、黄酒和芝麻油,有时也需要加一些佐料,如黑豆、腌萝卜、花生、芹菜等。这样做出来的菜形式简单,但其味无穷。

Guide: Would you recommend several Shanghai local snacks to us?

王: 当然可以。这里好吃的东西太多了。首先,我要说的是,在上海,有些最好吃的东西不是在大饭馆里,而是在街边的小店。有的一般在晚上7点左右开始一直开到午夜,如黄浦区的云南路就很值得一看。我特别建议你们去品尝臭豆腐。这臭豆腐闻着臭,吃起来香,将之小块油炸,外表酥脆,内层鲜嫩,再淋些酱油、醋、蒜汁,撒上葱花,加上一些腌制的泡菜,便是一盘又香又酥的臭豆腐了。其实,在上海不同的区有不同的风味小吃。

Guide: They all sound so delicious. I can't wait to taste them all.

王: 是呀,还有好多我没有提到呢。上海菜从不缺乏想象力。品尝一次你会终生难忘的。

Guide: Thank you so much Mr. Wang.

王: 不用客气。祝你们在上海过得愉快。

## 课文注释  Notes on the Text

1. He is both... and quite a scholar on Shanghai culinary culture:如果按字面意思直译成"他既是……,又是上海饮食文化的大学者",听起来不通顺,补译成"对上海饮食文化颇有研究",说起来上口,意思更到位。

2. 非常高兴有机会跟你们谈我们上海的饮食文化:翻译时,根据上下文和英语的习惯,只要译成 With pleasure 就足以表达原意了。

3. 从本质上来说比较简单,具有乡土味,充分利用了丰富的自然原料:rustic cuisine which makes the best use of the most naturally abundant ingredients. "充分利用了丰富的自然原料"本来就是解释"简单和具有乡土味"的含义,因而作为 rustic cuisine 的定语从句的结构译出,既表达了原意,也很符合英语的语感。

4. 排在海鲜后第二位的当数猪肉了:按英文习惯,用介词 after,整句译为 After seafood, pork is the second most popular meat.

5. 在上海,人们也吃鸡肉、牛肉和羊肉,但不像吃鱼或吃猪肉那么频繁,量也没有那么大:Chicken, beef and lamb are eaten but not... 汉语习惯用主动句,英文中被动句的使用频率比汉语高,特别在不强调或不知道动作是由谁发出的时候,更是这样。本句的主语"人们"是极模糊的主语,因而译成被动句非常合适。

6. "外来影响"译成 international influences,强调上海的饮食受到了全世界饮食的影响。

7. 到处都是经营……:用 Shanghai is filled with... 非常形象地译出原句中"到处"的意思。

8. 我特别建议你们去品尝臭豆腐……:译成"chou dou fu" which means smelly bean

curd. 各个民族都有自己独特的文化。在汉译英时,可以先用拼音的方式,标出读音,然后再做一些解释。解释的粗略和详细程度视具体场合而定。

# 词语扩展 *Developing Vocabulary and Expressions*

- 炒/爆炒/炸/煎/清炒 sautéing /quick-frying/ deep-frying/frying/ plain-frying
- 清蒸/焙/红烧 steaming/ roasting；broiling/ braising with soy sauce
- 煲/焖/烫 braising；stewing；simmering/ scalding
- 泡/腌 pickling/salting/ marinating
- 切丁/柳/片 dicing/cubing；filleting；slicing；shredding
- 臭豆腐 stinky tofu (smelly tofu)
- 春卷/蛋卷 spring rolls ；egg rolls/chicken rolls
- 蛋炒饭/糯米饭 fried rice with egg/ glutinous rice
- 蛋花汤/鱼丸汤 egg & vegetable soup/ fish ball soup/
- 紫菜汤/牡蛎汤 seaweed soup/ oyster soup
- 刀削面/乌龙面/麻辣面 sliced noodles/ seafood noodles/ spicy hot noodles
- 饭团/水饺/油条 rice and vegetable roll / boiled dumplings/ fried bread stick
- 火锅 hot pot
- 皮蛋/咸鸭蛋 preserved egg/ salted duck egg
- 肉丸/虾球 rice-meat dumplings / shrimp balls
- 调味品/原料 seasonings/ ingredients
- 辣椒油/蚝油/鱼露/香油/芝麻酱 chilli sauce/oyster sauce/fish sauce/sesame oil/sesame paste
- 生姜/醋/酱油/黄酒/番茄酱 ginger/vinegar/soy sauce/yellow rice wine/tomato sauce
- 味精 gourmet powder; monosodium glutamate
- 芥末粉/咖喱粉/花椒 ground mustard/curry powder/Chinese prickly ash
- 茴香/桂皮/五香粉/丁香 fennel/cassia bark/the five spices powder/cloves
- 高热量食品 high-calorie foods
- 速冻食品 instant frozen foods
- 烘烤食品 bakery products
- 谷类食品 cereal-based foods
- 转基因食品 GM food (genetically modified good)
- 色、香、味 color, aroma and taste
- 适时烹调 timing the cooking
- 把握火候 controlling the heat
- 佐料的调配 the blending of seasonings
- 南丹北咸,东甜西辣 the light southern (Canton) cuisine, and the salty northern (Shangdong) cuisine; the sweet eastern (Yangzhou) cuisine, and the spicy western (Sichuan) cuisine.
- 鲁菜通常较咸,汁色普遍较浅 Shandong cuisine is generally salty, with a prevalence of light-colored sauces.
- 鲁菜注重选料,精于刀工,善于炊技 Shandong dishes feature choice of ingredients/ materials, adept technique in slicing and perfect cooking skills.
- 川菜选料范围大,调味及炊技变化多样 Sichuan cuisine features a wide range of

115

ingredients, various seasonings and different cooking techniques.
- 川菜最大的特点是品种多,口味重,以麻辣著称 Sichuan food is famous for its numerous varieties of delicacies and strong flavors, and is best known for being spicy-hot.
- 粤菜强调轻炒浅煮,选料似乎不受限制 Cantonese cuisine emphasizes light cooking with seemingly limitless range of ingredients.
- 扬州菜注重选料的原汁原味 Yangzhou cuisine emphasizes the original flavors of well-chosen materials.

## 译操练 *Interpreting Practice*

1. 听译 ▶▶ Listening Interpreting

    A. Listen to the sentences and interpret them into English.
    Sentences 1—10

    B. Listen to the paragraphs and interpret them into English.
    Paragraphs 1—2

2. 视译 ▶▶ Sight Interpreting

    A. Interpret the following sentences into English:
    (1) 菜系的差异由多种因素所致,其中包括地理位置、气候条件、交通状况、人口迁移、海外文化。
    (2) 华人在饮食方面所持的价值观与西方人有很大的不同。
    (3) 近几年来,随着中国经济的迅猛发展,中国的饮食文化从传统的中餐食物向着中餐快餐连锁店发展了。
    (4) 在食物的新口味方面,上海人也表现出无穷的好奇心。
    (5) 上海的啤酒屋最受年轻一代的青睐。
    (6) 华人的饮食文化可追溯到几千年以前。
    (7) 在上海,能品尝到中国各个地区地道的烹调风味。
    (8) 湖南菜口味很重,用烟熏肉的做法是最为显著的特点之一。
    (9) 中国饮食的一个显著特点是,一年中不同的季节可用不同类型的药品原料做滋补食品。
    (10) 如今,到中餐馆就餐并使用筷子的外国人越来越多,同时许多中国人拿起刀叉吃顿西餐也轻松平常。

    B. Interpret the following paragraphs into English:
    (1) 在漫长的历史发展过程中,中餐逐渐分化为南北两大口味。一般来说,南方菜讲究鲜嫩,而北方由于天气寒冷油重一些,菜中常加醋和大蒜。北方的主食是面条、饺子以及其他用面粉做的食物,而大多数南方人则以米饭为主食。
    (2) 山东菜的特色是:清香、鲜嫩、味纯;江苏菜选料严格,制作精细,讲究造型,酥烂可口;安徽菜重油、重色、重火功;湖南菜口味重酸辣、鲜香、软嫩;浙江菜讲究刀功,味道鲜脆软滑,保持原味;广东菜用料广泛,除了通常用的肉、禽类外,还用蛇、猴、猫等制成菜肴,菜的特点多以清淡、生脆、爽口、偏甜为主;福建菜以海产品为主要原料,注重甜酸咸香、色调美观,滋味清鲜；四川菜以麻辣、味厚著称，调味品众多。

## 3. 情景练习 ▶▶▶ Situational Interpreting

Interpret the following speech into English.

> **Roles**
> 市长先生
> 陈小姐：翻译

尊敬的各位来宾，女士们、先生们、朋友们：

经过几个月的紧张筹备，第五届上海国际美食节就要开幕了。今晚，我们很荣幸地邀请到来自海内外的各位宾朋，在这里欢聚一堂，共度良宵。在此，我谨代表美食节各主办、承办单位和上海市政府，向前来参加美食节的各位来宾表示热烈的欢迎和衷心的感谢！

随着人们的生活水平不断提高，旅游已成为社会关注的热点。我们上海市民热情好客，这里的饮食文化源远流长。本届美食节的举办，必将进一步推动饮食文化的创新，为旅游业发展增添新的光彩。我们愿同各位一道，共同致力于美食业的创新与发展，让美食香溢千家万户，让旅游繁荣现代生活，为弘扬中华美食做出新的贡献。

生活如花似锦，美食五彩缤纷。我们端出了最好的美酒佳肴热情款待各位嘉宾。让我们共同举杯，为美食节圆满成功、为我们的友谊地久天长、为各位领导和朋友的健康和幸福，干杯！

## 译常识与技巧  *Interpreting Tips and Skills*

**数字翻译（Interpreting Numbers）(2)**

（1）分数（Fractions）

分子用基数词，分母用序数词。当分子为1时，分母用单数；当分子为2或2以上时，分母用复数。

二分之一：a/ one half 　　四分之一：a/ one quarter 　　四分之三：three quarters
五分之一：one-fifth 　　十分之九：nine-tenths 　　百分之六：six-hundredths

当分子和分母的数目很大时，可用 over 将分子、分母隔开。

九十分之四十八：forty-six over ninety
二十八分之一十三：thirteen over twenty-eight

带分数的表达方式：整数后面用 and 连接。

五又三分之二：five and two-thirds
十五又四分之一：fifteen and one quarter

（2）小数（Decimals）

小数点的英语为 point，小数点前面的数如果是零的话，可读成"zero（美式）"或"naught（英式）"，或者省略不读。小数点后面的数字都读成个位数，如果是零的话，就读成"O /ou/"，例如：

0.5：point five; zero/naught point 5
0.357：point three five seven; zero/naught point three five seven
0.004：zero/naught point o o four
78.34：seventy-eight point three four

汉语里常常在表示大数目的时候,用小数点表示,译成英语时,一般还原为英语的数字表达法。例如:

零点九万（0.9万）:nine thousand
零点三亿（0.3亿）:thirty million
五点八四万（5.84万）:fifty-eight thousand and four hundred

**（3）模糊数字（Indefinite Numbers）**

大约,大概,……左右:about / around/ some / approximately / roughly
少于、小于、低于、不到、不足、以下:fewer than / less than / under / below
多于、大于、高于、超过、以上:more than / over / above / … and more
将近、接近、差不多、几乎、差一点:nearly / almost / toward / close on
数十/ 几十 / 好几十/ 数十年:tens of (20－99); dozens of ( 24－99);
　　　　　　　　　　　　　　　scores of (40－99) decades of ( 20－99)
数百 /数以百计 /好几百:hundreds of (200—999)
数千/ 数以千计/ 好几千: thousands of (2,000—9999)
数万/ 数以万计/好几万:tens of thousands of (20,000—99,999)
数十万/好几十万:hundreds of thousands of (200,000—999,999)
数百万/好几百万:millions of (2,000,000—9,999,999)
数千万/好几千万:tens of millions of (20,000,000—99,999,999)
数亿/好几亿/亿万:hundreds of millions of (200,000,000—999,999,999)
数十亿/好几十亿:billions of (2,000,000,000—9,999,999,999)

## 技巧练习 Exercises for Skills

**Read aloud the following numbers in English.**

| 五分之四 | 七分之四 | 七十分之三十五 | 七又八分之三 |
| 0.3 米 | 0.78 公斤 | 0.008％ | 9.481 |
| 99.21％ | 30.50 公里 | 23.49 吨 | 789.12 亩 |
| 4.5 万 | 10.8 万 | 9.59 万 | 0.8 万 |
| 678.12 万 | 0.3 亿 | 24.58 亿 | 238.04 亿 |
| 五十五岁上下 | 两百人左右 | 不到一千公斤 | 将近一百万 |
| 好几百人 | 数以万计 | 千千万万 | 几十亿 |

# 第 10 单元 时代潮流

## Unit 10　New Trends

# 第1部分 Section 1

 **Vocabulary Work**

| | | | |
|---|---|---|---|
| studio | 演播室,工作室 | fabric | 布料 |
| artistic touch | 艺术元素 | outfit | (全套)衣服 |
| wardrobe | 衣服,行头 | follow in one's footsteps | 效法某人 |

 **Text Interpreting**

**Interpret the following talk alternatively into Chinese and English:**

### An Interview with a Fashion Designer

主持人： 谭女士,谢谢您来演播室接受我们采访。

Ms. Tam: Thank you for having me.

主持人： 我们都知道您在美国是一位著名的华裔时装设计师。您最初怎么会决定以后成为设计师呢?

Ms. Tam: I wasn't thinking about becoming a designer, I just loved to make dresses for myself when I was younger. I loved especially dressing up for the Chinese New Years with the dresses I made. I also played with my brothers and sisters using sheets and blankets to put around them. Even though in high school we had to wear uniforms, I still wanted to try to be different so I would design my hair differently.

主持人： 您给自己的日常生活增添了不少艺术元素,那么之后您是否也想到要进入时尚设计领域呢?

Ms. Tam: No, gradually it became my path. I have never changed my path and I am so lucky that fashion gradually came to me. My mother always said to me that we do not have enough money to buy clothes, but we can buy the fabric from the market and create an original style that nobody has.

主持人： 我想是您的母亲极大地鼓励了您。那么您如何搭配自己选择的色彩?

Ms. Tam: It is all magical. I always look at nature and I think nature has the most beautiful colors. I wanted to give life to my design. It is hard to explain how I choose the colors, but it all comes from within.

主持人： 女性着装时,应该如何选定最适合自己的衣服呢?

Miss Tam: It depends upon the occasion. They should choose the color depending upon their skin complexion, hair color and personality, which is how I choose which model should wear which outfit during my fashion shows. People should learn about their own styles and know more about themselves.

主持人: 女性顾客穿着以您的名字命名的品牌时装时,你希望带给她们什么感觉?

Ms. Tam: I want them to feel very special, beautiful and spirited.

主持人: 准备一季时装展很花时间吧?

Ms. Tam: It does take a lot of time. The first time you see everything put together, you finally say, "Oh my God, it works!" Because it has been a long process, when it is finished you think, "Finally, it is done!"

主持人: 您不仅是女装设计师,也为纽约一些知名餐厅的员工设计工作服。您是如何设计工作服的?

Ms. Tam: It was all based on the theme and the colors of the interior. They also wanted a Chinese feeling, which was another important aspect. We talked about different concepts and the ideas they had in mind. It was very interesting; I was able to learn about each person's position and type of work. I had to find out if their jobs required them to move around or not, so that I can make their outfits comfortable. Another important element is the type of fabric. They need to wash the clothing often, so the fabric I choose must not lose its color and always stay in good condition.

主持人: 您想对年轻一代,尤其希望和您一样成为知名设计师的年轻人说些什么呢?

Ms. Tam: They should go deep inside themselves and find what they really love to do. If you do things from your heart, you can make things happen. You can change the world because you have the power and the power comes from within you. They say that if you work hard, even a rusted rod can become a fine needle.

主持人: 谭女士,谢谢您与我们分享这么多有关时装的想法。现在我想请在场的观众朋友们向您提一些问题。

Ms. Tam: Ok, I'd like to talk with you all.

# 课文注释  Notes on the Text

1. Thank you for having me. 根据语境,这句感谢的话应该译成"也谢谢您/你们邀请我",与前一句对应。"Thank you for having me"也常用于到别人家做客临走之前表示感谢之意,相当于表示"谢谢您款待我"或"谢谢您邀请我过来"。

2. I wasn't thinking about becoming a designer... 我从来没想过能成为设计师……。这里的过去进行时结构表示曾经一直想做某事。请注意英汉语表达时态的方式不一样,汉语主要通过"过""了""曾经"等词或说话语气表示过去时,不一定只用"以前""过去"这些明确表示过去含义的词。

3. I also played with my brothers and sisters using sheets and blankets to put around them. 和兄弟姐妹们玩耍时,我给他们裹上床单和毯子。此句需要灵活翻译,play with,use 和 put around 在英语句子中是按照主次结构安排的,语法功能

各不相同。但按照汉语描述动作和事件发生的习惯,"裹上床单和毯子"成了主要动作。

4. 您给自己的日常生活增添了不少艺术元素,那么之后您是否也想到要进入时尚设计领域呢？After the artistic touches that you added to your everyday life, did it then strike you that you wanted to be involved in the world of design and fashion? 原句中的"艺术元素"最好不要直译,artistic touch 更规范,表示艺术品位、格调、风格或感觉;"想到"强调突然想起或隐约觉得,用 it strikes sb. that... 更合适。另外,"进入(时尚设计领域)"也不宜直译为 enter 或者 step into,这是一个渐进的过程,be involved in...更准确。翻译本句时,也需注意句型处理,分清主从。英语句子把原句的后半句作为主句,这样处理更符合英语句子的表达逻辑。

5. 我想是您的母亲极大地鼓励了您：I think your mother is your inspiration. 原句可以直译为 I think your mother has inspired/encouraged you,但把动词"鼓励"译成英语名词 inspiration,表达更简洁,更地道。

6. 女性着装时,应该如何选定最适合自己的衣服呢？When a woman is looking for something suitable to wear, how should they choose the outfit most suitable for them? 原句中的"着装"是指挑选自己要穿的衣服,不能直接译成 get dressed 或 put on their clothes(穿上衣服)。因此,译文处理成 looking for something suitable to wear,语义更准确。

7. 准备一季时装展很花时间吧？Does the preparation of a season's collection take time? 通常,国际知名时装展都在每年的春夏(9、10月上旬)和秋冬(2、3月)举行,因此,season 表示"(时装)季"。"时装展"可以译成 fashion show,但是对设计师本人而言是 fashion collection,表示要展示自己所有的作品。collection 用于艺术设计领域时有时不能直译成"收集",而是指一系列作品或成套产品。

8. 您是如何设计工作服的？What approaches did you have when you began designing the workforce's wardrobe? 原句若直译显得非常唐突,译文较委婉,用 approach 表示"方法、路径",说明主持人更想了解设计师的思路或理念。

9. 您想对年轻一代,尤其希望和您一样成为知名设计师的年轻人说些什么呢？What do you have to say to the next generation, particularly for those hoping to follow in your footsteps? 译文将原句处理为定语从句,符合英语句式结构,避免重复。另外,"希望和您一样成为知名设计师"用固定表达 follow in one's footsteps 令译文增色不少,表达简洁而生动。

10. They should go deep inside themselves and find what they really love to do. If you do things from your heart, you can make things happen... 本部分多次出现人称代词 they 和 you,注意英、汉语人称代词的差异,其实 Ms. Tam 说的话都是针对年轻人的,但是为了拉近距离,人称代词一直在变化。译成汉语时,需灵活处理,有的可直译,有的省略,还有一些需变换人称。请参考译文。

# 词语扩展 Developing Vocabulary and Expressions

- body measurements　　　　　　三围
- catwalk show　　　　　　　　　时装展示
- customizing clothes　　　　　　量身定做服装
- de rigueur　　　　　　　　　　时尚的,合乎社会礼仪的
- designer's vision　　　　　　　设计师的设计理念

- fashion magazine 时装杂志
- Generation X/Generation Xers 新新人类
- Generation X/Gen-X women 新新女性
- guiding concept for fashion 时装的主流理念
- high-end buyer 识货的顾客,会买东西的顾客
- hippie chic 嬉皮风格
- hot fad 火爆的时尚
- impulse buy 即兴购物
- individual way of dressing 个性化的着装方式
- knee-length skirt 齐膝短裙
- luxury goods giant 奢侈品市场
- midriff baring shirt 露脐装
- peasant shirt 乡土式衬衫
- prominent shades 流行色
- self-expression 自我展现
- spike heels 细长的高跟鞋
- style consultant 时装顾问
- stylish and fashion-forward 时尚且前卫
- behind the times 落伍的,赶不上时代的
- tie-dye pattern 扎染图案
- look chic 穿戴得时髦雅致
- up-to-the-minute style 最新的款式

## 译操练 Interpreting Practice

### 1. 听译 ▶▶ Listening Interpreting

A. Listen to the sentences and interpret them into Chinese.
   Sentences 1—10

B. Listen to the paragraphs and interpret them into Chinese.
   Paragraphs 1—2

### 2. 视译 ▶▶ Sight Interpreting

A. Interpret the following sentences into Chinese:

(1) Pierre Cardin has become a household name on products around the world from couture clothing to alarm clocks.

(2) We have entered the era of dress correctness, in which women's clothes are purchased less to attract male sexual attention and more to match rising professional ambitions.

(3) Jeans represented the American West and when they started to be worn as casual wear, they were a symbol of rebellion.

(4) Lots of people are interested in fashion and like to look at clothes in magazines. And they take care of how they look.

(5) People are now more relaxed in our approach to dressing, mixing summer with winter clothes, and labels such as T. C. are not limited

# 第 10 单元  时代潮流 New Trends

  to trends and seasons.
（6）This idea appeals to new customers who are younger, trendier and not label-led.
（7）Trashion (a blend of "trash" and "fashion") is a term for art, jewelry, fashion and objects for the home created from used, thrown-out, found and repurposed elements.
（8）"Human society puts a great deal of emphasis on female appearance and this will inevitably result in more clothes being purchased for girls than boys," said the professor of psychology.
（9）Looking good in Italy is a national obsession. Forget football, fast cars and food. This nation's favorite pastime is style.
（10）Lady Gaga dramatically won the attention of the MTV Video Music Awards when she took to the stage in a matching dress, boots, hat and purse apparently made from raw meat.

**B. Interpret the following paragraphs into Chinese：**
（1）Granny chic denotes a fashion style which consists of old-fashioned items worn in a stylish way. Granny style cardigans, floral dresses and flesh colored tights were seen walk down the catwalks of Paris, New York, London and Milan and the trends have now filtered down to the high street.
（2）Many fashion models look very skinny. I think it isn't right to set a beauty standard of fashion models for all women. Many women wish to be thin only because it's a beauty standard and perceived as desirable. Some of them worry way too much about losing weight, but being average is as good as being thin. Bigger women shouldn't obsess too much over their weight.

## 3. 情景练习 ▶▶ Situational Interpreting
**Interpret the following conversation alternatively into Chinese and English：**

> Roles
> Michelle: hostess of a radio program
> Leo: editor of a famous fashion magazine

Michelle: We're in Paris Fashion Week. I also brought Leo, editor of *Jolie* with me to present On the Town!
Leo: Michelle，你好。大家好！欢迎收听我们从巴黎时装周为你带来的《时尚快车》节目。
Michelle: Well, we're obviously in the right place because as I look around me I can see nothing but extremely fashion-conscious people walking around. You must feel at home, Leo.
Leo: 是啊，也觉得很兴奋。巴黎时装周和伦敦时装周、米兰时装周、纽约时装周并称为世界著名的四大时装周。全世界的顶级时装设计师们几乎每一个都是通过巴黎走进了世界的视野。
Michelle: In recent years, China's passion for fashion is on full display at

Paris Fashion Week. Chinese stars are taking front row seats at the runway shows of France's most famous fashion houses. And not surprisingly Chinese designers are also a growing force in the world's fashion capital. The *Chinois* presence in Paris is a sign that the haute-couture industry is increasingly turning its gaze on China's booming economy.

Leo: 法国的时装界也渴望中国最出名的面孔出现在他们的时装秀上。中国是一个急速发展的奢侈品牌市场，法国设计师渴望确立他们在利润丰厚的中国市场的地位。

Michelle: Yes, you're right. The "China in Paris" showroom also gives young Chinese designers the chance to introduce their work to the world's fashion capital. Some designers said that Paris, for them, is the international fashion stage and the place where they really want to present their clothes.

Leo: 希望国际时尚界中的中国面孔越来越多。好，现在我们为听众朋友们介绍一下今年巴黎时装周的趋势吧！

Michelle: Ok, let's introduce to you the top 10 trends we have gathered from the fashion week.

# 第2部分 Section 2

## 词汇预习  Vocabulary Work

| 工信部 | the Ministry of Industry and Information Technology | 商用牌照 | commercialization license |
| --- | --- | --- | --- |
| 可穿戴设备 | wearable device | 实时 | in real time |
| 无处不在 | ubiquitous | 超低延迟连接 | ultra-low-latency connections |
| 虚拟现实游戏 | VR games | 超高速无线技术 | ultra-fast wireless technology |
| 系统容量 | system capacity | 大规模设备连接 | massive device connectivity |
| 智能城市基础设施 | smart city infrastructure | 无缝连接 | seamless connectivity |
| 物联网 | internet of things | 传输基地 | transmission base |
| 发射器 | transmitter | | |

## 口译实践  Text Interpreting

**Interpret the following talk into English:**

### 5G 网络技术意味着什么

"5G"一词近期成了社会关注的焦点。今年 6 月 6 日,国家工信部宣布将发放 5G 商用牌照,这意味着基础电信运营商将开始提供 5G 服务。在不久的将来,5G 技术将会进入我们的生活。

那么,什么是 5G? 它又会给我们的生活带来什么样的变化呢?

"5G"中的"G"指的是移动通信网络技术的时代。1G 能让我们与他人打电话交谈,2G 能让我们发信息,3G 为我们提供了移动数据和互联网,4G 令上述所有功能更快速。

现在,5G 有望带来更快的数据上传下载速度,以及更稳定的网络连接。这意味着你能在几秒之内下载完一部高清电影,发送和接收数据之间只存在一些较短的延时。比如,当你和朋友视频聊天时,在 4G 网络下大概会有 100—200 毫秒的延时,而 5G 网络则会将延时缩短至1毫秒甚至更短,几乎接近实时。

据报道,5G能够改进许多先进技术,如无人驾驶汽车、可穿戴设备以及休闲娱乐体验。5G将带来的最显著和最令人兴奋的革命性变化是运输业。在5G网络下,车辆几乎能够实时交换信息。无处不在的超低延迟连接,意味着汽车、公共汽车和道路都可以实时地相互交谈,在自动驾驶汽车的世界里,提醒驾驶员已发生的堵塞、事故或完全实现无人驾驶。信息交换的短延时会令无人驾驶汽车在行驶时更为安全,从而避免潜在的危险。与此同时,使用5G网络的可穿戴设备能随时向医生们提供病人的最新健康状况,并在出现问题时即时通知医生。除此之外,5G的短延时会令游戏体验更加真实,虚拟现实游戏将更受欢迎。

5G是下一代超高速无线技术,可提供更快的数据速率、更短的延迟、节能、降低成本、提高系统容量和大规模设备连接。它有望推动智能城市基础设施和工业互联网等新技术的发展。5G有望实现为几乎所有东西提供无缝、超快速的连接,这将使各种不同的功能蓬勃发展。一些最常见的应用将围绕着基础设施的连接展开,从灯柱和道路,到垃圾箱和自行车停放架,一切都变成了智能对象。换句话说,实现"物联网"。

尽管5G令我们的生活更加方便快捷,但这一技术并不完美。

5G网络的传输距离并不远。你能在距离最近的传输基地10公里处使用4G网络,几乎不会出现没有信号的情况。但5G的覆盖范围大约只有300米,这意味着我们需要更多的发射器才能获得信号。在向智能手机用户提供广泛的5G服务之前,电信运营商需要时间来建立网络基础设施。而为了能接入5G网络,我们也需要购买专为5G设计的价格不菲的新产品。

## 课文注释  Notes on the Text

1. 超低延迟连接:ultra-low-latency connections;超高速无线技术:ultra-fast wireless technology.
2. 5G有望实现为几乎所有东西提供无缝、超快速的连接,这将使各种不同的功能蓬勃发展。这句可译成典型的非限制性定语从句:5G is expected to promise seamless, superfast connectivity for practically anything, which will enable all sorts of different functions to flourish.
3. 5G是下一代超高速无线技术,可提供更快的数据速率、更短的延迟、节能、降低成本、提高系统容量和大规模设备连接。原句并列项在翻译成英语时要注意词性的一致性;5G is the next generation of ultra-fast wireless technology, offering faster data rates, reduced latency, energy savings, cost reductions, higher system capacity and massive device connectivity.
4. 在向智能手机用户提供广泛的5G服务之前,电信运营商需要时间来建立网络基础设施。此处"建立"可处理成get in place,很贴切;"广泛的"译为 a wide suite of,即"一系列、一整套":Telecoms operators will need time to get the network infrastructure in place before they can offer a wide suite of 5G services to smartphone users.

# 第10单元 时代潮流 New Trends

## 词语扩展 Developing Vocabulary and Expressions

|  |  |
|---|---|
| ❖ 保护主义 | protectionism |
| ❖ 后脱欧时代 | post-Brexit UK |
| ❖ 歧视性举措 | discriminatory measures |
| ❖ 广泛讨论 | on everyone's lips |
| ❖ 利益共同体 | everyone has a stake in it |
| ❖ 对话机制 | dialogue mechanisms |
| ❖ 核心网络 | core network |
| ❖ 增强现实 | augmented reality |
| ❖ 移动游戏 | mobile gaming |
| ❖ 电脑犯罪 | cyber-crime |
| ❖ 网络界 | cyber community |
| ❖ 电脑文化 | cyber culture |
| ❖ 电子出版物 | e-journal |
| ❖ 电子会议 | e-meeting |
| ❖ 电子商务 | e-commerce/e-business |
| ❖ 电子邮件网关 | e-mail gateway |
| ❖ 互联网接力聊天 | IRC(Internet Relay Chat) |
| ❖ 电脑迷 | computer nerd/digit head |
| ❖ 电脑能手 | digiteer |
| ❖ 电脑专家 | digerati |
| ❖ 交互式电视 | interactive TV |
| ❖ 垃圾邮件 | junk e-mail |
| ❖ 网络爱情 | cyber romance |
| ❖ 网络电话 | web phone |
| ❖ 网络攻击 | cyber attack |
| ❖ 网络经济 | webnomics |
| ❖ 网络空间 | cyberspace |
| ❖ 网络礼节 | netiquette |
| ❖ 网络新闻 | cyber journalism |
| ❖ 网络新闻 | net news |
| ❖ 网络杂志 | webzine |
| ❖ 网络诈骗 | cyberfraud |
| ❖ 网络治疗专家 | cybertherapist |
| ❖ 网虫 | cyber cult |
| ❖ 网迷 | cyber addict/ Webaholic |
| ❖ 网民 | netizen |
| ❖ 网民身份 | cytizenship |
| ❖ 网上超市 | cyber mall |
| ❖ 网上大学 | cyber university/college |
| ❖ 虚拟图书馆 | virtual library |
| ❖ 虚拟现实/世界 | virtual reality/virtual world |
| ❖ 以太网 | Ethernet |
| ❖ 因特网盲 | internot |

**Interpreting Practice**

### 1. 听译 ▶ Listening Interpreting

A. Listen to the sentences and interpret them into English.
   Sentences 1—10

B. Listen to the paragraphs and interpret them into English.
   Paragraphs 1—2

### 2. 视译 ▶ Sight Interpreting

A. Interpret the following sentences into English：
   (1) 为了准备好一个可能没有安卓系统的未来,据说华为正在开发可以在自己的智能手机上运行的移动操作系统。
   (2) 普遍认为,名牌衣服比平价衣服更结实,但研究发现,快时尚品牌的T恤和牛仔裤通常比名牌衣服更耐穿。
   (3) 据说,来年网上促销的一种趋势是将会越来越多地使用数据开发,为网上购物者提供更加个性化的服务。这一切将给购物者带来更好的购物体验。
   (4) 在有些服装零售商网站,消费者可以根据他们自己的身体特征创建一个可以"试穿"各种服装的虚拟模特。
   (5) 根据美国食品公司一项新的调查显示,28%的快递员在送餐前吃了客人点的食物,这让普通消费者难以接受。
   (6) 与驾车去商场购物相比,在家中网上购物可以减少许多污染。但是,如果人们既在网上购物又去逛传统的商店,那么结果则会是能源消耗的全面增长。
   (7) 你走进商店能摸到、感觉到商品,但是在网上你必须看清楚商品后才能确认那是否是自己需要的东西。
   (8) 营销经理称,公司的流媒体短视频应用软件抖音在中国每月拥有3亿用户。抖音的国际版TikTok在印度、东南亚和北美要越来越受欢迎。
   (9) 国家邮政局的数据显示,2018年,中国快递行业共处理了505亿件包裹,同比增长近26%,该行业的总收入同比增逾21%。
   (10) 华为技术有限公司表示,其在全球范围内供货20多万个5G基站,在5G超高速网络技术领域,华为仍牢牢占据全球供应商领头羊地位。

B. Interpret the following paragraphs into English：
   (1) 讲求实效的网络营销者们绝不是简单地把平面广告抄送到网页上。成功运作的网站把促销宣传与其他内容融为一体,巧妙地把广告信息传递给受众。为了提高网站访问率,培养顾客对产品的信赖度,各企业不断更换产品信息并提供许多互动机会。
   (2) 因特网改变着许多事物。它已对商务领域产生了巨大的影响。公司能够把他们的系统与其产品供应商和合作伙伴直接相连,可以在网上24小时地进行交易,可以比以往更多地了解他们的顾客。经济的运作因此将更加富有成果。

## 第 10 单元 时代潮流 New Trends

### 3．情景练习 ▶▶▶ Situational Interpreting

**Interpret based on the information given. Add any information when necessary.**

> **Roles**
> Mr. Jackson：美国 F＆C.com 公司在上海分部的销售部经理
> 夏小姐：网上购物者
> 白先生：翻译

Mr. Jackson 想对中国的网上购物者进行一次市场抽样调查。他首先选择了在该公司网站上购物积分最高的购物者夏小姐作为访问对象。谈话地点是在该公司的接待室。

Mr. Jackson 主要询问了三方面的情况：一、夏小姐对该公司提供的网上销售服务切身感受如何；二、夏小姐认为该公司的网上销售有哪些其他网站服务所没有的特点与优势；三、夏小姐对该公司网上服务的批评或建议。

夏小姐对 Mr. Jackson 的调查一一做了回答：首先，她描述了自己的购物体验，认为该公司网站的商品大部分物美价廉、时尚舒适（与该公司的网站名很相符：Fashion and Comfort），定购方便，送货快捷，信誉较高；其次，她认为该公司网上促销的手段比较新颖有效，不但提供了每件商品的 3D 画面，而且允许网上消费者根据其自身身体特征创建自己可以"试穿"各种服装的虚拟模特；最后，夏小姐建议该公司再多提供一些非常具有上海时尚特色的服饰，另外是否可以增加男士用品的种类和数量。

## 译常识与技巧  Interpreting Tips and Skills

**习语与引语（Idioms and Interpreting Quotations）**

口译时常碰到发言人引用习语、古典诗词和经典佳句，特别是为政府首脑、高级官员、文化人士、社会名流做口译的译员对此感受颇深。在这些场合，这些名人常在演讲中引用一些习语或名言，以表达自己的感情、观点和立场，或表示对对方国家的文化传统的欣赏和赞扬。因此，口译人员一方面要尽可能地了解和记忆一些常用的习语和引语，同时还要培养自己根据上下文语境进行准确而灵活的翻译的能力。

从广义上说，习语包括俗语（colloquialism）、谚语（proverb）、俚语（slang expression）、成语（fixed expression）、歇后语（two-part allegorical saying）等。引语则是指引用自经史子集或名人专家的话语，往往言简意赅，含义隽永。习语和引语的翻译可以采用直译法，以保持原汁原味的表达，例如：

易如反掌 as easy as turning over one's hand/palm
君子动口不动手 A gentleman uses his tongue, not his fists.
千里送鹅毛，礼轻情义重。The gift itself may be as light as a feather, but sent
　　　　　　　　　　　from afar, conveys deep feelings.
Behind the mountains there are people to be found. 山外有山，天外有天。
Speech is silver, silence is gold. 雄辩是银，沉默是金。

将汉语引语译成英文可以解释其意，例如：

　　孟子说过："穷则独善其身，达则兼济天下。" An ancient Chinese philosopher Mencius used to say, "In the time of hardships, a man should seek self-development through efforts of his own. Once becoming well-off, he should help others with a big heart."

但是英文中引用了中文的名言,则一定要找到与中文对应的语句,这对译员的文化素养是很大的考验,如美国前总统里根 1984 年访华时在欢迎宴会上引用了《易经》中的一句话,他说道:

And as a saying from *The Book of Changes* goes, "If two people are of the same mind, their sharpness can cut through metal."(二人同心,其利断金。)

再如美国前总统克林顿 1998 年下旬访华时在人民大会堂的国宴上致辞时用了孟子的一句话,他说道:

In so many different ways, we are upholding the teaching of Mencius, who said: "A good citizen in one community will befriend the other citizens of the community; a good citizen of the world will befriend the other citizens of the world."(一乡之善士斯友一乡之善士,天下之善士斯友天下之善士。)

习语和引语无法直译时,译员首先需要考虑使用目标语中已有的表达代替,采用形象替代法,尽量能让对方明白其意,也可以考虑意译法和增补法,例如:

入乡随俗 When in Rome, do as the Romans do.(形象替代法)
The leopard cannot change its spots. 江山易改,本性难移(形象替代法)
你讲的这个例子很风趣,但是跟我讲的风马牛不相及。I think you have made a very vivid and interesting example. But I think it is dramatically different from the main part that I was talking about.(意译法)
as cool as a cucumber 镇定自若(意译法)
解铃还须系铃人 Let him who tied the bell on the tiger take it off, meaning, whoever started that trouble ends it by himself.(增补法)
三个臭皮匠,赛过诸葛亮。Three cobblers with their wits combined surpass Zhuge Liang the mastermind — Two heads are better than one.(增补法)

## 技巧练习  Exercises for Skills

A. Interpret the following idioms:
Walls have ears.
The die is cast.
a thorn in the flesh
to move heaven and earth
to steal the show
心急吃不了热豆腐。
十五个吊桶打水——七上八下。
班门弄斧
狼狈为奸
南水北调

B. Interpret the following paragraphs into Chinese:
(1) Our pleasure now is something which you and your distinguished delegation will recognize. For one of the first remarks in *The Analects of Confucius* is: "Is it not a delight that friends should visit from afar?" We wish you and all your delegation a very warm welcome to No. 10 Downing Street and to

Britain.

(2) The question is, where do we go from here? How do we work together to be on the right side of history together? More than 50 years ago, Hu Shi, one of your great political thinkers and a teacher at this university, said these words: "Now some people say to me you must sacrifice your individual freedom so that the nation may be free. But I reply, the struggle for individual freedom is the struggle for the nation's freedom. The struggle for your character is the struggle for the nation's character."

C. **Interpret the following paragraphs into English:**
(1) 我们的先哲通过观察宇宙万物的变动不居,提出了"天行健,君子以自强不息"的思想,成为激励中国人民变革创新、努力奋斗的精神力量。
(2) 中华民族历来尊重人的尊严和价值。还在遥远的古代,我们的先人就已提出"民为贵"的思想,认为"天生万物,唯人为贵"。

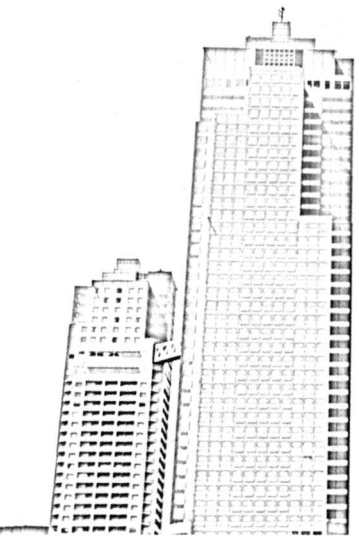

业务洽谈

第十一单元

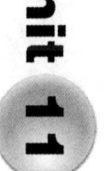

Unit 11

**Business Talk**

# 第11单元 业务洽谈 Business Talk

# 第1部分 Section 1

 **Vocabulary Work**

| | | | |
|---|---|---|---|
| catalogue | 产品目录 | model | 型号 |
| quotation | 报价 | indication prices | 参考价格 |
| light aluminum alloy | 轻型铝合金 | after-sales service | 售后服务 |
| lubricant | 润滑油 | make | 品牌 |
| discount | 折扣 | structured deal | 阶段式协议 |
| receipt of invoice | 发货收据 | CIF (Cost, Insurance & Freight) | 到岸价（成本、保险加运输） |

 **Text Interpreting**

Interpret the following conversation alternatively into Chinese and English:

### Price Bargaining

A: I have seen your exhibits in the showroom and studied your catalogues. I'm particularly interested in your racing bicycles. I think some of the models will sell well in the States.

B: 谢谢您对我们的产品感兴趣。我们的自行车在全球市场确实很有竞争力。请问，您对哪些车型特别有兴趣呢？

A: Here's a list of my requirements. I'd like to have your lowest quotation, CIF New York.

B: 谢谢您的询价。请告诉我们你们的订货量，以便我们计算报价。

A: I'll do that. Meanwhile, could you give me an indication of the prices?

B: 这是我们的最新价目单，请过目。

A: My goodness. I'm really surprised to see the prices you're asking.

B: 您觉得我们的价格太低吗？

A: That's not exactly what I had in mind. They're much more than what we expected. In fact, you'll find your prices compare unfavorably with those of other makes. I can show you others' quotations that are lower than yours.

B: 我们的报价有根有据。我们的赛车都是新产品，比老的车型轻多了。轻型铝合

· 137 ·

金赛车只有10公斤重。而且,我们在各地的分公司会提供良好的售后服务,你们根本不用担心技术问题。另外,我们还提供各种配件,包括润滑油。

A: I know your research and service costs are high. But we're large dealers in racing bicycles and I'm sure there's a promising market in our area for moderately priced bicycles of the models mentioned. This will slash your costs, right?

B: 你说得对。折扣的大小取决于订单的大小。如果你们能保证跟我们长期合作,并且订货量大,比如说半年达到800件,那我们会给贵方九二折。另外,每超出100件,我们增加九九折。

A: What if we place orders over 2,000 pieces for 12 months, with a guarantee? May I suggest we sign a contract at a 16% discount on your quoted prices? That would help to introduce your products to our customers. You know, when we're launching a product in a new market, we usually start with low prices, so as to compete with the dominant makes. You don't price yourself out of the market.

B: 八四折似乎有点太高了,那样我们就没什么赚头了。为了做这笔生意,我们打算给你们八六折。这可是我们的底价,恐怕没回旋的余地了。不然,我们就没多少利润可言了。

A: It's unwise for either of us to stick to one's own price. Let's meet each other halfway so as to conclude the business. What about a structured deal? I mean 16% for the first six months and 14% for the next six months.

B: 那就前半年八五折,后半年八六折。我们只能让到这个地步了。不然,过不了多久,我就会到贵公司找工作了。

A: Good. What if we pay within 10 days from receipt of invoice?

B: 我们通常按实价打九零折。

A: Sounds interesting! Now shall we come to the next issue?

## 课文注释  Notes on the Text

1. sell well 的意思是"有销路,卖得好"之义,其反义词为 sell badly。例如,Anti-age creams always sell well.(抗衰老面霜的销路总是很好。)

2. 您对哪些车型特别有兴趣呢? What is it in particular you're interested in? 其中 in particular,相当于 particularly 或者 especially,意思是"特别地"或者"尤其"。例如,Is there anything in particular that you want to talk about?(你有什么特别想谈的吗?)

3. 请过目:Please take/have a look at it。"过目"也可以为 run through;例如,There's a document for you to run through.(有份文件请您过目。)

4. 您觉得我们的价格太低吗? 这句话直译为 Do you think our prices are too low? 显然没有 You think we should be asking for more? 更为地道,更能体现出原句所具有的幽默感。

5. In fact, you'll find your prices compare unfavorably with those of other makes: 事实上,跟其他厂家的价格相比,你们在价格上没有优势可言。其中 compare favorably/unfavorably (with) ... 的意思是"(和……相比较)有/没有优势";例如,The fabrics imported from China are 20% cheaper and compare very favorably in quality.(从中国进口的布料价格便宜两成,而且质地上也很有优势。)这一句也

# 第11单元 业务洽谈 Business Talk

可以翻译为：Compared with those of other makes, your prices are not competitive.

6. 恐怕没回旋的余地了：I'm afraid that we can't make any further reduction.（恐怕我们再也不能降低价格了。）同样的说法还有：I'm afraid that we can't make any further concessions in price.（恐怕我们再也不能让步了。）
7. Let's meet each other halfway so as to conclude the business：我们各让一半，生意就成交了。也可以说 If we can reach some middle ground, we might have a deal.
8. 我们就没多少利润可言了：这是生意场上很常见的一种策略，英文可以说 That would leave us a much lower margin, 也可以说 That would slash our profit margin.

## 词语扩展 Developing Vocabulary and Expressions

- offer(or) 报盘，发盘，报价（人）
- counter-offer 还盘，接盘
- offeree 还盘人，接盘人
- buying offer 买方报盘
- selling offer 卖方报盘
- firm offer/offer with engagement 实盘
- non-firm offer/offer without engagement 虚盘
- break-even price 保本价格
- net price 净价
- unit price 单价
- floor price 底价
- minimum/lowest/rock-bottom price 最低价格
- C & F (cost and freight) 成本加运费价
- FOB (free on board) 船上交货价格，离岸价格
- terms of payment/payment terms 付款条款
- profit margin 毛利（率）
- bottom line 底线
- margin 利润，盈余
- (prices) to remain constant 保持稳定
- underquote 要价低（于他人）
- (offers) to be valid/firm for ... days 报价有效期为……天
- hold/keep ... offer open for ... days 报价有效期为……天
- entertain/accept ... offer 接收……还盘
- raise ... offer by 2% 把报盘提高2%
- cannot make any further concession 不能再作让步
- accept/cancel/confirm an order 接受/取消/确认订单
- allow/grant ... a discount of ... 给……打……折扣
- lead to a temporary rise in sales 导致销售量暂时增长
- result in a slight fall in sales 导致销售量有所下降
- suggest a comprise/propose an alternative 提出一个折中方案/另一种方案
- (prices) go down/fall/drop gradually/steadily （价格）逐渐下跌
- (prices) be/come in line with the international market （价格）跟国际市场相一致

- （prices) be out of line with the international market（价格）跟国际市场相左
- （counter-offer) be not up to the present market level（还盘）达不到现行市场价格水平
- （prices) go up/increase sharply/rapidly/drastically/dramatically（价格）急剧上涨
- （counter-offer) not to be in keeping with the current/prevailing price（还盘）跟现行价格相左

## 译操练 Interpreting Practice

### 1. 听译 Listening Interpreting

A. Listen to the sentences and interpret them into Chinese：
Sentences 1—10

B. Listen to the paragraphs and interpret them into Chinese：
Paragraphs 1—2

### 2. 视译 Sight Interpreting

A. Interpret the following sentences into Chinese：
(1) Our lowest price is $500 per unit, and we can't go down below that.
(2) We can't take a cut in the size of the order, because that means our profit margin will be slashed to below 5%.
(3) This deal promises big returns for both sides. Let's hope it's the beginning of a long and prosperous relationship.
(4) There is little scope for further reducing the price because that is the best we can do in price.
(5) The quality of our personal computer enjoys a high reputation in overseas markets.
(6) Our investigation reveals that the majority of American consumers prefer to buy low-priced new models with additional features.
(7) They have recently entered European markets and have gained a market share of 10% in three months.
(8) The company proposed a six-month contract at a 14% discount of the quoted price and was waiting for a positive react.
(9) It's hard to see how you can place such a large order. How can you turn over 1,000 pieces in such a short period of time?
(10) Let me run through this again: 2,000 units at a discount of 15%; the shipment for first 500 units to be delivered in 20 days, by the 21st.

B. Interpret the following paragraphs into Chinese：
(1) The international market for our sensors is fast growing, and you might have noticed there has been a constant rise in price in the past ten months. There is every indication of a further increase in the near future. Meanwhile, I must point out that our offer is only valid until the end of May. You'd better place an order with us in a week, because we may have to raise the prices when the present stocks run

# 第 11 单元 业务洽谈 Business Talk

out. By the way, delivery in May is the best we can do for you if the order is placed at once, since the demand for our products has kept increasing. Anyway, it's up to you to decide.

（2） In the past five years, our unit sales have gone up steadily—by 300%, and profits have increased almost by 250 percent. However, most of our sales—more than 80%—were made in Shanghai, and the rest came from the nearby places. We're entering Guangzhou, Nanjing, and Hangzhou markets since January, and gaining more and more market shares. We now have more salespeople in these areas, and we're planning to run good advertising campaigns. By the end of this year, our sales in the new areas are expected to reach about 40% of the total in terms of unit sales.

## 3. 情景练习 ▶▶ Situational Interpreting

**Interpret the following conversation alternatively into Chinese and English. Add any information when necessary.**

> **Roles**
> Mr. King: manager of a sneaker company
> Mr. Johnson: businessman from Australia

Mr. Johnson: Good morning, Mr. King, I came to visit you in the hotel today to discuss the price of your sneakers.

Mr. King: 欢迎！欢迎！Johnson先生。请坐。你看过我们的报价吗？

Mr. Johnson: Yes. The price you quoted is AU＄150 per pair CIF Sidney.

Mr. King: 不错。你觉得这个价格如何？

Mr. Johnson: Oh, I'm afraid it is too high. Now, sneakers from other Asian producers are available in Australia and their prices are much lower than that of yours. They range from AU＄100 to 120. We've been doing business with each other for more than five years and your sneakers enjoy popularity in Australia. But I'm afraid other producers are drawing business away from us.

Mr. King: 我们的鞋子质量上乘,当然价格要高一点。

Mr. Johnson: Yes, I understand. This is the main reason why we continue to import from you. We also sell sneakers from other producers and the prices are usually 10% to 15% lower, but the quality is similar to yours. I only hope you can make your price comparable to those of others.

Mr. King: 那好吧,为了生意,我们愿意做出一些让步。你觉得降价2%如何？

Mr. Johnson: Are you kidding? 2% amounts to nothing compared with 10% to 15%.

Mr. King: 你的意思是让我们降价10% to 15%？

Mr. Johnson: Not as much as that, but at least 6%.

Mr. King: 对不起,我们达不到那个程度。最多也只能到4%。

Mr. Johnson: Let's say 4% for 1,000 pairs.

# 第2部分 Section 2

## Vocabulary Work

| 支付条款 | terms of payment | 保修 | warranty |
|---|---|---|---|
| 信用证 | Letter of Credit (L/C) | 不可撤销信用证 | irrevocable L/C |
| 保兑信用证 | confirmed L/C | 汇票 | draft |
| 发票 | invoice | 保险单 | insurance policy |
| 产地证明 | certificate of origin | 托收支付 | payment by collection |
| 汇款支付 | payment by remittance | 提货单 | bill of lading |
| 保修期 | period of warranty, warranty period | 交货日期 | time/date of delivery, delivery time/date |
| 承兑交单 | D/A (document against acceptance) | 付款交单 | D/P (document against payment) |

## Text Interpreting

Interpret the following conversation alternatively into English and Chinese:

### 保险、交货和支付条款

A: Fillmore先生,我们已经谈妥了价格和订货量问题,现在我们该谈保修问题了吧?这些型号的赛车保修期多长时间?

B: It's 6 months, but I can make an exception in your case and give you a one-year warranty period.

A: 也就是说,在一年时间内如果任何一辆车子出了问题,你们会免费维修。听上去不错。但是,那一年后出了问题怎么办呢?你知道,赛车不同于普通的自行车,在训练和比赛中什么事情都可能发生。

B: Well, we have a special scheme: it's $400 or so for a year's cover. And we guarantee to carry out any repairs on site within 24 hours provided the bicycles are used within the city. If you phone our local office before ten o'clock in the morning, we usually come out to your place the same day. Outside the city it will obviously take longer. Of course you can send the faulty bikes to our local office.

# 第11单元 业务洽谈 Business Talk

A：明白了。那交货日期呢？我们希望你们能在31日之前履行第一批订单。我们的这批货要的很急，你知道现在是赛车的销售旺季。

B：You mean in 25 days? We usually deliver within 40 days from receipt of your order—30 days at most. But if you decide now and let me have a firm order with a 10 percent deposit, I think we can promise to get the vehicles to you by the 5th next month—that'll be 30 days. We'll give your order top priority. And remember you can have a 10 percent discount of net price provided we receive the full amount in ten days from now.

A：现在该谈付款了。你们通常的做法是什么？

B：In our export business, we demand payment by confirmed, irrevocable Letter of Credit payable against documents.

A：你们也使用其他付款方式吗，如托收、汇款和银行担保书？你也知道，使用信用证便意味着增加我们的进口成本。我们去银行开信用证，要付一笔押金的。你们能否破例接受承兑交单或者付款交单呢？

B：I'm afraid we cannot accommodate you there. We have been doing business with all other buyers on 100% confirmed, irrevocable L/C. I suggest you consult your bank and see if they can reduce the required deposit to a minimum amount.

A：谢谢，我会看看他们能降低多少。请问你们会提供哪些单据呢？

B：Together with the draft, we'll send you a complete set of Bills of Landing, an invoice, an export license, an insurance policy, a certificate of origin, and a certificate of inspection.

A：我们需要一式三份的发票，要有签字；保险单一式两份，包括海洋险和战争险，投保金额为发票金额的110％。

B：That's right. We'll do that. And now let's iron out the remaining details...

## 课文注释 Notes on the Text

1. 我们已经谈妥了价格和订货量问题：We've settled questions of price and quantity. "谈妥了价格"也可以翻译为 have settled the question of price，当然也可以处理为 The terms of price have been agreed upon.

2. It's 6 months, but I can make an exception in your case...保修期是6个月，但我可以给您破例。make an exception 是"把……当作例外"之义，例如 I don't usually lend people money, but in your case I'll make an exception.（我一般不借钱给他人，但你的情况例外。）

3. 也就是说，在一年时间内如果任何一辆车子出了问题，你们会免费维修。So free repairs if any bicycles develop a fault within one-year period. 谈判的时候，经常会重复对方所讲的内容，以便得到对方认可，目的是为了避免不必要的误解。"也就是说"在这种情况下可以翻译为 you mean 或 that is to say。"（车子或机器）出了问题/故障"最常见的说法是 break down 或 develop a fault，例如，The truck broke down/had a breakdown on the road.（卡车在路上出了问题。）

4. 那一年后出了问题怎么办呢？What happens if a bicycle breaks down after a year? 在口语中，我们会使用 what's going to happen/what happens/what will happen...？询问"会有什么结果"或"该怎么办"。例如，What will happen if she finds out?（她要是发现了，该怎么办？）

5. 在训练和比赛中什么事情都可能发生：You never know what will happen in training or racing. 当然，也可以说，Anything can happen in training or racing.

6. And we guarantee to carry out any repairs on site within 24 hours provided the bicycles are used within the city：在市区内，我们保证在 24 小时内到指定地点进行维修。其中 on site 的意思是"就地的"；同样的说法还有 on the spot 或 on field。

7. 你知道现在是赛车的销售旺季：This is the season for racing bicycles in our market, you know. "旺季"是 peak period, busy season, midseason 或 the height of the season。Don't travel there at the height of the season.（旅游旺季别去那个地方。）但是，in season 或 out of season 其实就是"旺季"或"淡季"。例如，Hotels charge more in (peak/busy) season and less out of season.（宾馆在旺季收费较高，淡季则比较便宜。）

8. We'll give your order top priority：我们会优先处理你们的订单。give sth. top/high priority 就是"把……置于优先考虑的位置"。

9. And remember you can have a 10 percent discount of net price provided we receive the full amount in ten days from now：不要忘了，十日内支付全部货款我们会给 10％的实价折扣。net price 是"实价"，打过折扣的价格。

10. I'm afraid we cannot accommodate you there：这个我们恐怕不能破例。accommodate 的意思是"迁就，容忍"。

## 词语扩展  Developing Vocabulary and Expressions

- 保兑行                          confirming bank
- 光票信用证                clean L/C
- 跟单信用证                documentary L/C
- 可撤销信用证           revocable L/C
- 可转让信用证           transferable L/C
- 不可转让信用证      non-transferable L/C
- 预支信用证                anticipatory L/C
- 议付信用证                negotiation L/C
- 承兑信用证                acceptance L/C
- 集装箱                         freight/cargo container
- 分批装运                   partial shipment
- 转运                             transshipment
- 装运单据                   shipping document
- 装运                             shipment
- 预付运费                   freight prepaid
- 保险费                         premium rate
- 海洋险                         marine risk
- 战争险                         war risk
- 平安险                         free from particular average (F.P.A.)
- 附加险                         extraneous risks
- 短量险                         risk of shortage
- 破损险                         risk of breakage
- 运输险                         risk of carriage
- 渗漏险                         risk of leakage

## 第 11 单元 业务洽谈 Business Talk

- ❖ 目的地 destination
- ❖ 提货 take delivery
- ❖ 提货通知 cargo delivery notice
- ❖ 提前/推迟装运 advance/postpone the shipment
- ❖ 离岸检验 inspection at the port of shipment
- ❖ 到岸检验 inspection at the port of destination
- ❖ 开箱检验 open-package visual inspection
- ❖ 退款 refund
- ❖ 一式两份的 in duplicate
- ❖ 一式三份的 in triplicate

## 译操练 *Interpreting Practice*

### 1. 听译 ▶▶▶ Listening Interpreting

A. Listen to the sentences and interpret them into English.
   Sentences 1—10

B. Listen to the paragraphs and interpret them into English.
   Paragraphs 1—2

### 2. 视译 ▶▶▶ Sight Interpreting

A. Interpret the following sentences into English：
   （1）我们会免费修你的车,因为它还在保修期内。
   （2）说到售后服务,你们在洛杉矶有维修点吗?
   （3）我们会在两个星期内开出以你方为受益人的不可撤销信用证。
   （4）这笔生意,我们就破例接受付款交单。
   （5）如果你们能在十天内下订单,我们可以在3月份装运。
   （6）我们要了解贵方的市场推广计划,然后才能给你们独家代理权。
   （7）你知道,有些食品是季节性的,我们必须在8月底以前上市,不然会错过季节的。
   （8）如果你们坚持8月底之前交货,那你们就要接受分批装运,也就是说8月份交一半,九月份交另外一半。
   （9）我们的产品保证质量。一旦发现假货,我们会退款的。
   （10）请准备中英文合同各一份,两份同样有效。

B. Interpret the following paragraphs into English：
   （1）因为这是我们的第一笔生意,我希望我们在付款方面按照惯例行事,也就是说使用即期信用证付款。我知道你们恐怕有自己的难处:信用证付款程序有点复杂,费用也高,而且你们还要付押金。但我们也存在不能按时收回货款的困难。我们大家做生意都不容易。如果可能的话,我也想给你们破例,但是数额在3000美元以下我才接受付款交单。你们的情况不同。所以,很遗憾,我们只能接受保兑、不可撤销信用证。
   （2）得知你们对100号订单的货物质量不满,我们深感遗憾。我们准备给你们进行合理的赔偿,但是赔偿金额不会达到你们所提出的总价值的40%。我们建议降价25%,你方接受货物。

145

## 3. 情景练习 ▶▶ Situational Interpreting

Interpret based on the information given below. Add any information when necessary.

> Roles:
> 刘先生：北京佳美家具公司
> Edward Frank：美国 Frank 兄弟家具公司总经理
> 陈先生：翻译

北京佳美家具公司的展厅给 Edward Frank 留下了深刻的印象。Frank 首先在价格上同佳美家具公司的刘先生讨价还价并最终达成协议，进而就发货日期、保险和支付条款等问题进行商谈。下列信息可供参考：

- Frank 认为佳美家具不仅美观大方，而且结实耐用，在美国市场上肯定有潜力，但其价格高于同类产品；
- 刘先生说，佳美家具属于目前市场上的畅销产品，科技含量高，采用上等东南亚木材；
- Frank 提议佣金增加 5%，但在刘先生的妥协下双方同意增加 3%；
- 刘先生同意在收到货款后立即发货到纽约港；
- 保险包括海洋险和战争险，投保金额为发票金额的 110%。

## 译常识与技巧  Interpreting Tips and Skills

### 缩略语（Abbreviations）

做笔记可以用符号夹杂缩略语。因此，译员也需要记忆一定数量的缩略语，如用"工"表示"工业"，"G"表示"政府"，"E"代表"经济"。译员常常自己发明一些缩略语，但我们不鼓励无休止地设计新的缩略语，因为记忆和识别新符号可能给表达带来额外的负担。

下面是一些常用的英文字母和汉字所代表的信息：

| 缩略语 | 信息意义 | 缩略语 | 信息意义 |
| --- | --- | --- | --- |
| ACPT | 接受 | GNP | 国民生产总值 |
| ATTN | 注意 | GDP | 国内生产总值 |
| CLSD | 关闭 | SOE | 国有企业 |
| CONC | 有关 | R&D | 研究和发展 |
| DBL | 两倍并购 | M&A | 企业并购 |
| EXCL | 排除 | ROI | 投资回报率 |
| Hon. | 尊敬的 | JV | 合资企业 |
| INT | 兴趣，利息 | SEZ | 经济特区 |
| IOU | 欠条 | UNESCO | 联合国教科文组织 |
| I/O | 替代 | VPN | 虚拟专用网 |
| MTKS | 十分感谢 | RM | 房间 |
| NLT | 不迟于 | ACK | 承认 |
| O/S | 出售 | 改开 | 改革开放 |
| PLS | 请 | 社保 | 社会保险企业 |
| ASAP | 尽快 | 国标 | 国民经济发展指标 |

## 第11单元 业务洽谈 Business Talk

| | | | |
|---|---|---|---|
| THO | 尽管 | 野区 | 野生动物保护区 |
| WT | 等待 | 5yP | 五年计划 |
| AF | 如下 | 优x | 优越性 |
| ICO | 假如 | 现h | 现代化 |
| FYI | 供参考 | 政j | 政治家 |

英语中的一些常用后缀也可用缩略形式：

ing → G
  speaking = speakG              building = BLDG
ed → D
  accepted = ACPTD            agreed = AGRD
ment → T/MT
  shipment = SHPT              agreement = AGRMT
able/ible/ble → BL
  available = AVLBL               possible = PSBL
ful → FL
  handful = HNDFL               meaningful = MNGFL
er/or → R
  debtor = DR                       better = BTR
est/ist → ST
  soonest = SNST                latest = LATST
less → LS
  worthless = WTHLS           regardless = RGDLS

# 第 12 单元　商务谈判

## Unit 12　Business Negotiation

# 第12单元 商务谈判 Business Negotiation

# 第1部分 Section 1

## 词汇预习  Vocabulary Work

| | | | |
|---|---|---|---|
| sole agency | 独家代理 | submit | 提交 |
| income bracket | 收入等级 | proposal | 建议书 |
| switch | 转移 | initial work | 前期工作 |
| promote | 推销 | commission | 佣金 |
| turnover | 营业额 | sample contract | 合同草案 |

## 口译实践  Text Interpreting

Interpret the following conversation alternatively into English and Chinese:

### Sole Agency

王先生： 史密斯先生,我一直期待着在上海与您会面。

Mr. Smith： Me too. It's been almost a year since I saw you last time in the States. That's a great year for both of us and you are now one of the most important dealers of our products in Asia. We have been doing business with each other for four years and we have built up trust and a strong working relationship. By the way, please call me Bill.

王先生： 你说得对,史密……哦……比尔。通过我们的代理商,四种型号的产品去年销售总额已达20万美元。如果我们没有估算错的话,这已经占到你们在亚洲销量的百分之二十多。嗯……你也知道,我们在北京、上海和天津的办事处在过去几个月内陆续开业,正在逐渐赢得市场。

Mr. Smith： I understand you're coming to the request to act as our sole agent in China, which you made in one of the recent emails to us. Our opinions, you know, have been positive. But... but our research shows most of your sales are made in Shanghai. Of course we have noticed your work in other parts of China.

王先生： 不错,但是我们对销售额还是很满意的。毕竟是新产品,要求太高也不现实。我相信我们今年的销售成绩会比去年高出很多,因为我们在其他地区的销售网络会发挥作用。我们做过调查,那些地区的消费者对这些产品很感兴趣,特别是在城市,因为城市里高收入人群的比例较高。

151

Mr. Smith: I know the Chinese market has great potential. We all know the size of population has always been an important factor for any product. That means you have a lot to do; it's not easy to persuade customers to switch to a new product.

王先生: 你说得很对。但是,我们的得力武器是在上海销售你们的产品的经验。还有,我们更了解中国人。我的意思是,我们对本地很了解。一旦我们签了在中国整个地区的独家代理协议,我们就可以做大量工作,大力推广你们的产品,让消费者相信他们真的需要你们的产品。

Mr. Smith: Your analysis is quite convincing, and I'm sure an active, experienced agent is able to develop a successful regional business. But as an agent, your orders must be big enough. Furthermore, we need to know your sales volume during the past three years, your plans for promoting the products, and the possible annual turnover.

王先生: 我们会给你们提交一份详尽的计划书。不过现在我可以肯定地告诉你,要是我们成为你们在中国的代理,年销售量会翻一番。

Mr. Smith: I hope your sales will increase sharply.

王先生: 只要你们提供全力的技术和市场支持,我们不会令你们失望的。现在,我想谈谈佣金问题。一份两年的代理期,佣金是多少?

Mr. Smith: Our usual practice is 10 per cent. And as you know commissions depend on the quantity of goods ordered. You get a higher rate if you order a bigger quantity.

王先生: 我觉得百分之十是不行的。你肯定知道,为了打开局面,在上海以外的地区我们得做大规模的广告宣传。你刚才也说到,为了从其他厂家抢生意,要做大量的前期工作。你们必须把广告费用考虑在内。另外,我们还得培训不少销售人员。我感觉佣金要达到百分之十五才行。

Mr. Smith: That's too much for us. To tell you the truth, we're taking the initial work into consideration. Tell you what, the best I can do is 12 per cent for one year if your sales reach ＄400,000.

王先生: 这个想法不错。如果行的话,我们再讨论下一年的佣金。

Mr. Smith: And, I must make it clear that as our agent you shouldn't sell similar products from other manufacturers.

王先生: 当然不会,除非得到你们事先同意。

Mr. Smith: Major issues seem to be set. I will bring in a sample contract tomorrow. If you like, we can sign it then.

## 课文注释  Notes on the Text

1. 毕竟是新产品,要求太高也不现实。It's a new product, you know. How could you do better? 这句中的"要求太高也不现实"可以灵活处理为 How could you do better? 这样显得既口语化,也表达了原句的含义。

2. ……城市里高收入人群的比例较高。... in cities that have a higher than average proportion of people in the higher income brackets. "高收入人群"这里指和乡村比较而言的城市高收入人群的比例,所以可以译成 have a higher than average proportion of people in the higher income brackets。其中,income bracket 指"收入等级",例如 people in the ＄100,000 to ＄150,000 bracket(收入在 10 万到 15 万美

元的人)。

3. It's not easy to persuade customers to switch to a new product. 要让顾客放弃自己熟悉的产品,转而购买一种新的产品,并不容易。原文中的 switch to a new product 指的是"转而使用一种新产品",言下之意是放弃自己原先使用的产品。在翻译中,应该把这个隐含意义表示出来显得更地道一些。

4. 你肯定知道,为了打开局面,在上海以外的地区我们得做大规模的广告宣传。Surely you'll agree that a big advertising campaign will be needed to pave the way in the new areas for the products. "打开局面"的意思是有一个良好的开端,所以可以译成 to pave the way for the products。

5. 你刚才也说到,为了从其他厂家抢生意,要做大量的前期工作。As you indicated just now, a lot of initial work has to be done to draw business away from other producers. "抢生意"可以译成 to draw business away from other manufacturers 或者 to compete with other dealers for business。另外,这里我们可以使用被动语态,避免太多的句子以 we 开头,从而避免使谈话显得单调。

6. 另外,我们还得培训不少销售人员。The training adds to the expenses too. 王先生说这句话的意思是:培训也要花钱。所以,如果把这句话直译为 In addition, we have to train salespersons,就显得拐弯抹角而含义不清。

## 词语扩展  *Developing Vocabulary and Expressions*

| | |
|---|---|
| ❖ agency agreement | 代理协议 |
| ❖ agent service | 代理业 |
| ❖ general agent | 总代理(商) |
| ❖ selling agent | 销售代理(商) |
| ❖ sales representative | 销售代表 |
| ❖ insurance agent | 保险代理(商) |
| ❖ import agent | 进口代理(商) |
| ❖ landing agent | 卸货代理(商) |
| ❖ distributor | 经销商 |
| ❖ entrust | 委托 |
| ❖ binding | 有约束力的 |
| ❖ business connection | 业务关系 |
| ❖ draft agreement | 协议草案 |
| ❖ effective period | 有效期 |
| ❖ intermediary | 中间人,中间商 |
| ❖ invoice value | 发票值 |
| ❖ letter of confirmation | 确认书 |
| ❖ market share | 市场份额 |
| ❖ marketing ability | 销售能力 |
| ❖ advertising campaign | 广告攻势 |
| ❖ marketing campaign | 营销攻势 |
| ❖ publicity material | 宣传资料 |
| ❖ selling season | 销售季节 |
| ❖ sales volume | 销售量 |
| ❖ sales network | 销售网 |

- packaging 包装
- outer packing 外包装
- purchasing power 购买力
- term of validity 有效期
- deposit 保证金，押金
- letter of guarantee (L/G) 保证书
- terminate 终止

## 译操练 Interpreting Practice

### 1. 听译 Listening Interpreting

A. Listen to the sentences and interpret them into Chinese：
Sentences 1—10

B. Listen to the paragraphs and interpret them into Chinese：
Paragraphs 1—2

### 2. 视译 Sight Interpreting

A. Interpret the following sentences into Chinese：

（1）We have spacious, well-equipped showrooms where you can display the full range of your samples.

（2）Your agency has the experience we need, and we have the best-quality products.

（3）I think it premature for us to discuss the question of agency at the present stage.

（4）The commission rate will be increased in proportion to your annual turnover of the sales.

（5）We hope our handling of this first order will lead to a permanent agency.

（6）Thank you for your offering us the agency in our market for your products and we really appreciate the confidence you have placed in us. We'll make greater efforts to push the sales.

（7）If you can push the sales of our products successfully for the next quarter, there will be a very good chance of our working out a mutual beneficial agency agreement.

（8）I want to make it clear that we have no intention to consider exclusive sales in your market at present.

（9）We are interested in your proposal to make advertisements for our products in China, but we feel that the market conditions may not make worthwhile the expense of even a modest advertising campaign.

（10）We're now representing several other manufacturers and have enjoyed sales results above average.

B. Interpret the following paragraphs into Chinese：

（1）The agent may use the trademarks of the seller during the effective period of

## 第 12 单元 商务谈判 Business Negotiation

the agreement only in connection with the sale of the stipulated products. Even after the termination of the agreement the agent may continue to do so to sell the products held in stock. However, the agent acknowledge that the patents, trademarks, copyright and other industrial property rights used in the products remain to be sole properties of the seller and shall not dispute them in any way.

（2）Disputes arising from the performance of the agreement should be settled through friendly negotiations. If no settlement is reached in negotiations, the case shall then be submitted for arbitration to the local international economic and trade arbitration commission and the rules of the commission will be applied. The award of the arbitration will be final and binding upon both parties. The arbitration fee shall be borne by the losing party unless otherwise awarded by the arbitration organization.

## 3. 情景练习 ▶▶▶ Situational Interpreting

**Interpret the following conversation alternatively into English and Chinese. Add any information when necessary.**

> **Roles**
> 张先生：an agent
> Mr. Green：a customer

张先生： 我们现在是不是该谈谈代理的细节问题了？

Mr. Green： All right. The territory to be covered of the sales agency will be the whole of Asia.

张先生： 我同意。那代理时间多长呢？

Mr. Green： Two years, and renewable for a further period of two years if both parties agree.

张先生： 行。佣金问题呢？

Mr. Green： We usually allow a commission of 5% on the invoice value.

张先生： 我觉得5%低了点儿。你也知道,在亚洲微波炉市场的竞争相当激烈。我们得花大量资金去做广告宣传。若5%的佣金,那我们就没有利润可言了。但如果你们承担广告费用,我们就接受你们的建议。

Mr. Green： Generally we don't take advertising expenses. Our price is worked out according to the cost. If we put advertising expenses on our account, it means an increase in our cost.

张先生： 我得告诉你,你们的竞争对手提出的佣金可要比这个高。

Mr. Green： Well, to our mutual benefit we shall allow 2% of your sales to be appropriated for advertising purposes.

张先生： 如果你们不能再提高的话,我们就接受你说的吧：佣金5%,加上销售额的2%作为广告宣传费。

Mr. Green： The draft for agreement will be ready tomorrow. As soon as you receive your firm's confirmation we'll make out a formal one.

张先生： 行呀。谢谢！

# Section 2 第2部分

 **Vocabulary Work**

| | | | |
|---|---|---|---|
| 推销员 | sales people | 行业 | line of business |
| 办公设备 | office equipment | 短缺 | scarcity |
| 盈余;剩余 | abundance | 买方市场 | buyer's market |
| 强行推销 | hard sell | 分部 | branch |
| 咨询式销售 | consultative selling | 双向交流 | two-way communication |
| 产品目录 | catalogue | 善意,友好 | goodwill |

 **Text Interpreting**

Interpret the following speech into English：

### 如何做成功的推销员

女士们、先生们：

　　下午好！今天我想谈一谈在我们这一行，也就是办公家具行业，优秀的推销员应该具备哪些素质。你们知道，各国经济已经从短缺期进入剩余期。现在的商品交易量比历史上任何时候都要大。当下的市场为买方市场，消费者要求的是服务而不是强行推销。那我们怎样才能与众不同呢？当然，答案就是推销员的素质和服务质量。我们公司在世界各地有成千上万的优秀推销员，而你们是我们在这个地区的新鲜血液，也会成为我们本地区分部中最重要的成员。

　　我们作为推销员的首要任务是什么呢？为顾客服务。你们一定注意到我没有用"向顾客推销"这个说法，因为我们所做的事情远远不只是"推销"。通过"咨询式销售"，我们帮助顾客做出明智的决定。我们的方式是同顾客平等对话，在这个过程中我们了解信息，同时提供信息。咨询型的推销员不以居高临下的方式和顾客讲话，不会去主宰他们。相反，他们通过双向的交流，去了解消费者的需求。询问顾客很有必要，不然你怎么真正了解他们的要求？在销售一套办公用品的时候，我们销售的远不止于几件家具。我们销售的可能是一种新形象。顾客想让人一走进他们的办公室就能认可他们的能力。办公室必须体现出主人想要的一种成功的氛围。

　　咨询式销售强调的是信息的供给和协商，而不是让顾客适应我们的思维方式。有了信息的交流，有了对顾客需求的反应，我们就取得了顾客的信任。如今的客户对自

# 第 12 单元　商务谈判　Business Negotiation

已要购买的东西希望有更多的、更全面的了解。这就意味着,优秀的推销员必须了解自己的产品。在这间展室里面,我们只有为数不多的几种款式,你们必须对这些款式非常熟悉。而且,你们还要知道我们还能提供哪些选择,有什么颜色,送货要花多长时间,以及最终的花费会有多少等。你们不可能是万事通,什么都懂,那是不可能的。但是,你们每个人都要尽可能地去了解,身边要有产品目录和产品介绍,不知道就去查阅。

对顾客、对自己要诚实。如果你自己了解自己推销的产品,那你就不会不诚实。要真心诚意地去帮助顾客购买他们中意的产品。顾客满意了,我们就成功了一半。满意的顾客会对我们的公司产生信任感,是我们的活广告,因为他们会在朋友和同事那里给我们做宣传。

优秀的推销员在销售的过程中总是很有计划。咨询式销售是一个有计划的过程,可以清楚地分为四步:

1. 了解顾客需求;
2. 帮助顾客选择合适的产品;
3. 向顾客说明这款产品如何达到了他们的要求;
4. 顾客购买后,要确保货物会准时、完好无损地送达,并保证顾客对货物完全满意。

同时,优秀的推销员很讲求职业道德。你们应该自始至终以顾客需求为中心。职业推销员总是把顾客的利益放在首位。你们必须真心诚意地去了解并去满足顾客的需求,不要刻意夸大购买产品后得到的利益。产品销售之后,回访顾客也很重要,这样可以建立友情,确保顾客真正对所购买的产品称心如意。

最后,一位优秀的推销员明白他们不经意之间也许会破坏自己的销售形象。你们要为自己和自己的产品树立正面的形象。不要穿会给人留下错误印象的衣服。讲话不应太快或太慢,更不能高声介绍。握手时坚定有力,会显示出你的力量和诚意。微笑会让顾客敞开心扉,说出他们对所需产品的真实想法。最后一点是,要充满自信。有自信心的推销员能提高销售量。有了自信,成功就不远了。

谢谢大家!

## 课文注释  Notes on the Text

1. 你们知道,各国经济已经从短缺期进入剩余期。You see, economies have moved from a period of scarcity to one of abundance. "进入"一词可以直接译成 move from ... to ... 或者 enter。例如 enter a new phase/move to a new stage(进入一个新的阶段)。

2. 当下的市场为买方市场,消费者要求的是服务而不是强行推销。It's a buyer's market and the buyer demands service rather than hard sell. 汉语的"而不是"常可以译成 rather than 或者 instead of。例如,Rather than criticizing his wife, he tried to find out if there was something wrong. (他试图去了解到底出了什么问题,而不是去批评妻子。)

3. 你们一定注意到我没有用"向顾客推销"这个说法,因为我们所做的事情远远不只是"推销"。You must have noticed that I don't say *sell to the customer*, because we're doing far more than just selling. 英语中修饰形容词比较级形式时,常用 much, far, a great deal, a lot 等。例如,An agent has to do much/far more than selling a product in an area. (代理的工作远远不止于在一个地区销售一种产品。)下文"在销售一套办公用品的时候,我们销售的远不止于几件家具"一句也可以如

157

法炮制,翻译为: In selling new office equipment we're selling far/much more than pieces of furniture.

4. 顾客满意了,我们就成功了一半。Half the battle is customer satisfaction. 这句话可以用英文中的俗语 half the battle, 其意思是"接近成功/胜利"。例如, If you can get an interview, that's half the battle. (得到了面试的机会, 你就接近成功了。)

5. 满意的顾客会对我们的公司产生信任感,是我们最好的活广告,因为他们会在朋友和同事那里给我们做宣传。A satisfied customer develops company loyalty and provides our best advertising, because they tell their friends and colleagues about our business. 这里把"我们最好的活广告"翻译为 our best advertising 准确地表达了原句的意思,没有必要硬译"活"字,反而影响理解。

6. 同时,优秀的推销员很讲求职业道德。Good sales people are also ethical in their sales. "职业道德"的英文表达是 professional ethics。例如, His professional ethics are suspect, but he is within the law. (他的职业道德令人怀疑,但他并没有违法。) 但是, "讲求职业道德"可以直接译为 be ethical。在翻译时,我们有时要 translate the meaning, 而不能拘泥于词和句子的表面形式。这一点在口译中更为重要。

7. 你们应该自始至终以顾客需求为中心。You should always concentrate on the customer's needs. "以……为中心"可以用动词 concentrate/focus (one's attention) (on)。例如, We must concentrate/focus our attention on the quality rather than quantity of the products. (我们必须把重心放在产品的质量上,而不是数量上。)

8. 最后,一位优秀的推销员明白他们不经意之间也许会破坏自己的销售形象。Finally, a good sales person is conscious of the fragile nature of their sales image. 这句话的翻译完全是根据意义翻译,并没有拘泥于原文的字词。如果忠实于原文,这句话可能被译为"a good sales person understands that they would harm/tarnish their sales image easily",就显得很主观,好像是推销员有意破坏了自己的形象,而 the fragile nature of their sales image 则体现出销售形象的脆弱性这一客观特点。

9. 微笑会让顾客敞开心扉,说出他们对所需产品的真实想法。Smiling encourages the customer to tell you what they really want. 汉语句子中的"敞开心扉"和后面的"讲出他们对所需产品的真实想法"其实所指相同,因此在英文中翻译为 tell you what they really want 就表达了原句子的含义。

## 词语扩展  Developing Vocabulary and Expressions

- ❖ 销售总代理　　　　general sales agent
- ❖ 销售策略　　　　　marketing strategy
- ❖ 销售淡季　　　　　slack sales season
- ❖ 销售预算　　　　　sales budget
- ❖ 销售利润　　　　　selling profit
- ❖ 销售合同　　　　　sales contract/agreement
- ❖ 销售税　　　　　　sales tax
- ❖ 销售渠道　　　　　marketing channel
- ❖ 销售总额　　　　　gross sales
- ❖ 商标　　　　　　　trade mark
- ❖ 品牌名　　　　　　brand name
- ❖ 国内市场　　　　　home market

## 第12单元 商务谈判 Business Negotiation

- ❖ 坚挺　　　　　　　strong (market)
- ❖ 疲软　　　　　　　weak (market)
- ❖ 经济衰退　　　　　economic recession
- ❖ 经济危机　　　　　economic crisis
- ❖ 零增长　　　　　　zero-growth
- ❖ 免税　　　　　　　zero rate of duty
- ❖ 软推销　　　　　　soft sell
- ❖ 书面确认书　　　　written confirmation
- ❖ 推荐　　　　　　　recommend
- ❖ 妥协　　　　　　　compromise
- ❖ 免费　　　　　　　be free of charge
- ❖ 有效合同　　　　　valid contract
- ❖ 无效合同　　　　　void contract
- ❖ 宣传费　　　　　　publicity expense
- ❖ 广告媒体　　　　　media of advertisement
- ❖ 广告策略　　　　　advertising strategy
- ❖ 报刊广告　　　　　press advertisement
- ❖ 报纸广告　　　　　newspaper advertisement
- ❖ 车身广告　　　　　transportation advertisement
- ❖ 户外广告　　　　　outdoor advertisement
- ❖ 广告代理　　　　　advertising agent
- ❖ 总公司　　　　　　home office
- ❖ 预付款　　　　　　down payment
- ❖ 指导价格　　　　　guiding price

## 译操练  Interpreting Practice

### 1. 听译 ▶▶▶ Listening Interpreting

**A. Listen to the sentences and interpret them into English.**
Sentences 1—10

**B. Listen to the paragraphs and interpret them into English.**
Paragraphs 1—2

### 2. 视译 ▶▶▶ Sight Interpreting

**A. Interpret the following sentences into English：**

（1）我们公司经营进出口业务长达30年多年，在亚洲各地有着广泛的影响。
（2）在上海，我们是化妆品领域最主要的进口商之一。我们想了解与你们建立经贸业务关系的可能性。
（3）我已经收到你们发来的你们电脑新产品的产品介绍和价目表。我今天来的目的是想和你们谈谈你们新产品的销售问题。
（4）全世界范围内，我们这一行业的竞争都非常激烈。但是只要经营方法得当，我们会打开市场的。
（5）我们的政策一直很优惠。我们会送给你们20台免费电脑样机，供展示使用，而且你们可以享受3%的佣金。

（6）在国际贸易中，卖方不可能和世界上每一位可能的买方直接打交道。因此，中间商起着很重要的作用。中间商要么从卖方买来货物卖给买方，要么在卖方和买方之间引线搭桥。

（7）如果未能及时回复客户的询问，他们对你本人和你经销的产品的信任感就可能遭到破坏。

（8）如果我们想要销售量不断增加，市场份额越来越多，那我们就要让顾客满意，以此来同客户建立长期合作关系。

（9）为客户服务就意味着你得真心诚意地去了解客户的需求和要求。

（10）个性化服务的好处之一，就是可以让顾客对推销员和他们的产品产生一种长期的信任感。

B. Interpret the following paragraphs into English：

（1）"一带一路"已发展为超大规模合作平台和增长驱动。已有126个国家和29个国际组织同中国签署了合作协议。中国同沿线国家贸易总额超过6万亿美元，对沿线国家投资超过800多亿美元，上缴东道国税费20多亿美元，为当地创造了将近30万个就业岗位。

（2）你说得很对，在过去几年里我们从来没有向你们提过佣金的问题。那并不是我们不想要佣金。我们前几次的订货量不大，因为我们担心货物的销路问题。这几年，我们投入不少资金做宣传和促销，经过几番努力终于打开了市场。现在，我们的订货量每次都不会少于两千台。现在你们如果还不给我们佣金就说不过去了吧。

## 3. 情景练习 ▶▶▶ Situational Interpreting

Interpret based on the information given below. Add any information when necessary.

> Roles：
> 黄女士：成功的电脑推销员
> Larry Smith：《销售》(Marketing) 杂志编辑
> 陈小姐：翻译

Larry Smith 在采访黄女士，内容主要涉及她的推销经历和推销经验。下列内容可供参考：

- 黄女士从事该行业10年，成功推销电脑10万台；
- 她的推销方式主要是在公众场合和大小公司做免费讲座；
- 她认为一位推销员应该热情、诚实、自信，对所推销的产品做到如数家珍，把客户需求永远放在第一位。

##  译常识与技巧　Interpreting Tips and Skills

**顺译 (Linear Interpretation)**

顺译是指尽可能按照句中概念或意群出现的先后顺序将原语整体意思译出。顺译可以减轻记忆的压力。因此，顺译的特点是快。当原句与译出语的语序相同时，顺译就比较方便。当英汉两种语言在语序和词序上有较大差异的时候，在不影响原句意

## 第 12 单元 商务谈判 Business Negotiation

思的情况下,一般也可以使用顺译。试比较:

(1) I am happy to see you again.
    顺译法:我很高兴又见到你了。
    一般译法:又见到你了,我很高兴。

(2) Please allow me to say something on behalf of my colleagues of BE Company.
    顺译法:请允许我说几句话,来代表我们 BE 公司的同事们表达我们的心意。
    一般译法:请允许我代表我们 BE 公司的同事们说几句话,表达我们的心意。

(3) The plane crash occurred at about 8 in the morning of 12 January, 2003, near the small town of Cavendish.
    顺译法:这起飞机失事发生在 2003 年 1 月 12 日上午 8 时左右,地点是卡文迪什小镇附近。
    一般译法:这起飞机失事于 2003 年 1 月 12 日上午 8 时左右发生在卡文迪什小镇附近。

(4) Is there any possibility of my taking the first flight to Shanghai?
    顺译法:有没有可能我搭头班飞机去上海?
    一般译法:我搭头班飞机去上海,行不行?/可以吗?

必须注意的是采用顺译法翻译时,要将切分开的意群在尽可能减少移位的前提下连贯起来。在以下例句中,斜线表示断句处,"+"表示补充信息:

(5) There are still 5 minutes / before we end the meeting.
    还有十五分钟,我们就散会。

(6) Tens years have passed / before I met him again.
    十年+以后我+才+再次见到他。

(7) My visit to your university comes on an important anniversary, as Mr. Zhang mentioned.
    我对贵校的访问,+正+逢一个重要的周年纪念,这正如张先生刚才说的+那样+。

(8) Macao people sincerely hope / that the Portuguese side will continue / to cooperate with the Chinese side in a friendly way / and promote the satisfactory resolution of all issues / relating to the transfer of power and a smooth transition.
    澳门人民真诚地希望,葡萄牙方面继续与中国方面友好合作,促使各种问题的顺利解决,+实现+政权的顺利交接。

有时,顺译法译出来的句子未必很符合习惯,但在视译和同声传译等特定的场合却是译员必不可少的翻译技能。

## 技巧练习 Exercises for Skills

A. Interpret the following sentences alternatively into Chinese and English:
   (1) I am not pleased with what he told me, to take his manuscript to the publishing house.
   (2) I decided not to do the job, knowing it would take me several days to do it all by myself.
   (3) The answer to the question of whether we should continue to hold the

meeting as planned depends in part on when the epidemic disease is curbed.

（4）大学生求职，实际就是求职信息传播，就是大学生通过书信、上网、登门或引见等渠道，向可能的聘用单位表达求职的意愿。

（5）干扰大学毕业生正常求职的因素目前还不少，如不正之风、设骗欺诈、信息泛滥等等。

（6）女士们，先生们，人类现在仍然面临着许许多多的困难，又要保护环境，又要发展经济，真是任重而道远呀。

**B. Interpret the following paragraphs alternatively into Chinese and English：**

（1）Mr. President, may I thank you for the privilege of speaking here? I should also thank you for ensuring me such an attentive audience. May I wish you and your faculty colleagues every success in your future work? And to the students, I should like to wish you good fortune with your studies and a satisfying and successful career ahead.

（2）中国过去几千年的社会，非常讲究"忠""孝"二字。有关的故事、谚语很多，即使是不识字的普通老百姓也深受影响。在古代，"忠""孝"是治国治家的有力手段，统治者和家长强调忠心和服从。"忠""孝"里积极因素固然不少，但也不乏消极的东西。我们今天就是要取其精华，去其糟粕。

# Unit 13 第13单元 节日风俗

## Festivals and Customs

# 第13单元 节日风俗 Festivals and Customs

# 第1部分 Section 1

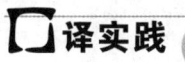 

| | | | |
|---|---|---|---|
| rewarding | 富有成就的 | absence | 缺席，不在 |
| presence | 在场 | ongoing | 持续不断的 |
| unconditional love | 无条件的爱 | structure | 塑造 |
| self-discipline | 自律 | ref | 裁判 |

**Interpret the following speech into Chinese:**

Hi, everybody. This Father's Day weekend. I'd like to spend a couple of minutes talking about what's sometimes my hardest, but always my most rewarding job—being a dad.

I grew up without my father around. He left when I was two years old, and even though my sister and I were lucky enough to have a wonderful mother and caring grandparents to raise us, I felt his absence. And I wonder what my life would have been like had he been a greater presence.

That's why I've tried so hard to be a good dad for my own children. I haven't always succeeded, of course—in the past, my job has kept me away from home more often than I liked, and the burden of raising two young girls would sometimes fall too heavily on Michelle.

But between my own experiences growing up, and my ongoing efforts to be the best father I can be, I've learned a few things about what our children need most from their parents.

First, they need our time. And more important than the quantity of hours we spend with them is the quality of those hours. Maybe it's just asking about their day, or taking a walk together, but the smallest moments can have the biggest impact.

They also need structure, including learning the values of self-discipline and responsibility. And above all, children need our unconditional love—whether they succeed or make mistakes; when life is easy and when life is tough.

We also know that every father has a personal responsibility to do right by our kids as well. All of us can encourage our children to turn off the video games and pick up a book. All of us can pack a healthy lunch for our son, or go outside and play ball with our daughter. And all of us can teach our children the difference between right and wrong, and show them through our own example the value in treating one another as we wish to be treated.

Our kids are pretty smart. They understand that life won't always be perfect, that sometimes the road gets rough, that even great parents don't get everything right. But more than anything, they just want us to be a part of their lives.

So recently, I took on a second job: assistant coach for Sasha's basketball team. On Sundays, we'd get the team together to practice, and a couple of times, I'd help coach the games. It was a lot of fun—even if Sasha rolled her eyes when her dad voiced his displeasure with the refs.

I was so proud watching her run up and down the court, seeing her learn and improve and gain confidence. And I was hopeful that in the years to come, she'd look back on experiences like these as the ones that helped define her as a person—and as a parent herself.

In the end, that's what being a parent is all about—those precious moments with our children that fill us with pride and excitement for their future; the chances we have to set an example or offer a piece of advice; the opportunities to just be there and show them that we love them.

That's something worth remembering this Father's Day, and every day.

Thanks, and Happy Father's Day to all the dads out there.

## 课文注释  Notes on the Text

1. I felt his absence. 这句话的英语表达非常简洁,完整的译文应是:"他不在,我感到是种缺憾。"在上下文意思十分充分的情况下,可以简略地译为:"我仍然觉得缺憾。"

2. And I wonder what my life would have been like had he been a greater presence. 这句话是虚拟语气,翻译时要注意把虚拟的语气表达清楚,可以译为:"我常常想假如他陪伴着我,我的生活会有怎样的不同啊。"

3. I haven't always succeeded, of course. 这句话反过来译,可以使句意更加顺畅,可以译为:"当然,我也常常做得不好。"

4. And all of us can teach our children the difference between right and wrong, and show them through our own example the value in treating one another as we wish to be treated. 这句话的翻译中可以适当地选用汉语中一些约定俗成的表达方式,如"以身则""己所不欲,勿施于人"等。整句话可以译为:"我们都能够告诉孩子什么是对,什么是错,以身作则告诉他们'己所不欲,勿施于人'的道理。"

5. But more than anything, they just want us to be a part of their lives. more than anything 就是最高级的意思表达,to be a part of their lives 可以灵活地处理,整句话可以译为:"但是,最重要的是,他们只是希望我们走入他们的生活。"

# 第 13 单元 节日风俗 Festivals and Customs

## 词语扩展 Developing Vocabulary and Expressions

**American major holidays:**
- \* New Year's Day 元旦(1月1日)
- \* Martin Luther King, Jr.'s Birthday 小马丁·路德·金诞辰(1月15日)
- Inauguration Day 总统就职日(1月20日)
- Lincoln's Birthday 林肯诞辰(2月12日)
- Valentine's Day 情人节(2月14日)
- \* Washington's Birthday 华盛顿诞辰(2月22日)
- St. Patrick's Day 圣帕特里克节(3月17日)
- Easter Friday 复活节(3月或4月)
- April Fools' Day 愚人节(4月1日)
- Planting Day 植树节(5月第二个星期五)
- Mother's Day 母亲节(5月第二个星期日)
- \* Memorial Day 阵亡将士纪念日(5月30日)
- Flag Day 国旗节(6月14日)
- Father's Day 父亲节(6月第三个星期日)
- \* Independence Day 独立纪念日(7月4日)
- \* Labor Day 劳工节(9月第一个星期一)
- \* Columbus Day 哥伦布纪念日(10月12日)
- Halloween Day 万圣节前夕(10月31日)
- \* Veterans' Day 退伍军人节(11月11日)
- \* Thanksgiving Day 感恩节(11月第四个星期四)
- \* Christmas Day 圣诞节(12月25日)

\* 有星号者为法定全国假日,其中小马丁·路德·金诞辰、华盛顿诞辰和哥伦布纪念日定于最临近上列日子的星期一。多数州以2月第三个星期一为总统日(President's Day),同时纪念华盛顿和林肯的诞生。

**Some important international days:**
- World Consumer Right Day 世界消费者权益日(3月15日)
- World Water Day 世界水日(3月22日)
- World Health Day 世界卫生日(4月7日)
- World Earth Day 世界地球日(4月22日)
- International Secretary Day 国际秘书节(4月25日)
- International Red-Cross Day 国际红十字日(5月8日)
- International Nurse Day 国际护士节(5月12日)
- World Telecommunications Day 世界电信日(5月17日)
- World No-Smoking Day 世界无烟日(5月31日)
- World Environment Day 世界环境日(6月5日)
- World Population Day 世界人口日(7月11日)
- World Tourism Day 世界旅游日(9月27日)
- World Post Day 世界邮政日(10月9日)
- World Grain Day 世界粮食日(10月16日)
- World Aids Day 世界艾滋病日(12月1日)
- World Disabled Day 世界残疾日(12月3日)

**Interpreting Practice**

### 1. 听译　Listening Interpreting

A. Listen to the sentences and interpret them into Chinese.
   Sentences 1—10

B. Listen to the paragraphs and interpret them into Chinese.
   Paragraphs 1—2

### 2. 情景练习　Situational Interpreting

Interpret the following speech into Chinese.

Roles
Mr. Rivers: a speaker;
Miss Chen: an interpreter

## The Spirit of Christmas

Ladies and Gentlemen,

　　Christmas, as you know, is the festival for young children. It is for their sake that we decorate our homes with holly and mistletoe. It is for their sake that we put on paper hats and play jolly games. It is for their sake that we eat turkey and Christmas pudding and a whole variety of other good things. It is for their sake alone—that we drink port and smoke cigars on this occasion.

　　Please do not think I am opposing the idea that Christmas is primarily a children's festival. On the contrary, its great merit is that it makes children of us all. It is the one time in the year when we can forget our grown-up dignity and have a good time. This, I think, is the spirit of Christmas, and I ask you to join me in drinking to it.

# 第13单元 节日风俗 Festivals and Customs

# 第2部分 Section 2

 **Vocabulary Work**

| 阴历 | Chinese Lunar Calendar | 兽窝 | lair |
| 记载 | archive | 工匠 | craftsman |
| 技艺 | feat | 吉祥的 | auspicious |
| 自发性地 | of one's own accord | 高跷 | stilts |
| 耍龙灯 | dragon dance | 狮舞 | lion dance |
| 鞭炮 | firecracker | 对联 | antithetical couplet |

 **Text Interpreting**

Interpret the following speech into English:

### 春 节

女士们,先生们:

很荣幸有机会给大家介绍中国的文化传统。今天我要讲的是中国最重要的传统节日——春节。

春节标志着阴历新年的开始。在汉语里,过春节也叫"过年",意思是避开"年"这个怪物。相传"年"是古时一种凶猛的怪物。它的样子像强壮的公牛,长着狮子一样的头。这个怪物通常待在深山里。但每到冬末春初,它在山里找不到足够的食物就会到村庄里吃东西。村民们非常害怕,于是纷纷搬家,逃离这个怪物。后来人们发现,"年"很害怕三样东西:红色、明亮的火焰和大声的吵闹。人们为了阻止"年"进村,就把大门漆成红色,还点火烧竹子,发出噼噼啪啪的响声。从此,"年"就再也不来村里了。这样,一个传统就形成了。爆竹的响声后来被鞭炮的响声所取代。这就是开始燃放鞭炮欢庆春节的来历。当然,出于安全方面的考虑,几年前中国的一些大城市禁止燃放鞭炮,使得现在这些城市过春节时比以前安静得多。

春节的食物也有一些讲究的。因为春节标志着新的一年的第一天,所以第一顿饭是相当重要的。饺子、汤圆和年糕是过年时家家户户必不可少的、最吉祥的食品。年糕表示人们希望生活"步步高"。香甜的汤圆是合家团圆的象征。

春节期间的娱乐活动多种多样,丰富多彩。耍龙灯和舞狮是春节期间的传统项目。表演者不一定是职业演员。有时是自发组织的农民、街头小贩们或工匠们。还有一种传统表演活动叫高跷。根据记载,中国的祖先开始使用高跷是为了从树上采集水果。如今,熟练的高跷表演者能够在高跷上表演非常惊人的技艺和极难的动作。

现在,随着人们生活水平的不断提高,特别在城市,人们已经采用了新的方式庆祝新年。比如,人们不再费心发贺卡,而是用电话或者手机短信表达对亲朋好友的问候。在新年假日期间出游是另一时尚的趋势。

但不管庆祝方式怎么变化,春节的精华不会变,那就是:人们为了祈求新的一年吉祥如意,家家户户都打扫得干干净净,门上都贴上对联,人人穿上新衣裳,拿出最精美的食物,欢聚在一起,互相说些吉利的话,表示祝贺。最重要的是,春节是一个合家欢聚的日子。出门在外的人们总要想方设法在除夕夜前赶回家中,吃一顿团圆饭。

我今天简要介绍了一下中国春节的来历、传统的春节食物和活动。很希望各位朋友有机会去亲身体验一下欢乐的节日气氛。

谢谢大家!

## 课文注释 Notes on the Text

1. 相传:也可译为 as legend goes。
2. 它在山里找不到足够的食物就会到村庄里吃东西:在译文中,加上了 it came out of its mountain lair and entered villages to eat whatever it could catch。加上前部分,与 entered villages 形成对称的句式,意义更加明确,而且朗朗上口,不失为佳句;后部分加上 to eat whatever it could catch, 也使怪物的凶猛可怖的形象跃然纸上,生动地译出了原文。
3. 春节的食物也有一些讲究的:在这里"讲究"的意思就是"春节有特别的食物",因此可译为...has its special food as well。
4. 饺子、汤圆和年糕:就用中文的拼音即可,有必要的话,再加上一些解释,如 Nian gao or New Year Cake。
5. 年糕表示人们希望生活"步步高":"步步高"的"高"与"年糕"谐音,因此,学汉语的人很容易理解它们之间的关系。翻译时,如果时间或场合不允许,就用意译为: Nian gao conveys the hope of improvement in life year after year.
6. 互相说些吉利的话:也可译为 wish each other Happy New Year。

## 词语扩展 Developing Vocabulary and Expressions

**Chinese traditional festivals**
- 元旦 New Year's Day
- 除夕 New Year's Eve
- 春节 Spring Festival
- 元宵节 Lantern Festival
- 清明节 Qingming/ Tomb-sweeping Festival
- 端午节 Dragon Boat Festival
- 中秋节 Mid-autumn Festival
- 重阳节 Double Ninth Festival

**Related activities and expressions**
- 八宝饭 steamed sweet glutinous rice pudding
- 拜年 paying a New Year call
- 出入平安 Safe trip wherever you go.

# 第13单元 节日风俗 Festivals and Customs

- 春联 Spring Festival couplets
- 辞旧岁 bid farewell to the old year
- 灯谜 lantern riddles
- 多福多寿 Live long and proper.
- 恭贺新禧 Best wishes for the year to come.
- 恭喜发财 Wish you prosperity.
- 观潮 watching the flood tide
- 国泰民安 The country flourishes and people live in peace.
- 红包 red packets (cash wrapped up in red paper, symbolizing fortune and wealth in the coming year)
- 吉祥如意 Everything goes well.
- 吉星高照 Good luck in the year ahead.
- 健康长寿 Wish you longevity and health.
- 金玉满堂 Treasures fill the home.
- 龙灯舞 dragon dance
- 龙舟赛 dragon-boat race
- 门神 door god
- 庙会 temple fair
- 年画 New Year picture
- 年夜饭 family reunion dinner on Lunar New Year's Eve
- 庆祝游行 gala parade
- 去晦气 get rid of the ill-fortune
- 扫墓 paying respect to the dead
- 赏月 viewing the full moon
- 生意兴隆 Business flourishes.
- 事业成功,家庭美满 Wish you success in your career and happiness of your family.
- 守岁 stay up late or all night on New Year's Eve
- 岁岁平安 Peace all year round.
- 团圆饭 family reunion dinner
- 心想事成 May all your wishes come true.
- 一帆风顺 Wish you every success.
- 祝您新年快乐幸福 Wish you happiness and prosperity in the coming year.
- 粽子 glutinous rice dumpling wrapped in bamboo leaves

## 译操练 Interpreting Practice

### 1. 听译 ▶▶▶ Listening Interpreting

**A.** Listen to the sentences and interpret them into English.
Sentences 1—10

**B.** Listen to the paragraphs and interpret them into English.
Paragraphs 1—2

171

## 2. 情景练习 ▶▶▶ Situational Interpreting

**Interpret based on the information given. Add any information when necessary.**

Roles：
张先生：台湾人
Mr. Blake：美国游客
陈小姐：翻译

**中秋节**

- 中国人在农历八月十五庆祝中秋节。
- 中秋节是观赏满月的日子。圆圆的月亮象征着圆满，进而象征着家庭团聚。人们喜欢登上亭台楼阁，并摆上食品或安排家宴，团圆子女，共同赏月叙谈。
- 中秋节的特制食品是一种圆形的月饼，内含核桃仁、蜜饯、豆沙或蛋黄等。
- 月饼有很多种，最受欢迎的是广式、苏式和台式月饼。广式月饼（Gantonese mooncake）比较油腻，苏式（Soochow mooncake）和台式月饼（Taiwanese mooncake）有一层脆皮（crisp skin）。
- 以月之圆兆人之团圆，以饼之圆兆人之常生，用月饼寄托思乡之情，思念亲人之情，祈盼丰收、幸福，都成为天下人们的心愿，月饼还被用来当作礼品送亲赠友，联络感情。
- 许多地方有烧斗香、点塔灯、舞火龙等风俗。

## 口译常识与技巧  Interpreting Tips and Skills

**句子翻译处理技巧（1）——分清主从**

在处理复杂句子的翻译时，分清主从、理顺关系十分关键。以汉英翻译为例，在处理汉语的"平行结构"时，我们往往要先仔细分析原句，区分主从关系，在正确理解原文的基础上，采用"分清主从"的技巧。

我们先看下面这个句子：

原文：总工程师急躁不安，两手插在裤子口袋里，踱来踱去。

初涉翻译领域的人可能会采用很多动词来翻译，因为汉语中确实使用了很多动词。

原译：The chief engineer was vexed and restless. He put his two hands into his trousers pockets and paced back and forth.

但是进一步分析该译文我们发现，句子的主体部分是"The chief engineer paced back and forth"，而"vexed and restless"和"hands in his trousers pockets"是从属结构，是用来解释原因和补充情境的。因此，句子应该译为：

Vexed and restless, the chief engineer paced back and forth, hands in his trousers pockets.

总的来说，在处理从属结构时，我们通常会采用以下几种模式：

1. 独立主格（Nominative Absolute）
   A. 名词＋现在分词短语（n. ＋ present participle phrase）
      原文：天气要是合适的话，我们明天要到西山去玩。
      译文：Weather permitting, we'll go on an excursion to the Western Hill tomorrow.
   B. 名词＋过去分词短语（n. ＋ past participle phrase）

# 第 13 单元 节日风俗 Festivals and Customs

原文:他脸朝天,头枕着手躺着。

译文:He lay on his back, his face up and his hands crossed under his head.

- C. 名词+形容词短语(n. + adjective phrase)
    原文:他鼻子冻得通红地走进房来。
    译文:He came into my room, his nose red with cold.
- D. 名词+副词短语(n. + adverbial phrase)
    原文:她伸出双手,掌心向上。
    译文:She put out her hands, palms up.
- E. 名词+名词(n. + n.)
    原文:数以千计的船民被淹死,其中许多是小孩。
    译文:Thousands of boat people were drowned, many of them children.
- F. 名词+不定式(n. + infinitive)
    原文:来客也不少,有送行的,有拿东西的,有送行兼拿东西的。
    译文:We also had quite a number of visitors, some to see us off, some to fetch things, and some to do both.
- G. 名词+介词短语(n. + prepositional phrase)
    原文:他们欢快地一手拿着鞭子,一手扯着缰绳,催马向前。
    译文:In jolly spirits, they urged the horses on, whip in one hand and reins in the other.
- H. with+上述模式(with + the above-mentioned patterns)
    原文:全班都瞧着他,他更感到不自在了。
    译文:He felt more uneasy, with the whole class staring at him.

2. 现在分词短语 (Present Participle Phrase)
    原文:我强做均匀的深呼吸,努力使自己镇静下来。
    译文:I tried to compose myself, forcing deep, even breath.

3. 过去分词短语(Past Participle Phrase)
    原文:我一直坐到十一点多钟,全神贯注地看书。
    译文:I sat until eleven, absorbed in a book.

4. 形容词短语(Adjective Phrase)
    原文:周总理是那样谦逊、随和、易于接近,使大家很快就不紧张了。
    译文:Modest, unassuming, easy to approach, Premier Zhou soon put everyone there completely at ease.

5. 名词短语(Noun Phrase)
    原文:他是一位天才的语言学家,同样精通法、德、英多种语言。
    译文:A gifted linguist, he was equally at home in French, German and English.

6. 不定式短语(Infinitive Phrase)
    原文:如果听到他讲英语,人们会以为他是英国人。
    译文:To hear him speak English, one would take him for an Englishman.

7. 相关短语(Co-operative Phrase)
    原文:运动会风雨无阻,照常进行。
    译文:The sports meet will be held, rain or shine.

8. 解释性或描述性短语(Explanatory or Descriptive Phrase)
    原文:他的妻子料理一切大大小小的事务。
    译文:His wife manages all affairs, big and small.

9. 延续否定(Continuative Negation)

原文:周围没有村庄,甚至连一棵可供遮蔽的大树也没有。

译文:There are no villages around, not even a big tree to take shelter under.

现在我们已经知道了该如何处理从属部分,至于如何区分主从关系,还需要注意一些翻译原则,如非必要信息从属于必要信息,否定部分从属于肯定部分,条件或原因从属于结果等。

由于汉英语言结构差别巨大,在翻译过程中要十分小心,切不可忽视主从关系的处理。

# 第 14 单元 旅游观光

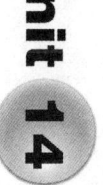 Unit 14 **Sightseeing**

# 第14单元 旅游观光 Sightseeing

# 第1部分 Section 1

 **Vocabulary Work**

| | | | |
|---|---|---|---|
| borough | 区 | Staten Island | 斯坦登岛 |
| Liberty Island | 自由岛 | Ellis Island | 埃利斯岛 |
| pedestal | 底座 | crime-ridden | 充满犯罪的 |
| be dedicated | 为……举行落成典礼 | Puerto Rican | 波多黎各人 |
| enclave | 小团体；居住地 | influx of immigrants | 移民涌入潮 |

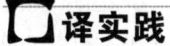  **Text Interpreting**

Interpret the following conversation alternatively into Chinese and English:

## Visiting New York City

Guide: Good morning, everyone! Welcome to New York City. I am Peter, the tour guide today. We are now on our way to Manhattan. Well, you know, New York City is composed of five boroughs: Manhattan, the Bronx, Brooklyn, Queens, and Staten Island. Manhattan is located on the Manhattan Island, covering about 58 square kilometers. It is taken as the symbol of New York City. You see, the Statue of Liberty, the Empire State Building, Broadway, Wall Street and many other places of interest are all at Manhattan. Now tell me, what you are most interested in and what you want to see most here?

游客：我一直想亲眼看到自由女神像。你能给我们介绍一下吗？

Guide: With pleasure! The Statue of Liberty is located on Liberty Island in New York Harbor. It was a gift from the people of France to the people of the United States to celebrate the 100th anniversary of the independence of the USA. It was originally called "Liberty Enlightening the World." It is 46 meters high and together with the pedestal it reaches 93 meters. The whole statue weighs 225 tons. The statue was designed by a young French sculptor, Frédéric-Auguste Bartholdi, while the steel framework was designed by Alexandre Gustave Eiffel, who was so famous for having designed the Eiffel Tower in Paris. The construction took ten years and was completed in 1884, and then it was shipped in 214 pieces from Lyon, France to New York in June, 1885. The Statue of Liberty was dedicated on October 26, 1886. The Statue was extensively restored for her spectacular centennial in 1986. When we get there, you will see its splendor yourself.

游客：我想看帝国大厦。我在很多美国电影里面都看到了。我觉得它非常浪漫。

Guide：That's true. The Empire State Building features in many films. It is a symbol of New York itself and one of the major attractions here. It is visited by more than 2 million tourists each year. The Empire State Building is situated in the center of Manhattan, away from the skyscraper clusters downtown in the financial district and midtown, so this is one of the few places in Manhattan where you have a great 360 degrees view. At the time it was built, it broke all records in the history of architecture and was dubbed "the 8th world wonder." It is 381 meters high, 102 storeys, and was built in only 14 months. It was the highest building in the world within 40 years after its completion.

游客：我也看了很多美国电影。纽约市好像是一个充满暴力的城市。我们在这里游览会不会安全呢？

Guide：Don't worry, you are quite safe. New York has had a reputation as a crime-ridden city, partly due to the hundreds of TV and movies with crime dramas set in it. However, in recent years, it has been ranked in the top ten safest large cities in the United States. In addition, New York has been growing safer for the last decade. New York City's crime rates are also varied by neighborhood and borough. With Staten Island as the safest borough in the city, Queens and Manhattan in the middle range, Brooklyn and The Bronx as the highest crime spots. But as Manhattan is the main tourist destination in the city, the New York Police Department has generated many schemes to make the City a safer place.

游客：纽约市也有很多移民吗？

Guide：Yes. New York has seemed more of an international city than an "American" city, due to the large influx of immigrants. Only Los Angeles receives more immigrants. Hundreds of languages are spoken in New York City. In many major cities in the world, immigrants tend to cluster into enclaves where they can talk and shop and work with people from their country of origin. In the United States, this is most pronounced in New York City. Immigrants of Irish, Italian, Chinese, Korean, Puerto Rican, African and Jewish origin all have enclaves within the city. If you are interested, you can go to Ellis Island where there is an Immigration Museum. Ellis Island lies next to Liberty Island. Ellis Island was the gateway through which more than 12 million immigrants passed between 1892 and 1954. Because of its unique historical importance, it was declared part of the Statue of Liberty National Monument in 1965. The Ellis Island Immigration Museum after renovation was opened to public in 1990. We will go to see the Statue of Liberty first. If time permits, we will go to the Immigration Museum.

# 第14单元 旅游观光 Sightseeing

 **Notes on the Text**

1. It was designed by a young French sculptor, Frédéric-Auguste Barthold. The steel framework was designed by Alexandre Gustave Eiffel. 这两句中有两个很长的外国名字,导游因为很熟悉,介绍了全称。作为口译人员,只需译出姓氏就可以了。

2. The Empire State Building features in many films：features 的意思为"使……有特色"或"使(演员)主演一部电影",在此可处理为"出现在许多电影里"。

3. where you have a great 360 degrees view：360度是指"环绕四周",因而译为"你能远眺四周的景色"。

4. Hundreds of languages are spoken in New York City：若根据结构译成"上百种语言被听到……",则不符合汉语习惯。特别在口语中,汉语习惯用主动句,因此,可译为："在纽约市,你可以听到上百种语言。"

5. Ellis Island was the gateway through which more than 12 million immigrants passed between 1892 and 1954. "gateway"是门户、通道的意思,在这里不需直接译词,应适当转换一下,把意思译出,可译为："1892年至1954年间,有一千二百万移民经由这里进入美国。"

6. Because of its unique historical importance：英语语言喜欢用大量的介词短语结构,而汉语语言习惯用动词结构,因而在翻译时,要注意适当转换。这里译为"由于它具有独特的历史意义"。

 **Developing Vocabulary and Expressions**

**Some scenic spots in New York City**
- Broadway                           百老汇
- Brooklyn Bridge                    布鲁克林大桥
- Central Park                       中央公园
- Ellis Island                       埃利斯岛
- Empire State Building              帝国大厦
- Federal Hall                       联邦大楼
- Madison Square                     麦迪逊广场
- Metropolitan Opera                 大都会剧院
- Rockefeller Center                 洛克菲勒中心
- Times Square                       时代广场
- Wall Street                        华尔街
- New York Stock Exchange            纽约证券交易所
- Washington Square Park             华盛顿广场公园
- United Nations' Headquarters       联合国大厦
- American Museum of Natural History 美国自然科学博物馆

**Some scenic spots in Washington D. C.**
- Washington National Cathedral      华盛顿国家教堂
- Arlington National Cemetery        阿灵顿国家公墓
- International Spy Museum           国际间谍博物馆
- Library of Congress                国会图书馆

179

- Lincoln Memorial 林肯纪念堂
- National Gallery of Art 国家美术馆
- Smithsonian Institution 史密斯松协会
- Thomas Jefferson Memorial 杰斐逊纪念堂
- US Capitol 美国国会大厦
- Vietnam Veterans Memorial 越战纪念碑
- Washington Monument 华盛顿纪念碑
- White House 白宫
- The John F. Kennedy Center for the Performing Arts 肯尼迪演艺中心

**Other famous scenic spots in USA**

- Blue Ridge Parkway 蓝色山脊公园道
- Disney World 迪士尼乐园
- Golden Gate Bridge 金门大桥
- Niagara Falls 尼亚加拉瀑布
- Rocky Mountain National Park 落基山国家公园
- The Apostles 使徒岛
- The Grand Canyon National Park 大峡谷国家公园
- The Olympic Rain Forest 奥林匹克雨林
- Yellowstone National Park 黄石国家公园
- Yosemite National Park 优胜美地国家公园
- Great Smoky Mountain National Park 大烟山国家公园
- Mountain Rushmore National Memorial 罗斯摩尔山国家纪念馆

## 译操练  *Interpreting Practice*

### 1. 听译 ▶▶ Listening Interpreting

A. Listen to the sentences and interpret them into Chinese.
   Sentences 1—10

B. Listen to the paragraphs and interpret them into Chinese.
   Paragraphs 1—2

### 2. 情景练习 ▶▶ Situational Interpreting—Role Play

Interpret based on the information given. Add any information when necessary.

> **Roles**
> Mr. Darcy: a native American
> Mr. Yu: a Taiwanese tourist
> Miss Chen: an interpreter

- **Washington, D.C.**

   1) Washington, D.C. — The nation's capital is more than the hustle of press conferences and international summits, power suits, policy and

politics. Just a 10-minute walk beyond the monumental corridor and government buildings will allow you to discover hometown Washington: a thriving, lively and cultured capital city.

2) What draws most visitors to Washington, D. C. again and again is the vibrant, accessible and world-class city from inspiring monuments to monumental arts and culture—and the stimulating, educated and diverse global communities among us.

3) Wherever you choose to visit Washington, D. C. , just remember to stay on the right side of the Metro escalators to avoid looking like a tourist!

- **White House**

The White House at 1600 Pennsylvania Avenue, NW, was originally constructed (in) 1792—1800, the work of James Hoban. It was reconstructed in 1815 after being burned by British soldiers during the War of 1812. It has been the home of every president of the United States since John Adams. The exterior of the main structure, despite some additions and minor changes, remains much as it was in 1800. The interior has been completely renovated using the historic floor plan. It is significant for its Federal architecture, as a symbol of the presidency, and for the important decisions made within its walls over the years.

# 第 2 部分 Section 2

##  Vocabulary Work

| | | | |
|---|---|---|---|
| 风景区 | scenic area | 景点 | place of interest |
| 海拔 | (at) an altitude of | 宫殿式庙宇 | temple of palace style |
| 必游之地 | must-visit spot | 瞻仰 | pay one's respect |
| 清幽 | tranquil and serene | 塔 | pagoda |

##  Text Interpreting

Interpret the following conversation alternatively into Chinese and English：

### 参观日月潭风景区

Guest： I have heard a lot about Sun Moon Lake in Taiwan. People say it is a paradise!

导游： 是的，的确很美。日月潭在南投县。它是个天然大湖，四周层峦叠翠。全潭以光华岛为界，南形如半月，北形如日轮，故名日月潭。

Guest： I see. So besides the lake, what else can we see?

导游： 主要有七大景点。有文武庙、孔雀园、光华岛、台湾山地文化中心、日月潭青年活动中心、玄奘寺和慈恩塔。

Guest： That sounds very interesting. I can't wait to see them all. Can you tell me more?

导游： 当然。文武庙位于潭北山的山腰上，因供奉古中国的著名学者孔子、著名将领岳飞及关羽而得名。庙分前、中、后三殿，占地广阔，色彩以金黄色为主，为中国传统宫殿式庙宇，气势雄伟壮观。孔雀园位于环湖公路北侧，园内分三个区：孔雀园、瑞鸟园和蝴蝶博物馆。园内饲养孔雀四百多只，各类飞禽及标本20多万只。然后是光华岛。光华岛位于日月潭中心。岛上有座月下老人亭，为旅客必游之地。

Guest： Why is it a must-visit spot? Is there anything special about that old man?

导游： 是的。月下老人可是专门为情人牵线搭桥的呀！这是个甜蜜的、幸运的小岛，特别是年轻人都向往着甜蜜的爱情。现在，人们都要来这个岛，祈求好运呢！

Guest： Great! I will surely go there to *koutou* to the old man.

导游： 台湾山地文化中心保存了台湾山地十个部族的文化及习俗，展示各族特有的建筑、雕刻、编织、渔猎等器物。日月潭青年活动中心设有会议厅、餐厅、宿舍，可供四百人集会。另外还有一个户外体育训练场可供使用。玄奘寺位于青龙山上,为纪念唐玄奘法师至西域取经,宣扬中华文化而建,寺内供有玄奘法师的灵骨以供瞻仰。最后是慈恩塔。它位于青龙山顶,高达海拔1000米,是日月潭最高点。采中国宝塔式建筑,共分九层。塔顶两层是王夫人灵堂,环境清幽,并设有石桌、石椅可供人休息。

Guest：Oh，thank you so much for such a nice introduction.
导游： 别客气,祝你玩得愉快。

## 课文注释 Notes on the Text

1. paradise,译成"人间仙境",因为在西方国家,paradise 即"天堂",是最美丽的地方,译为"人间仙境"即简洁又易懂,又十分神似。
2. 四周层峦叠翠:中文的美往往在于辞藻,浓墨重彩,而英文相比之下,则用词简约,口译"层峦叠翠"之类的四字成语时,译者无须深究汉语形义的美,而应以传递基本要义为原则,这里可以相应译为"surrounded by green mountains"即可。
3. 全潭以光华岛为界,南形如半月,北形如日轮,故名日月潭:这一句中文信息量较多,而且用词凝练,在口译时可以将整句话切分成小句,逐句译出,以求快速准确地表达,此句可以处理为,"The Guanghua Island on the lake marks the boundary. From the south, the island looks like a half moon. From the north, it resembles the outer shape of the sun. So it's called Sun Moon Lake."
4. 月下老人亭:在口译中,经常会遇到这种特有的文化,有其专有的名称,在口译时,最好先将名称说出,然后再附上解释"meaning..."等等,但注意解释不要过多过繁。
5. 玄奘寺位于青龙山上,为纪念唐玄奘法师至西域取经,宣扬中华文化而建,寺内供有玄奘法师的灵骨以供瞻仰。这句话十分复杂,在口译时,译员要将信息进行适当的整合,可参考译为：This temple is dedicated to Xuan Zang, the Tang Dynasty Buddhist monk, for his efforts in popularizing Chinese culture. You know he went to the Western regions on a pilgrimage for Buddhist scriptures. Inside the temple is an altar where Xuan Zang's ashes are placed for worshippers to pay their respect. 其中"寺内供有玄奘法师的灵骨以供瞻仰"这一部分,在译文中增加了一个词 altar,原文中说的很含糊,但译文可以根据常识加上"祭坛",用定语从句表示,使得句意更加充分。

## 词语扩展 Developing Vocabulary and Expressions

- 包价旅游 package tour
- 饱览绚丽风光 feast one's eyes on the scenery of the charming landscape
- 被列为重点文物保护单位 be put down on the list of the important historical sites to be given special protection
- 避暑胜地 summer resort
- 表现了中国古代劳动人民的聪明才智 show the wisdom and talent of the Chinese working people in ancient times
- 布局对称 symmetrical layout
- 苍翠繁茂的森林 verdant and lush forest

- 出境旅游市场 an outbound tourism market
- 春色满园 Signs of spring are visible everywhere in the garden.
- 春意盎然 Spring is very much in the air.
- 动感之都 city in move
- 洞天福地 blessed spot; fairyland; scenery of exceptional charm
- 独具匠心 show unusual ingenuity; original/ingenious design
- 繁花似锦 multitude of blossoming flowers; flourishing scene of prosperity
- 丰富的旅游资源 rich/abundant tourist resources
- 丰富多彩的民俗民风 rich and varied customs and styles
- 国内旅游市场 domestic tourism market
- 海天一色 the sea melted into the sky
- 湖光山色 landscape of lakes and hills
- 湖光山色，相映成趣 The lakes and mountains form a delightful contrast; The lakes and mountains contrast beautifully with each other.
- 画柱雕梁 painted pillars and carved beams
- 吉祥之地 propitious place
- 锦绣河山 land of charm and beauty
- 尽收眼底 have a panoramic view
- 景色宜人，令人心旷神怡 soothing and relaxing views of landscape
- 令人心旷神怡的疗养胜地 most refreshing health resort
- 名胜古迹 scenic spots and historical sites
- 秋高气爽 high autumn and bracing weather; fine autumn weather
- 曲径通幽 winding path leading to a secluded spot
- 人文景观 places of historic figures and cultural heritage
- "食、住、行、游、购、娱"一条龙的旅游服务体系 an integrated/comprehensive service system for tourism covering dining, accommodation, transportation, sightseeing, shopping and entertainment
- 文化/学术/疗养/商务旅游 cultural/academic/convalescence/business tour
- 野生动物保护区 wildlife preservation area
- 有导游的团体旅游 conducted tour
- 重峦叠嶂 range upon range of mountains; mountain peaks rising one after another

## 口译操练 Interpreting Practice

1. 听译 ▶▶ Listening Interpreting

    A. Listen to the sentences and interpret them into English.
       Sentences 1—10

    B. Listen to the paragraphs and interpret them into English.
       Paragraphs 1—2

## 2. 情景练习 ▶▶▶ Situational Interpreting

**Interpret based on the information given. Add any information when necessary.**

> **Roles**
> 李先生:台湾本地人
> George:美国游客
> 陈小姐:翻译

- 台湾的人口超过二千三百万,为全世界人口密度最高的区域之一。除了岛上的原住民外,大部分人民皆来自中国大陆,尤以福建人民为多。佛教、道教是台湾的主要宗教,如观音菩萨、海洋女神妈祖有众多信徒。基督教、天主教、伊斯兰教等也有不少教徒。地方虽小,但台湾却保留了古老的中国文化,从林立街头的古迹庙宇和故宫文物的收藏之丰富即可见一斑。
- 台北市位于台湾岛北部,台北盆地的中央,四周与台北县相邻。全市面积272平方公里,是全省的政治、经济、文化和教育中心,为台湾第一大城市。现今全市共划分中正、大同、中山、松山、大安、万华、信义、士林、北投、内湖、南港及文山12个行政区。
- 台北市是台湾的工商业中心,全岛规模最大的公司、企业、银行、商店都把他们的总部设在这里。以台北市为中心,包括台北县、桃园县和基隆市,形成了台湾最大的工业生产区和商业区。
- 台北市是台湾北部的游览中心,除阳明山、北投风景区外,还有省内最大、建成最早、占地8.9万平方米的台北公园和规模最大的木栅动物园。此外,由私人经营的荣星花园规模也相当可观。剑潭、北安、福寿、双溪等公园,也都是游览的好地方。台北市名胜古迹颇多。

## 口译常识与技巧  Interpreting Tips and Skills

**句子翻译处理技巧(2)——增减技巧**

本单元主要介绍口译中的增减技巧。从严格意义上来说,省略在口译中是误译,但是省略在口译实践中往往又是不可避免的,有时甚至是口译不可或缺的一种策略。此外,为了句子意思的完整,翻译时往往要增加一些词,因此增词也是口译常用的技巧之一。

**1. 口译中的省略**

口译中的省略是不可避免的,是因为人的处理能力是有限的。由于理解和记忆需要大量的处理能力,留给输出的处理能力非常有限,同时真正的口译现场还会有噪音等其他干扰,要求译员将原文完完全全地传达给译入语听众是非常困难的;加上语言中所含信息往往多于所需信息,这意味着一些信息可以删除或对其进行改动而不会造成交际中断。从对大量口译活动的分析中,人们发现省略是一个普遍现象。那么省略都在什么情况下产生呢?

(1) 因语言差异而产生的省略

英语重形合,汉语重意合。英语中句子段落之间的连接和关系主要是通过句子间显形的形态标志体现出来的,句子常常由一定的功能词(function words)或连接词(linking words)来连接,表示句子之间的关系,如 and 表示并列关系,but, yet, however 表示转折,if, unless 表示条件,as, because 表示原因等等。这些连接在英语中可以说是须臾不可离之。

汉语很少运用这些显形的连接手段,它虽然也有如"虽然……但是"等连接手段表示句子或分句之间的关系,但是汉语中的大多数句子或分句不分主从关系,它们并列在一起,连接它们的是意义而不是功能词。汉语句子或短句之间的连接是隐性的,常常隐没在上下文中,交际双方可以在一定的语境下根据上下文对它们的关系做出正确的判断。例如:

> 原文:Everyone can register with a doctor of his choice and if he is ill he can consult the doctor without having to pay for the doctor's service, although he has to pay a small charge for medicines. Those who wish may become private patients, paying for their treatment, but they must still pay their contributions to the national insurance and health schemes.
>
> 译文:每个人都可以在他所选择的医生处登记,生病了就可以请该医生看病而不必支付就诊费,只需付少量的药费。想请私人医生的人可以请私人医生看病,费用自理,但仍须交纳国民保险费和医疗保险费。

在该句中,连接词由原来的5个变成了1个,由此可以看出在英译汉时,省略掉连接词是完全可以的,这种省略对译文几乎没有任何影响,有时候甚至是必需的,所以在英汉翻译时可以按意思翻译,而不必拘泥于它的形式。

(2) 重复项的省略

在口语中,为了强调或争取时间构思最佳表达法,或考虑下面该说什么,说话者往往会用不同方式重复表达同一意思,口译时就没有必要重复。例如:

① Like, the Coca-Cola is a great example. They are available everywhere, in every single place, in every single spot.
   就好像可口可乐的产品一样,世界各地都有他们的产品。

② How do you get brand awareness of over 90% without using advertising?
   这个90%是从哪里来的呢?

例1中,everywhere 与 in every single place,in every single spot 意思相同,说者是为了强调自己的观点,翻译时只给出了一个综合的词汇"世界各地",这样省略,既可以表达意思,又可以节约时间来注意下面的内容。例2中的 get brand awareness 和 without using advertising 都没有翻译出来,可以猜想,本句的前面一句话中提到它们,翻译时不需重复,事实也正是如此,前一句话是 We have had experience that in some market we will be able to have the brand awareness over 90% without using advertising.

恰当地使用省略,可以使翻译更为简洁、集中、连贯,译员在输出阶段节省了精力和处理能力,便使更多的精力和处理能力用于理解和记忆,为输出做好准备。

必须指出的是,省略作为一项策略,不是困境中的权宜之计,而是应该成为译员内化了的口译技巧之一,译员省略一是出于处理能力管理的要求,二是因为听者可以根据已知的信息进行推断,经过省略的译文,尽管有时会遗漏一些次要信息,但可以使译文明晰,比起因追求内容完整而丧失明晰的译文更实用。

**2. 口译中的增加**

所谓增词法,是指翻译时依据意义或句法的需要增加一些词来更忠实、通顺地传达原文的思想内容。一般来说,增词法又分为以下几种情况:

(1) 增加连贯词

由于汉语句子间的连贯是隐性的,而英语句子的连贯是显性的,汉语翻译为英语常常要增加连贯词。例如:

原文:孔子的家里很穷,但他从小就发奋读书,刻苦学习。20多岁的时候,做了个小官。他很有学问，办事认真，工作出色，30岁左右就已经很出名了。

译文：Confucius was born of a poor family, but he worked very hard at his studies even when he was a child. He became a petty official in his early twenties. As he had great learning, worked in earnest and was outstanding in performing his duties, he had already earned a high reputation by the age of 30.

原文只有一个连贯词"但"，翻译为英语时，另外增加了两个连贯词 when 和 as。翻译并非是字字对译，这样做往往保留了形式却不能将内容准确完整地传达出去，所以翻译时，为了将原文的意思全面地表达出来，增词往往是必要的。

(2) 增加文化释义词

文化虽然有共性，但是差异是无所不在的，翻译中总会遇到一些文化词语，为了使听众理解，口译者对文化词语往往进行意译，但是为了保持源语的文化特色，直译有时也是行得通的，如果直译导致听众不理解的话，往往要增加解释性的词语。例如：

原文：According to the philosophy, the basic law by which man must live, in spite of his surface veneer of civilization, is the law of jungle.

译文：哲学认为，尽管披着文明的外衣，人类生存的基本法则是弱肉强食的丛林法则。

其中，the law of jungle 就是汉语没有的具有英语文化特色的表达法，直接将它们翻译出来可能会导致理解上的障碍，因此增加了补充解释。

增减译法是口译过程中必不可少的技巧。但是译者绝不能盲目使用，任意增减，而是应该因地制宜地进行恰当的处理，这样才能保证口译的质量。

# 第 15 单元

## 绿色城市

## Unit 15 Green City

# 第15单元 绿色城市 Green City

# 第1部分 Section 1

## Vocabulary Work

| | | | |
|---|---|---|---|
| garbage/trash/waste | 垃圾 | benign | 无害的 |
| chromium | 铬 | ammonia | 氨 |
| toxic waste | 有毒废物 | organic solvent | 有机溶剂 |
| lead compounds | 铅化合物 | throw out/toss out/dump | 倾倒 |
| genetic tinkering | 基因调整 | veteran | 资深人士 |
| alchemist | 炼金术士 | briefcase | 公文包 |
| biotechnology | 生物技术 | microbe | 微生物 |
| unprecedented | 无先例的 | emulate | 效法 |
| pose no threat | 不构成威胁 | nanotechnology | 纳米技术 |
| aluminum can | 铝罐 | fabrication | 制造 |

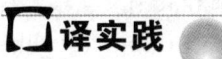  Text Interpreting

**Interpret the following report into Chinese:**

### Can We Make Garbage Disappear?

Welcome to "Today's Report." Our topic today is: can we make our garbage disappear? Whoever said "waste not, want not" hasn't had much influence on the 276 million Americans. In 2010 they threw out more than 195 billion kg of garbage. That means each man, woman and child tossed out an average of 725 kg of trash.

And that's just the benign solid waste. Each year American industries dump more than 1.1 billion kg of toxic wastes—like lead compounds, chromium, ammonia and organic solvents—into the air, water and ground.

The really bad news is that most of the planet's 6 billion people are beginning to follow the footsteps of the US and the rest of the developed world. "Either we need to control ourselves or nature will," says a veteran of recycling and solid-waste programs. As he sees it, garbage needs to become a thing of the past.

That may seem impossible, but it's not unprecedented. In nature, there is no such thing as waste. What dies or is discarded by one part of the ecosystem nourishes another part. Yet humanity can emulate nature's garbage-free ways, but it will require innovative technology and a big change in attitude.

Biotechnology is giving us additional tools to cope with waste—and turn it to our advantage. Microbes can take toxic substances in contaminated soil and convert them into harmless by-products. Scientists are working toward engineering corn plants with the kind of fiber content that paper companies would find attractive. So long as the genetic tinkering poses no ecological threat, that approach could tap into a huge stream of agricultural waste, turning some of it into industrial ingredients.

In consumer markets, recycling has already spawned an array of alchemists. Jackets are being made from discarded plastic bottles, briefcases from worn-out tires and belts from beer-bottle caps. Even though the US has barely begun to get serious about recycling, about 25% of its 195 billion kg of municipal garbage are now salvaged for some sort of second life.

There are limits to how many lives you can give to a pile of debris. In the long run, we have to reduce the amount of material we use in the first place. Some progress is being made—aluminum cans and plastic soda bottles have become thinner over the years, but more reductions will require a whole new kind of manufacturing process.

That is where nanotechnology plays a role. In this emerging field researchers expect to create products by building them atom by atom, molecule by molecule. This bottom-up nano-technological way of making things differs from the traditional fabrication methods that create so much waste along the way.

But technology is not enough. Just as critical are changes in attitudes and lifestyles. Brad Allenby, AT&T's vice president for environment, safety, and health, believes our move from the industrial age could help enormously. At present, he says, 29% of AT&T's management force telecommutes, meaning less reliance on cars. This could be part of something bigger—a shift in our view of what enhances our quality of life. Maybe we should put less value on things that use lots of materials and more on things that don't swallow up resources—like telecommuting and the Internet. Maybe downloading music from the Web will reduce the demand for CD cases. We still have an opportunity to use computers to cut consumption of paper and the trees it comes from.

As society becomes more information-rich, the easier it will be to find uses for discarded materials. One person's garbage is another's treasure. When that attitude goes global, the human beings of the new millennium may be able to look back on their former garbage-producing ways as a forgivable error of their youth as a species.

## 课文注释  Notes on the Text

1. "waste not, want not":为英语成语,课文参考译文为直译,比较简练:"不浪费,不愁缺。"也有人译为"勤俭节约,吃穿不缺",其中"约""缺"叠韵,正好与原文中押前韵的 waste 和 want 两词呼应,容易上口,便于记忆。注意这里 want 意为"缺乏",不是"想,想要"。

2. Either we need to control ourselves or nature will:此句为省略句,will 后面省略了宾语 control ourselves (us)。该句直译过来就是"要么我们要控制自己的行为,要

## 第15单元 绿色城市 Green City

么自然就会控制我们的行为"。根据汉语表达习惯,我们意译为:"我们如果不控制自己的行为,那我们就要听任自然界摆布。"

3. nanotechnology:纳米(nanometer),长度单位,符号为nm,1 纳米＝1 毫微米,即十亿分之一米,约为 10 个原子的长度。纳米技术,是指在 0.1～100 纳米的尺度里,研究电子、原子和分子内的运动规律和特性的一项崭新技术。纳米技术是一门交叉性很强的综合学科,研究的内容涉及现代科技的广阔领域。

4. AT&T:为 American Telephone & Telegraph 的缩写,中译名为美国电话电报公司。是一家美国电信公司,曾长期垄断美国长途和本地电话市场,现为美国最大的本地和长途电话公司。

5. telecommute:远距离工作,尤其指在家里通过使用与工作单位连接的计算机终端进行远距离工作。

6. information-rich:新闻报道作者常常为了语言精练构造新词或浓缩词,此即一例。再如:Nowadays, many people tend to be cash-rich and time-poor.

7. One person's garbage is another's treasure. 此句套用英语谚语 One man's meat is another man's poison.（对某人有利的未必对其他人也有利。）这种故意模仿现成的语句甚至篇章而临时创造新的语句或篇章的修辞手段在修辞学上称为仿拟或仿词(parody)。

## 词语扩展 Developing Vocabulary and Expressions

| | |
|---|---|
| ❖ afforestation | 绿化造林 |
| ❖ airborne pollutant | 气载污染物 |
| ❖ area emission source | 区域污染源 |
| ❖ city's environmental hygiene | 城市环境卫生 |
| ❖ common hygienic knowledge | 卫生常识 |
| ❖ cooperative medical system | 合作医疗制度 |
| ❖ disposal on land | 陆地废物处理 |
| ❖ domestic / household garbage / waste / refuse | 家庭垃圾(生活垃圾) |
| ❖ environmental degradation | 环境退化 |
| ❖ environmentalist | 环境主义者 |
| ❖ composite pollution | 混合污染 |
| ❖ garbage collection | 垃圾收集 |
| ❖ garbage disposal | 垃圾处理 |
| ❖ garbage incineration | 垃圾焚化 |
| ❖ greenbelt | 绿化地带 |
| ❖ household refuse processing plant | 家庭垃圾处理厂 |
| ❖ human exposure to pollutant | 人体接触污染物 |
| ❖ land-based pollution | 陆地来源的污染 |
| ❖ landfill treatment | 垃圾填埋处理 |
| ❖ liquid waste | 液体废物 |
| ❖ lower the incidence of complications | 减少并发症发病率 |
| ❖ noise abatement | 噪音治理 |
| ❖ noise control | 噪音控制 |
| ❖ noise screen | 噪音屏蔽 |
| ❖ open burning | 露天焚烧 |

- open dump 露天垃圾场
- pharmaceutical waste 医药废物
- popularize hygiene knowledge 普及卫生知识
- public health 公共卫生
- purify waste water 净化污水
- sanitary inspection; hygiene examination 卫生检查
- sewage disposal 污水处理
- sewage purification 污水净化
- utilization of industrial wastes 工业废物利用

## 译操练 *Interpreting Practice*

### 1. 听译 ▶▶ Listening Interpreting

A. Listen to the sentences and interpret them into Chinese.
   Sentences 1—10

B. Listen to the paragraphs and interpret them into Chinese.
   Paragraphs 1—2

### 2. 情景练习 ▶▶ Sight Interpreting

Interpret the following conversation alternatively into Chinese and English.

> **Roles**
> Mr. Jameson: an American spokesman at a press conference
> Miss Chen: a Chinese news reporter
> Mr. Wang: an interpreter

Jameson: Good afternoon, ladies and gentlemen, our second press conference concerning our environmental protection policies is now declared to begin. You are welcome to ask questions.

Chen: 您好，我是中央电视台的记者，我想就电子垃圾的处理提个问题。美国作为全球最大的电脑硬件的开发制造商之一，对于全球范围内因此而出现的新的"高科技"垃圾打算采取什么样的对策？

Jameson: Thank you for your question. It is a well-known fact that the high-tech revolution has inspired a seemingly endless stream of new and exciting electronic products that we just can't live without. The average life span of a personal computer has shrunk to around 18 months—and this has nothing to do with worn-out mice or damaged disk drives. And this has given rise to some problems indeed. For example, computer monitors can contain up to 3.5 kg of lead and can actually be considered hazardous waste once they are no longer in use. Circuit boards in electronic products contain cadmium, chromium and mercury, all of which are toxic substances that can leach into groundwater if left in a landfill. As to the measures to deal with all this techno-trash, many experts, scientists and policy-makers have spent a lot of time and money already. Firstly, I believe the most efficient way of solving a problem is to root out the very occurrence of that problem. So manufacturers and developers are working hard on new and "green" materials and technologies in the first place. And related legislation on using toxic material in the least degree is already in the works of our country. And secondly, another way to reduce waste is to avoid throwing things in the first place. We need to carry out much propaganda on raising customers' awareness to this. And many companies are reusing parts from old products in new models. This is not cheating—it makes both environmental and economic sense. Thirdly, the US should learn from other main manufacturing countries like Japan, and we should get involved in a global cooperation to tackle this problem. Thank you.

# 第2部分 Section 2

 **Vocabulary Work**

| 被动吸烟 | passive smoking | 电子烟 | e-cigarettes |
| 烟草税 | tobacco tax | 雾态物 | aerosols |
| 尼古丁 | nicotine | 蒸汽电子烟 | electronic nicotine delivery systems（ENDS） |
| 诱导 | lure | 加强监管 | intensify supervision |

 **Text Interpreting**

**Interpret the following report into English：**

早上好，朋友和同事们，女士们，先生们：

据世界卫生组织报道，全世界每年约有 100 万人死于吸烟导致的疾病，10 万人死于被动吸烟。而在中国有超过 3 亿烟民，几乎占全世界吸烟人口的三分之一。这是一个可怕的数字。鉴于此，中国政府近期公布了一系列全国范围内的禁烟措施。如在北京、上海等城市正式实施禁烟令，这适用于所有室内公共场所、工作场所以及公共交通。政府已将烟草税从 5% 上调到 11%，旨在抑制民众的吸烟行为，同时，对烟草广告的限制令也将于近期内实施。

然而现在有人鼓吹电子烟的健康风险远低于传统卷烟，然而事实真是如此吗？

那什么是电子烟呢？

第一类电子烟是非燃烧型烟草加热器。这类产品在加热后产生的雾态物含有尼古丁等高致瘾性物质，以及其他有害化学物质。

第二种电子烟是蒸汽电子烟。人体会在其加热雾化的过程中吸入液态剂释放的尼古丁和其他有害物质。一项新的研究表明，电子烟中使用的调味剂会损害血管细胞，从而增加患心脏病的风险。除了调味剂对健康的影响，研究人员还发现，电子烟使用者和传统烟民在吸烟 10 分钟后血液中的尼古丁含量是相同的。

然而不容乐观的是，近年来，吸食电子烟的人飞速攀升，尤其是年轻人。电子烟以时尚的方式诱导青少年先接触电子烟，之后他们很可能会吸食传统的烟草。

在美国，美国食品及药物管理局数据显示，几乎每 5 个高中学生中就有一个尝试过电子烟，目前有 360 万美国初、高中生在抽电子烟，这是一个令人震惊的数字。

大洋彼岸的中国也难以幸免。中国疾控中心今年的一项调查显示，去年我国电子烟使用者人数占总人口的0.9%,15岁及以上电子烟使用者的数量预计约有1000万。

女士们,先生们,世界卫生组织第七次发布的《全球烟草流行报告》确认电子烟毫无疑问是有害的,并呼吁各国政府和消费者不要轻信烟草企业关于电子烟等产品的宣传。我们必须严格加强电子烟的监管。随着电子烟在青少年中的使用增加,中国计划立法对电子烟进行监管,作为控烟行动的一个举措。

## 课文注释  Notes on the Text

1. 鉴于此,中国政府近期公布了一系列全国范围内的禁烟措施。此句中,"鉴于此"可用介词结构 in view of 处理,整句可译为 In view of this, the Chinese government recently announced a range of nationwide measures to try to curb the population's smoking habits.
2. 非燃烧型烟草/加热器蒸汽电子烟:heated tobacco products（HTPs）/ electronic nicotine delivery systems（ENDS）
3. 第一类电子烟是非燃烧型烟草加热器。这类产品在加热后产生的雾态物含有尼古丁等高致瘾性物质,以及其他有害化学物质。这两个句子不宜完全按照中文的语序来译,可分析其重点并灵活运用多种英文句式译为 Heated tobacco products（HTPs）are a particular type of e-cigarette. They are tobacco products that produce aerosols containing highly addictive substances such as nicotine, as well as toxic chemicals upon the tobacco being heated.
4. 第二种电子烟是蒸汽电子烟。人体会在其加热雾化的过程中吸入液态剂释放的尼古丁和其他有害物质。这两个句子不宜完全按照中文的语序来译,可以分析句子的语义中心并将之处理为一个主从复合句:Aerosols can also be created by another kind of e-cigarette, electronic nicotine delivery systems（ENDS）, through which liquid containing nicotine and other toxic chemicals can be inhaled after vaporization.

世界卫生组织、美国食品及药物管理局、中国疾控中心:the World Health Organization（WHO）/ the Food and Drug Administration （FDA）/the Chinese Center for Disease Control and Prevention. 这篇文章中机构和组织的专有名词较多,需在平时的学习中积累相关的词汇。

## 词语扩展  Developing Vocabulary and Expressions

- 二手烟 second-hand smoke
- 禁烟令 smoking ban
- 无烟缓冲区 smoke-free "buffer zone"
- 烟民 smokers
- 戒烟 quit smoking
- 电子烟 electronic cigarette, Electronic smoke, e-cigarette,
- 电子烟雪茄 E cigar, e-cigar
- 雾化器 atomizer
- 雾化烟弹 cartomizer
- 无尼古丁 no nicotine
- 低度尼古丁 low nicotine

- 中度尼古丁 middle nicotine
- 高度尼古丁 high nicotine
- 电子烟制造商 electronic cigarette manufacturer
- 环保友好型 eco-friendly
- 爱国卫生运动 patriotic public health campaign
- 暴病 sudden attack of a serious disease
- 并发症 complication
- 常见病发生 outbreak of common diseases
- 常见病普查 general survey of common diseases
- 常见病死亡率 mortality rate of common diseases
- 城市绿化 beautify the city by planting trees
- 除害防病 eliminating pests and preventing diseases
- 除四害 wiping out the four pests (mosquitoes, flies, rats and bedbugs)
- 传染病 infectious disease
- 传染媒介 contagion intermediary
- 传染途径 route of contagion
- 大流行病 pandemic disease
- 地方病 endemic disease
- 多发病 disease of frequent occurrence; frequently occurring disease
- 恶性病 malignant disease
- 防疫队 anti-epidemic team
- 防疫工作 anti-epidemic service
- 防治疾病 prevention and treatment of disease
- 妇幼保健 maternity and child care
- 妇幼保健站 health center for women and children
- 痼疾 chronic disease; obstinate illness
- 健康咨询站 health consultation center
- 救死扶伤 heal the wounded and rescue the dying
- 控制疾病流行 control the spread of diseases
- 疗养期 period of recuperation
- 疗养院 sanatorium; convalescent home
- 流行病 epidemic disease
- 顽症 chronic and stubborn disease
- 蚊蝇滋生地 breeding ground for flies and mosquitoes
- 细菌病毒传染媒介 germ infection carrier
- 婴儿死亡率 infant mortality rate
- 营养与保健 nutrition and health care
- 预防流行病 prevent epidemic diseases
- 职业病 occupational disease

# 第15单元 绿色城市 Green City

## 译操练  Interpreting Practice

### 1. 听译 ▶▶ Listening Interpreting

**A.** Listen to the sentences and interpret them into English.
Sentences 1—10

**B.** Listen to the paragraphs and interpret them into English.
Paragraphs 1—2

### 2. 情景练习 ▶▶▶ Situational Interpreting

Interpret the news based on the information given below.

> **Roles：**
> 吴先生：环境保护部门的负责人
> 冀小姐：翻译

女士们，先生们：

晚上好！

本次记者招待会主要公布我们现阶段环境保护政策目标、措施以及废弃物处理管理等方面的主要规定。欢迎各位记者和朋友提出建议和批评。

为达到"加强环境保护，提高生活品质"的目的，我们研究并推出"环境保护计划"；遵循可持续发展原则，落实发展计划；环境保护与经济发展兼顾；治标与治本并进：治标旨在改善现有公害污染，治本着眼预防环境受损于未然；采用一系列环保经济手段；加强环保投资民营化、合资化；强化与投资外商的纵横向协调与合作。

我们还拟定"环境保护计划"；加强环境影响评估，防范公害于未然；减少环境污染，解决人们日常生活环境问题，如垃圾、空气、水质污染改善、加强毒硅化学物质管理、环境绿化、美化和成立"可持续发展委员会"等。

依据废弃物清理法分成一般废弃物和事业废弃物两种，一般废弃物大部分指家庭垃圾。2012年，环保技术会议将垃圾焚化炉处理列为中长程垃圾处理方法，计划安排兴建垃圾焚化炉14座，迄今完工5座，施工6座，规划设计3座。我们于2004年底再制订"鼓励民营机构兴建营运垃圾焚化厂推动方案"，目前已核定8处兴建民营焚化炉。

下面是提问时间。谢谢大家。

## 译常识与技巧  Interpreting Tips and Skills

**句子翻译处理技巧(3)——转换技巧**

在本单元中，我们主要讲解口译中的转换技巧，其中又主要涉及词性的转换、语态的转换和语序的转换。

**一、词性的转换**

口译者在翻译中不要拘泥于源语的词性，要尽可能做到"得其意忘其形"。如名词就可以转换为代词、形容词、动词等。如：

原文：Every Englishman has some knowledge, however slight, of the work of our greatest writer.

译文：每个英国人都或多或少地了解我们这个伟大作家的作品。（名词转换为动词）

原文：There is probably no better way for a foreigner (or an Englishman!) to appreciate the richness and variety of English language than by studying the various ways in which Shakespeare used it.

译文：对于一个外国人，甚至是英国人，要欣赏到丰富多彩的英语最好的方法就是学习莎士比亚使用英语的种种方式。（名词转换为形容词）

## 二、语态的转换

汉语的谓语动词除了必要的情况一般多用主动语态；相比之下，英语的被动句用得比较多。英汉两种语言转化中，口译者必须要注意到英汉的这一差异，避免生硬的译文。例如：

原文：Individual rights and freedom are assured in the Constitution and are listed in the first 10 amendments.

译文：宪法保证了个人的权利和自由，并将它们载入前10个修正案。

原文：几乎所有的书店、旅馆、入境口岸、机场和旅游景点都能看到我们的出版物。

译文：Our publications can be found in nearly all the bookstores, hotels, ports of entry, airports and scenic spots.

## 三、语序的转换

语序的转换是本单元讲解的重点，它又分为以下几种情况：

### 1. 名词性结构口译

名词和名词性结构在句子中多数充当主语和宾语，懂得如何翻译名词和名词性结构对于正确口译是非常重要的。名词常常由形容词或其他名词来修饰充当定语，如何翻译名词从某种意义上来说就是如何翻译修饰名词的定语。

英语和汉语的定语位置有很大差别，英语的定语只有是单个的形容词和名词时才可以放在所修饰的中心词之前，其他都放在中心词之后；与之相反，汉语的定语无论多长都可以放在中心词之前。鉴于英汉定语的差异，汉英口译时，尤其要注意定语位置的转换。放在汉语中心词前的定语翻译时常常要放到英语中心词之后，可采用定语从句形式、介词形式、不定式形式等。

(1) 以介词形式放在中心词后

a comparatively complete financial market system with a fair size and much influence

规模适当，影响巨大，发展比较健全的金融市场体系

(2) 以形容词、现在分词、过去分词形式放在中心词后

有利于高新技术发展的资本市场

capital market beneficial to the new high-tech development

有比较优势的企业

enterprises enjoying comparative advantages

由国家旅游局批准的商务旅行社

a business travel agency approved by the National Tourism Administration

(3) 以不定式形式放在中心词后

第一个举办世界博览会的发展中国家

the first developing country to host the World Exposition

（4）以定语从句形式放在中心词后

那些将我们联系在一起并且强化我们关系的事务
issues that bind us and strengthen our relationship

**2. 动词性结构口译**

动词性结构口译指的是汉语句子中的动词及修饰该动词的状语的翻译。汉语中状语的位置是比较固定的，一般不是在句子前面，就是位于主谓之间，而英语中的状语位置比较灵活，可以在句子前面、中间或后面，放在句子中间的常常是在主谓之间，一般为单个的单词，如 usually，yet，hardly 等，如果状语是短语或分句，翻译时通常将其放到主语之前或句子尾部，例如：

就广泛领域里的合作以及建立新的亚欧伙伴关系交换我们的意见
exchange our views on cooperation in a wide range of areas and the establishment of new Euro-Asian partnership

**3. 整体把握句子结构**

英语和汉语的句子构成成分基本相同，有主语、谓语、宾语、定语、状语和补语，但是英汉句子在顺序、习惯用法上有许多不同之处。

英汉句子的基本结构是主谓结构，主语往往在句首，口译时有时句子的主语很长，译者一定要清楚地认识到所听到的只是主语，切不要只停留在对主语的理解和记忆上而忽略了后面的其他成分。例如，"几个小时以前，有位名叫汪小明的中国留法学生在巴黎的一个地铁车站冒着生命危险救了一个法国青年。"本句的主谓宾是"学生"、"救了"、"青年"，是句子的主干部分。主语相对较长，这就要求译者不仅要快速记下主语，同时还要认识到这仅仅是句子的一个成分，对即将到来的谓语、宾语等还应留有充分的注意。有的句子状语或定语很长。无论是什么成分偏长，译者一定要学会如何抓住句子主干。例如：

原文：我国改革开放和现代化建设事业的不断发展要求我们不断加强经济外交工作。

译文：The constant development in China's reform and opening up and the modernization drive requires us to further enhance economic diplomacy.

原文：The manager of the supermarket whose background I know quite well is 100％ honest.

译文：我对超市经理非常了解，他百分之百是诚实的。

除了句子主干外，句子的某个部分也有主次之分。例如：

原文：我们为顾全大局，在第三方的调停之下多次强烈要求贵方赔偿我们的一切损失。

译文：With the third party as an intermediary, to take the interest of the whole into account, we strongly demanded many times that you should compensate all our losses.

本句中状语"为顾全大局，在第三方的调停之下"放在句首，而"多次"放在谓语"要求"之后，"强烈"作为单个的词充当状语，放在主谓之间。

口译实战中译者经常需要对原文中的词性、语态和语序等进行调整。初学者需要在不断练习和实践中积累经验，才能灵活自如地完成汉英两种语言的转换。

第 16 单元

全球环境

Unit 16

# Global Environment

# 第16单元 全球环境 Global Environment

# 第1部分 Section 1

## 词汇预习 Vocabulary Work

| | | | |
|---|---|---|---|
| shine a spotlight on | 聚焦 | initiative | 动议 |
| think tank | 智囊团 | cardinal rule | 基本规则 |
| carbon emitters | 碳排放国 | resonate | 共鸣 |
| abstruse | 深奥的 | philanthropist | 慈善家 |
| nuclear reactor | 核反应堆 | cutting edge technology | 尖端技术 |
| uranium | 铀 | regulatory environment | 法律环境 |
| energize | 激活 | impetus | 推动力 |

## 口译实践 Text Interpreting

**Interpret the following speech into Chinese:**

I want to thank so many of my friends from China and from the United States who gather here. I'm very, very delighted that this session through the Brookings Institute is able to shine a spotlight on something as important as clean energy within the U.S.-China relationship. I want to thank John Thorton, who himself is a one-man think tank, for his friendship and for his vision and for his guidance, in particular a "thank you" for bringing us all here today.

Winston Churchill used to say famously, "You never kiss a person who's leaning away from you. You never climb a mountain that is leaning toward you. And you never speak to a group that knows a hell of a lot more about the subject matter than you do." This is the cardinal rule that I am violating this morning. My friends in China have another way to say it, "showing off one's skill or talent before an expert." You know more about this policy. I'm just learning from you.

The United States and China are the world's two largest energy users and carbon emitters. Cooperation on clean energy is a prime example of where we can further our common interests and benefit not only our people but also many throughout the world for decades to come.

Our two countries have had some successes in this area. You'll hear about them through the day. The problem is those successes don't necessarily resonate with average Americans or average Chinese. We have to humanize these accomplishments. We have to make them real in ways that citizens on both sides better see the benefits of supporting a strong U.S.-China relationship.

What does that mean? It means we can't just discuss these topics as abstruse or technical issues because they aren't. Ultimately we need to make clear that the U.S.-China relationship is one of the best opportunities we have to improve the quality of life for average American families and businesses, big and small, because the economic opportunities are increasingly very real.

So when people ask me why we should cooperate with China on clean energy initiatives, I say it's very simple. We are embarking on a technological revolution in clean energy like the space program or electronics of the 20th century that will dramatically expand high quality jobs, living standards, and our economy in the United States. We'll get better products, lower prices, and more jobs in both countries. I believe the possibilities in this particular area—clean energy—are unlimited.

Here's a good example. A few months ago I met the legendary innovator and philanthropist Bill Gates in Beijing. Now generally when Bill Gates mentions he has an idea for a new product, I listen. This time the product is a new kind of nuclear reactor, something that could operate for 40 to 60 years without refueling. Compare that to what we have today where reactors need to be opened up and refueled every 18 months or so.

So if this technology works, we would need a lot less uranium to create a whole lot more energy with far less nuclear waste. But why China? This is an American company, but the simple reality is right now the regulatory environment here in the United States means it would take decades just to certify the design. So by partnering with the Chinese they can move ahead and then commercialize the technology around the globe when it is proven. The end results—countries around the world would get cleaner, safer energy, and a joint U.S.-Chinese company could lead the world in nuclear reactor construction. That is a very big deal for so many involved.

Today with jobs being so needed, our cooperation on clean energy development is creating tremendous opportunities for new employment throughout the United States. Westinghouse is a prime example. I'm sure many of you are already familiar with their work in China where they're focused on four next generation nuclear reactors. What you may not know is those four reactors in China have already either saved or created 5,000 high quality jobs here in America and across 13 different states.

So as long as we continue to produce cutting edge technology and maintain our competitive advantage in management, services and education, the China market will loom very large. And as China continues its efforts in renewable energy, we're beginning to see Chinese companies launching operations in the United States, and that means even more investment and job creation here for us.

More broadly, our cooperation on clean energy is important and timely because of its impact on the environment, health and quality of life. The challenge now is where do we go from here? We're moving in a similar direction. The question is how do we ensure a common pathway for both the United States and China?

And that puts us back to where I started. These cooperative efforts will only work if we have the public behind us. We have to be relentless in demonstrating the benefits and speaking honestly about the challenges.

Our job, whether it's about clean energy or energizing the private sector, is to make the benefits of this relationship as clear as possible for the people of each country. We have to improve the lives of ordinary Americans just as the Chinese have to improve the lives of their citizens. If sustained common ground is to be found in the U.S.-China relationship, there is no better impetus than the strong desire on both sides to aggressively pursue a clean energy future. And by doing so, we will help each other, learn from each other and progress together.

Thank you all very much.

## 课文注释  Notes on the Text

1. My friends in China have another way to say it, "showing off one's skill or talent before an expert": 在这句话中，My friends in China have another way to say it 这一部分中限定了之后的翻译必须是汉语中约定俗成的习语，因此翻译 showing off one's skill or talent before an expert 时，可以在汉语中选取对等的表达方式，译为"班门弄斧"或"关公面前耍大刀"。

2. Cooperation on clean energy is a prime example of where we can further our common interests and benefit not only our people but also many throughout the world for decades to come. 在口译实践中，"词性转换"是一个十分常用的技巧，比如在此句中的 a prime example of 可以转译为"充分证明了"，这样一来，可以使口译员的表达更为轻松、明晰，整句可以译为："在清洁能源方面的合作充分证明了我们可以推进共同利益，并在未来几十年里，造福国民和世界各国人民。"

3. We have to make them real in ways that citizens on both sides better see the benefits of supporting a strong U.S.-China relationship. 在这句话中，make them real in ways that 指的是"在……方面让成绩落到实处"，口译表达时可以尽量简约，利用上下文的结构功能适当进行信息整合，此句可以译为"我们必须让这些成绩落到实处，让两国人民更清晰地看到支持一个强大的美中关系会带来什么好处"，其中的"在……方面"可以省去不译。

4. If sustained common ground is to be found in the U.S.-China relationship: 英语中的被动语态在译为汉语时，往往转为主动语态，在这里可以译为"如果要在美中关系中找到持久的共同点"。

5. Westinghouse: 美国西屋电气公司，总部设在宾夕法尼亚州匹兹堡市，是美国主要电气设备制造商和核反应器生产工厂。

## 词语扩展  Developing Vocabulary and Expressions

| | |
|---|---|
| ❖ at the expense of environment | 不惜以破坏环境为代价 |
| ❖ environmental monitoring system | 环境监测系统 |
| ❖ environmental organization | 环境保护组织 |
| ❖ environmental pattern | 环境模式 |
| ❖ environmental standard | 环境标准 |
| ❖ environmental survey satellite | 环境监测卫星 |
| ❖ environmentalist | 环境保护主义者 |
| ❖ environmental index | 环境指数 |

- green consumer　　　　　　　　　　　绿色消费者
- denude the land　　　　　　　　　　　破坏地力
- desertification　　　　　　　　　　　土地沙漠化
- the forestation project　　　　　　　防护林体系工程
- the Green Peace　　　　　　　　　　绿色和平组织
- the Green Revolution　　　　　　　　绿色革命
- cesspool　　　　　　　　　　　　　　污水池
- curb/control environmental pollution　控制环境污染
- major source of pollution　　　　　　主要污染源
- pollution/contamination of water sources　水源污染
- solid waste pollution　　　　　　　　固体废物污染
- total suspended particles　　　　　　总悬浮颗粒物
- tail gas discharge　　　　　　　　　　尾气排放
- domestic sewage　　　　　　　　　　生活污水
- domestic waste/house refuse　　　　生活垃圾
- burn away the refuse　　　　　　　　焚烧垃圾
- urban refuse　　　　　　　　　　　　城市垃圾
- enclose garbage with plastic garbage bags　垃圾袋装化
- electrolytic treatment　　　　　　　　电解处理
- nitrogen oxide　　　　　　　　　　　氧化氮
- hazardous waste　　　　　　　　　　有害废物
- industrial wastewater　　　　　　　　工业废水
- radioactive waste　　　　　　　　　　放射性废物
- solid industrial waste　　　　　　　　固体工业废物
- vicious circle　　　　　　　　　　　　恶性循环
- virtuous circle　　　　　　　　　　　良性循环

## 口译操练  Interpreting Practice

### 1. 听译 ▶▶ Listening Interpreting

A. Listen to the sentences and interpret them into Chinese.
　Sentences 1—10

B. Listen to the paragraphs and interpret them into Chinese.
　Paragraphs 1—2

### 2. 情景练习 ▶▶ Situational Interpreting

Interpret based on the information given. Add any information when necessary.

> Roles：
> Mr. Glenn：the chairman，from the US
> Mr. Li：a professor from China
> Mr. Blaire：a professor from Britain
> Miss Chen：an interpreter

# 第16单元 全球环境 Global Environment

Mr. Glenn: Ladies and gentlemen, may I have your attention please? The program for this morning's session will be concerned with the broad heading of "Global Warming and Renewable Fuels." We are going to divide the sessions into two major groups, which are respectively under the charges of Mr. Li and Mr. Blaire. Now let's invite them to brief us on the arrangement. Mr. Li, would you like to be the first one?

Mr. Li: 谢谢主席,大家好,第一组由我负责。我们组主要讨论二氧化碳与"温室效应"问题,具体包括:大气中二氧化碳浓度增加的历史记录;二氧化碳的主要排放来源;二氧化碳如何导致"温室效应";"温室效应"将给地球带来的灾害以及我们应该采取的对策。对该议题感兴趣的人员可以到我这登记,欢迎大家踊跃参加,谢谢。

Mr. Glenn: Thank you, Mr. Li. Now let's welcome Mr. Blaire to say something about Group II.

Mr. Blaire: Thanks a lot. The theme our group will cover is "The Discovery and Development of Renewable Fuels." Specifically, the theme can be subdivided into the following parts: the crisis of traditional fuels, especially fossil ones; possible alternative energy sources including wind power, solar power, tidal power and etc. You are welcome to join us in Room 102.

Mr. Glenn: Thank you, Mr. Blaire. Do you have any questions? If none, please go on with your discussions, which will be suspended at eleven a.m. After lunch and a break at noon, let's gather together at the Video Room on the second floor at two p.m.

# 第2部分 Section 2

## 词汇预习 Vocabulary Work

| | | | |
|---|---|---|---|
| 回顾过去 | retrospect the past | 协调 | reconcile |
| 生态恶化 | ecological deterioration | 再生 | regeneration |
| 承载能力 | carrying capacity | 一蹴而就 | be accomplished overnight |
| 令人瞩目的成就 | noticeable achievement | 无情的 | merciless |

## 口译实践 Text Interpreting

**Interpret the following speech into English:**

亲爱的朋友们,女士们、先生们:

早上好!

在这个阳光明媚的早晨,21世纪城市建设和环境国际会议在成都召开。来自世界各地的代表们相聚在此,回顾过去,展望未来,交流有关21世纪城市开发和居住问题的看法、意见。这是协调经济社会发展和环境保护过程中意义深远的重要会议。我谨代表中华人民共和国建设部向与会的所有朋友们表示热烈欢迎。

历史告诉我们,20世纪工业化和都市化使人们享受到前所未有的物质和文化的成就,与此同时,也对自然环境造成了巨大的压力,出现了许多严重问题,例如:生态恶化,人口激增,自然资源日益枯竭。经济社会发展对自然资源的需求日益增加,加剧了自然资源长期再生和生态系统有限的能力之间的矛盾,甚至威胁到人类自身的存在和发展。

在这个重要时刻,人类应该心平气和地、小心谨慎地思考该做些什么。在通过正确处理人类和自然的关系解决环境问题的基础上,实现经济社会可持续发展,这是人类面临的共同任务。我们必须以尊重和维护自然为前提,以人与自然、人与人、人与社会和谐共生为宗旨,以资源环境承载能力为基础,以建立可持续的产业结构、生产方式和消费模式为内涵,以引导人们走上持续和谐的发展道路为着眼点,强调人的自觉与自律,人与自然环境的相互依存、相互促进、共处共融。建设生态文明,是长期艰巨的过程,不会一蹴而就,也不会一劳永逸。

中国是四大文明古国之一。安居乐业是2000年前的中国哲学家老子崇尚的理想,也是我们所有人的共同目标。但是,由于中国现代化工业起步晚,许多城市在工业化和都市化过程中面临着生态环境问题。所以中国政府在发展经济的同时把环境保护作为首要任务之一。多年来,我们一直致力于控制空气污染、垃圾污染、噪音污染和人口爆炸。我们试图减少城市供水、能源、住房、交通方面的问题,扩大绿化面积,提高环境质量。我们取得了惊人的成就。成都是中国西南的中心城市,有着2300多年的悠久历史,在改善城市环境方面已取得了令人瞩目的成就。

自然是慷慨的,它为人类的生存和发展提供了适宜的条件。自然也是无情的,它对无尽的掠夺予以报复。今天,世界范围的生态环境问题是人人关注的,所有有责任心的人都应该行动起来,献身于提高环保意识、保护环境的高尚的活动中。

今天,由联合国人类住区委员会、中华人民共和国建设部和成都市政府联合举办的成都21世纪城市建设和环境国际会议为我们提供了互相学习、交流、合作的机会,我们愿意利用这个机会,学习别人的长处,我们将继续努力,改善人类居住环境,创造人类更美好的未来。

祝愿大会取得圆满成功。

谢谢大家!

# 课文注释  Notes on the Text

1. 在这个重要时刻,人类应该心平气和地、小心谨慎地思考该做些什么。在处理诸如"心平气和""小心谨慎"等四字格联合词组时,应遵循英语崇简的原则,避免用词累赘、重复,在这里这两个词处理为 calmly and carefully 即可。
2. 在通过正确处理人类和自然的关系解决环境问题的基础上,实现经济社会可持续发展,这是人类面临的共同任务。这句话的主语太长,翻译时必须选用形式主语"it"的结构,减轻口译表达过程中的压力。整句可以译为:It is a common task facing mankind to achieve economic and social sustainable development on the basis of solving the environmental problems by dealing with the relationship between mankind and nature properly. 这样对原文的重组可以使得翻译的过程更为顺畅、有条不紊。
3. 我们必须以尊重和维护自然为前提,以人与自然、人与人、人与社会和谐共生为宗旨,以资源环境承载能力为基础,以建立可持续的产业结构、生产方式和消费模式为内涵,以引导人们走上持续和谐的发展道路为着眼点,强调人的自觉与自律,人与自然环境的相互依存、相互促进、共处共融。汉语作为意合的语言,往往在一个完整的句子中包含较多信息。这句话就是典型的例子。在这一整句中,众多小分句连绵而下,一逗到底,构成一层完整的含义。在翻译时,必须在适当的地方进行断句,以符合英语表达习惯。
4. 强调人的自觉与自律,人与自然环境的相互依存、相互促进、共处共融。"人的自觉与自律,人与自然环境的相互依存、相互促进、共处共融"这一部分都是"强调"的宾语部分,因此翻译为名词性结构为好,"相互依存""相互促进""共处共融"三个四字短语,在英语中可以转化为 the mutually dependent and complementary relationship,信息没有减少,但是表达更简洁,更到位。
5. 建设生态文明,是长期艰巨的过程,不会一蹴而就,也不会一劳永逸。遇到"一蹴而就""一劳永逸"等成语时,译者不必慌乱,可以先将这些高度凝练的词语用普通的现代白话文加以理解,再进行诠释,全句可以译为:This will be a long-standing and formidable process, neither accomplished overnight, nor guaranteed once and for all.

## 词语扩展 Developing Vocabulary and Expressions

- 会员大会 general meeting, general assembly
- 执行委员会 executive council, executive board
- 常设机构 standing body
- 附属委员会 subcommittee
- 总务委员会 general committee, general officers, general bureau
- 预算委员会 budget committee
- 起草委员会 drafting committee
- 专家委员会 committee of experts
- 顾问委员会 advisory committee, consultative committee
- 名誉主席 honorary president
- 临时主席 interim chairman
- 文书,秘书 rapporteur
- 列入议程 place on the agenda
- 要求发言 ask for the floor
- 发言 take the floor, to address the meeting
- 同意……发言 give the floor to（美作：to recognize）
- 提出异议 raise an objection
- 逐字记录 verbatim record
- 散会 adjourn the meeting, to close the meeting
- 我被委任这个会议的主席。I will serve as the chairman of this meeting.
- 根据今天议程的安排,我负责主持这个会议,我希望能得到你们的良好合作。According to the order of our program today, I will be responsible for this session. I would like to ask for your kind cooperation.
- 我想对从世界各地来参加这次会议的诸位,表示热烈的欢迎。I wish to extend a warm welcome to you who have come from all parts of the world to attend this meeting (symposium, gathering).
- 我宣布这次会议现在开始。I would like to declare this conference open.
- A 博士今天不能出席,我谨代表他…… As the substitute of Dr. A who is unable to be here with us today, ...
- 这次召开的……第六届世界大会的主要议题是…… This Sixth World Conference of ... has been convened to treat especially the topic...
- 今天我们想首先讨论改善……方面的计划。Today we would like first of all to discuss the plan for improvement of ...
- 我代表执行委员会,想报告一下到今天为止能取得的进展。Representing executive members, I would like to report the progress up till now.
- 我想报告一下,根据……送来的资料,我们慎重地审议的结果。I would like to report on the results of our careful deliberations based on the materials presented by...
- 以上的报告完了。看来没有提出什么问题,那就让我们继续进行下一个议程吧。Thus far the business report. Since there seem to be no questions, let's proceed to the next agenda.
- 我为……深受感动。感谢你们的启发性的意见。我想让这次会议就此闭幕。I am deeply impressed by... Thank you for your enlightening opinions. I would like to

## 第 16 单元 全球环境 Global Environment

close this meeting now.
- ❖ 因为所有的议案都通过了,这个会议将于今天结束。Since all proposed resolutions have been passed (approved), the meeting will be closed for today.
- ❖ 既然今天的提案都已被采纳,那今天的会议暂告结束。All of today's proposals have thus been adopted, and today's session is hereby adjourned.
- ❖ 看到这个大会不断地取得进展和成功,真使我由衷地感到高兴。It is truly a cause of great joy to see this convention continually growing and prospering.
- ❖ 衷心地祝福这次会议将会结出硕果和获得丰收。I sincerely hope that this conference reaps fruitful results.

### 译操练 Interpreting Practice

**1. 听译 ▶▶ Listening Interpreting**

A. Listen to the sentences and interpret them into English.
   Sentences 1—10

B. Listen to the paragraphs and interpret them into English.
   Paragraphs 1—2

**2. 情景练习 ▶▶ Situational Interpreting**

Interpret based on the information given. Add any information when necessary.

环保局主要领导和 23 位市民坐在一起,听取大家对城市环保工作的意见和建议。
参与座谈会的市民希望政府能拿出更有效的措施,真正改善当地居民的生存环境,保障生活健康。大家表示,并不是一定要这些企业搬家,但是要求他们拿出切实有效的解决方法、解决步骤来,给大家一个希望,什么时候才能把废气污染问题解决好。
环保局领导听取市民意见后表示,大家的发言情真意切,自己也确实感到了肩上的担子重,任重而道远。到环保局当局长后自己一直关注北部废气污染问题,去年市环保局也联合经济开发区管委会进行了相关治理,目前成效是有的,环保监测超标的情况有明显下降,但与大家的愿望相比,差距还比较大,一些企业在废气治理方面采取了不少措施,但是也有部分企业确实动作比较慢,甚至有点敷衍。

### 译常识与技巧 Interpreting Tips and Skills

**口译中突发问题的解决**

一般情况下,特别是正式场合的翻译,口译人员在事先都对背景材料、有关知识和翻译内容做了充分的准备。但在口译过程中,往往会出现一些预料不到的情况,这就要求译员灵活地处理。

(1) 口译时没有听清怎么办?

在口译中,由于人多嘴杂或发言人发音不清楚或语速过快等原因使译员没有听清的情况时有发生。那么译员应该判断这个词、短语或句子是否重要。如果不译出也不会影响原句的意思,就可以忽略。

如果不能忽略(如数字、地名、人名等),就要问发言人。如:

发言人说:About 150,000 full- and part-time students attend Australia's 18 universities last year...

假设没有听清这个数目,译员可以说:You mean 150,000 ? 或 Did you say how many?

但在询问的时候译员要注意,不要很笼统地问一句 I beg your pardon,这样讲话者一定会一脸疑惑,不知道译员到底是哪里没有听清楚。

(2) 遇到听不懂的词怎么办?

任何一位译员,无论其专业基础多么扎实,知识底蕴多么深厚,都无法保证自己的听力百分之百地不出问题,毕竟口译所涉及的主题繁杂多样,再加上讲话者的发音、语速等各不相同,译员没有听懂个别单词的情况也是有的。那么,经验丰富的译员通常是如何妥善处理这一问题的呢?

处理办法是:首先,译员应该判断这个词、短语或句子是否重要,如果不译出是否会影响原句的意思。其二,有经验的译员会根据上下文,根据对整个讲话精神的体会,对未听懂的部分猜测出来,如:

原文:Another environmental event took place in the United States in 1993. 400,000 people in Milwaukee, Wisconsin, became sick from the drinking water. More than fifty people died. An organism in the water called cryptosporidium was to blame.

译文:另一次可怕的环境污染事件发生在1993年。美国威斯康星州弥尔沃基市40万人因饮用水污染生病,50多人死亡。水中的一种有机物是罪魁祸首。

这里 cryptosporidium 的专业术语是"隐形担孢子"。译员不懂这个词,一则可以音译,直接读出,二则用一个笼统的描述性词语"有机物"来说明一下。

这种情况还常出现在文化差异所引起的"词汇缺省",如中国文化中特有的食物名称、节日、习俗等,在英语语言文化中没有。也可以用音译或描述的方式。

最后,译员可以就某个听不懂的部分问发言人。如:

发言人说:Currently, the developed countries are plagued by economic stagnation and inflation.

其中,stagnation 是个生词,译员认为有必要弄清该词的意义,就可以问:stagnation? (用升调),或 What does "stagnation" mean? 发言人一定会做出解释的。但这种方式不宜多用,会影响交流的顺畅进行。因此,要求译者事先做好充分的准备,平时注意积累大量的词汇和各方面的知识。

(3) 口译中译错了怎么办?

译员工作中面临巨大的精神压力,尤其是知道有懂双语的听众或负责监听翻译质量和录音人员在场时,再加上较长时间集中注意力以求快速和准确地传译,难免发生漏译和误译。如何大大方方地在现场纠正错误也是一门技巧。

译员发现自己译错后,若是小错,只要是不影响大局,则不必急于把句子重译一遍。如:

原文:And we know that stability will be improved in the short term and growth prospects will be enhanced over the medium term by a wide range of structural reforms. We've seen evidence of this in countries like Brazil and Turkey where, for example, banking sector and other structural reforms have helped reinforce the fiscal and monetary policy frameworks that have been established.

译文:我们也知道广泛的经济结构改革将有利于短期的经济稳定和中期的经济发展。我们在巴西等国已经看到了这一点。(这里译员由于疏忽而漏译了"土耳其",但该错误无伤大局,则没太大必要进行刻意的更正。)在这些国家,银行业和其他结构性改革都有助于巩固已有的财政和货币政策体系。

但如果发现自己的内容出现了大的错误,则必须立即纠正,千万不能顾及自己的面子而给交流双方造成损失。如:

译错后,译员可以使用一些缓冲表达语:I mean, or rather, that is...,或者明确地说:"刚才这点翻译错了,应该译为……"

如果发现同事译错,而且错误比较严重的话,最好的办法是把自己的看法写在一张纸条上,悄悄递给同事,切忌越俎代庖。

(4) 遇到了发言人语速过快或有严重口音怎么办?

当讲话者语速过快时,译员可以请其讲得慢一些。但有些人早已养成讲话快的习惯,短时间内可以克服,时间稍长又开始快了起来。遇到这种情况,译员最重要的是稳住,千万不能慌乱,仔细分析语段的中心思想,力求将核心内容尽可能正确完整地传达出来。

此外,英语是世界上分布最广的语言,各个地区的人难免会有一些自己的口音,这就需要译员在平时多加积累,了解并熟悉不同地区人们的不同发音特点。

通常而言,英国人讲英语时喜欢将每个音节都发得清清楚楚,十分注意区分长韵元音和短韵元音,而美国人讲英语则显得有些模糊不清,且大部分的长韵元音都被缩短,如 grass 中的长韵元音 a。英国人发音较为完整,而美国人则发成短音,如同 had 中的 a 音。在英音中,字母 r 只有在元音前才发音,在元音后一般不发音,而在美音中,一般均发卷舌[r]。但这也并不是绝对的,如许多美国中西部人习惯将 hard 中的 r 音发得很夸张,而美国南方人则习惯将其隐去不发,使 hard 听上去更像 haahd [ha:(h)d]。字母组合 wh 在英音中为[w],美音则为[hw]。

此外,history, factory 等词在很多音标标注中 o 的发音(是一个浑元音)都是打了括号的。英式英语受文言文的影响喜欢省略这个 o,而在美式英语中,这个 o 常常是发音的。

澳大利亚人习惯省略辅音 h,如 how 听上去更像 ow;字母 a 在澳大利亚人的口音中常常发成[ai],于是,today 听上去更像 to die。

印度人的英语口音往往更加难懂,他们的语音中没有爆破音和清辅音,喜欢将 r 发成颤音,t 的发音又近似于 d,因此 thirty 听上去更像 dirty。

其实,不仅仅是各地的人讲英语有口音,中国不同地区的人讲中文时也常常带有浓重的地方口音,如南方人的"日"读作/ni/,北方人听起来像"年";四川人的"鞋子"听上去像普通话的"孩子"等等。这些都给译员的理解和口译带来了不少困难。

在实际口译进程中,突发状况是难以避免的。译员都需要在平时的训练中多加观察,善于总结,并培养自己遇事不慌的良好心理素质,这样才能镇定自若地处理口译实战中出现的各种突发状况。

# 口译教学测评

语言技能测试是了解学习成果和检验教学效果的必要手段,口译教学也不例外。

口译教学的测评可以采用两种形式,一种为"口译学习进展测试",采用课堂测试的方法,按教程单元进行。教师可依据单元主题,选择教材中部分内容,按教学大纲的要求编写考题,通过事先录音或课堂口述,请学生当堂口译。其间教师可以将学生的口译过程录音,以供评分之用。

另一种为"口译能力资格测试",采用标准化水平测试的方法,在学期结束时进行。教师可以参考一些较成熟的口译资格考试的做法,如"上海市英语口译岗位资格证书考试"。"上海市英语口译岗位资格证书考试"分为"基础口译""中级口译"和"高级口译"三个层次,在此我们将"中级口译考试"和"高级口译考试"这两个层次的考试要求、题型及形式做一简要介绍,并各附三套考卷,供本教程使用者参考。

## 上海市英语中级口译考试的要求、题型及形式

### 考试要求

"上海市英语中级口译资格证书考试"要求凡获得"上海市英语中级口译资格证书"者均具有良好的口语能力和基本口译技能,可从事一般的生活翻译、陪同翻译、国际研讨会翻译以及外事接待、外贸业务洽谈等工作。

英语中级口译考试旨在测试考生的"英译汉"和"汉译英"的口译能力以及对口译基本技巧的掌握程度。考生在口译时应能准确传达原话意思,语音、语调正确,表达流畅、通顺,句法规范,语气恰当,用词妥切。

### 考试题型

口译考试采用微型演讲文翻译的形式。翻译总量为四篇短文,其中两篇为"英译汉",两篇为"汉译英"。短文题材与本教程的课文题材大体吻合,体裁一般为介绍、宣传、发言、演讲、祝词、报告等。每篇短文的篇幅大致为 80～100 个词。每个考生的口译测试时间约 10 分钟。

### 考试形式

口译考试采用个别面试的形式。考生逐句听事先录制好的原文,然后逐句将原文的内容准确而又流利地从来源语翻译成目标语。测试顺序通常以"英译汉"部分为先,然后再做"汉译英"部分。每部分均含两篇短文,每篇短文一般含四个句子,每个句子的长度一般不超过 30 个单词。口译均以句子为单位进行。考生可得到一张口译记录纸,用以在听录音时做一些必要的笔记。考生听完一句话后约有 20 秒左右的间隙供口译。口译时间的长短由口译录音信号控制,即考生必须在"始译信号"和"止译信号"之间完成有关句子的口译。

以下为三套口译模拟试卷,其题材、形式与要求同"上海市英语中级口译资格证书"的口译部分相吻合。

# 中级口译模拟考试

## Model Test One

### Part A（E—C）

**Directions**: *In this part of the test, you will hear two passages in English. Each passage consists of four sentences. After you have heard each sentence, interpret it into Chinese. You will start at the signal ... and then stop at the signal ... You may take notes while listening. Now let us begin Part A with the first passage.*

**Passage 1**

Since we arrived, the gracious hospitality with which we have been received has been truly heartwarming. // A Chinese proverb best describes my feeling: When the visitor arrives, it is as if returning home. // One of the purposes of my visit was to make new friends, but I'm very pleased to find that instead of making friends, I am among friends. // And I'm also very pleased with our cooperation in the joint venture which has been very successful: We both gained and profited, and we both survived the fierce competition in the world market.

**Passage 2**

Ladies and gentlemen, I suppose you've all read the report about the restructuring of the group's organization, which has given rise to the problem of relocating the new group. // One possibility is to move all the head offices to Shanghai, and that is basically what the report recommends. // Alternatively, we could continue to run the two companies quite separately in their present locations with the smaller company in Shanghai. // I'm not sure how efficient the second option would be, but I'd like to hear your ideas on the subject.

### Part B（C—E）

**Directions**: *In this part of the test, you will hear two passages in Chinese. Each passage consists of four sentences. After you have heard each sentence, interpret it into English. You will start at the signal ... and then stop at the signal ... You may take notes while listening. Now let us begin Part B with the first passage.*

**Passage 1**

中国有一句话是这么说的，"上有天堂，下有苏杭。"// 这句话毫无夸张之意,苏杭这两座邻近上海的历史名城以其秀丽的景色每年吸引了数以百万计的海内外游客。// 例如,中国南方园林建筑艺术之典范、迷人的苏州造景园林在有限的空间里造就了无数自然景观。// 园林的池塘、河水、石头、花朵、树木给游客带来了如诗般的意境,是赴苏州观光客的必游之地。

**Passage 2**

女士们、先生们,进入新世纪的上海正在迅速发展为世界经济、金融和贸易中心之一。// 上海金融业的发展尤为引人注目,现已逐渐形成了一个具有相当规模与影响的金融市场体系。// 浦东新区近年来的崛起使这块黄金宝地成了海外投资的热点，投资总额已达980亿美元。// 上海这颗璀璨的东方明珠以其特有的魅力召唤富有远见卓识的金融家和企业家来此大展鸿图。

# Model Test Two

## Part A（E—C）

**Directions**: *In this part of the test, you will hear two passages in English. Each passage consists of four sentences. After you have heard each sentence, interpret it into Chinese. You will start at the signal ... and then stop at the signal ... You may take notes while listening. Now let us begin Part A with the first passage.*

### Passage 1

Permit me to say again this evening: Let us act according to the principle of mutual respect and mutual benefit, to the principle of both dignity and fairness. // It is certainly in the fundamental interest of our people to trade and be friends with the Chinese people. // We are very impressed by your modernization program, an ambitious undertaking which makes our future cooperative relationship very promising. // China today, I understand, is taking a practical and effective approach and we wish you success and offer you our cooperation in this great endeavor.

### Passage 2

We know that the human brain is divided into two roughly symmetrical hemispheres, which are comparable in size and form, but not in function. // The left hemisphere is primarily responsible for linguistic communication, i.e., the language center is located in the left side of the brain in most people. // The right hemisphere, on the other hand, controls one's visual and spatial activities, including also musical perception. // The most important differences between humans and other animals are the creative aspect of human language and man's sophisticated cognitive abilities.

## Part B（C—E）

**Directions**: *In this part of the test, you will hear two passages in Chinese. Each passage consists of four sentences. After you have heard each sentence, interpret it into English. You will start at the signal ... and then stop at the signal ... You may take notes while listening. Now let us begin Part B with the first passage.*

### Passage 1

欢迎科林斯先生和太太来上海。我叫孟诗琪，是上海联华制衣（集团）公司海外营销部的经理。// 我很高兴能代表公司总经理陈先生在此接待您和夫人。// 我受陈先生的委托，代表公司在今后的几天里同您进行业务洽谈。// 我将同科林斯先生商谈有关建立上海联华制衣（集团）公司海外销售网的事宜。请您多多指教。

### Passage 2

"远亲不如近邻"是中国人民推崇的、经得起时间考验的信条。// 这一广为人们所接受的信条很有意义地表明了相互照顾在中国社区生活中所起的重要作用。// 中国现有350万左右的义务工作者为年老体弱者、残疾人以及所需要帮助的人士提供服务。// 这些来自社会各界的社区服务自愿助工出于"人人为我，我为人人"的信念为社区服务。

# Model Test Three

## Part A（E—C）

**Directions**：*In this part of the test, you will hear two passages in English. Each passage consists of four sentences. After you have heard each sentence, interpret it into Chinese. You will start at the signal ... and then stop at the signal ... You may take notes while listening. Now let us begin Part A with the first passage.*

### Passage 1

I am delighted to extend this personal welcome to Chinese visitors to the Sydney Agricultural Technology Exhibition. // Here we present to our Chinese friends a comprehensive display of Australian agricultural achievements and advanced technology in farming that we have to offer. // I greatly value the friendship and confidence that we enjoy as your trading partner. // I am certain that this Exhibition will strengthen our economic cooperation and contribute directly to our further trade expansion.

### Passage 2

As an American manager of a Sino-American joint venture for two years, I have to say that there are differences in business management between Chinese and Americans that we American businessmen in China should try to understand and respect. // We are more direct and straightforward than most Chinese colleagues due to our different cultural traditions. Often times they consider our way of business practice is rather aggressive and we consider their process of decision-making time-consuming. // I can't say our way of doing business is absolutely superior. After all, there are merits and demerits inherent in both types of management. // It must be pointed out that in recent years, more and more American business executives have recognized the merits of the more humane Oriental way of Chinese management. It seems to offer something that we are lacking in.

## Part B（C—E）

**Directions**：*In this part of the test, you will hear two passages in Chinese. Each passage consists of four sentences. After you have heard each sentence, interpret it into English. You will start at the signal ... and then stop at the signal ... You may take notes while listening. Now let us begin Part B with the first passage.*

### Passage 1

今晚，我们很高兴在北京大学接待格林博士和夫人。我代表学校的全体师生员工向格林博士和夫人及其他新西兰贵宾表示热烈的欢迎。// 中新两国教育界人士的互访，增进了相互间的了解和学术交流。// 我相信格林博士这次对我校的访问，必将为进一步加强两校的友好合作关系做出重要的贡献。// 明天，贵宾们将要赴南京和上海访问,我预祝大家一路旅途愉快。

**Passage 2**
　　我很高兴应邀参加本届中外文化交流节,向诸位介绍中国书法这一人类文化财富和中国宝贵的旅游资源。// 中国有这么一句话,叫作"山不在高,有仙则名;水不在深,有龙则灵。"// 各位在中国旅游胜地所看到的包括铭文石碑在内的中国书法笔墨,就好比高山上的仙,大川中的龙。许多汉字属象形文字,我们可以从字形猜测词义。// 无论是刀刻书法还是笔墨书法都可以通过字形的夸张产生引人入胜的艺术效果。书法是一门研究艺术,观赏旅游景点的古代书法遗迹自然是一种艺术享受。

# 中级口译模拟考试参考译文

## Model Test One

### Part A (E—C)

**Passage 1**
　　自我们抵达这里时起,便一直受到暖人心房的盛情款待。// 中国有一句俗话最能表达我的感受,那就是"宾至如归"。// 我此次访问的目的之一是结交新朋友。然而我很高兴地发现,我不用结交朋友,我已处在朋友中间。// 我们合资企业成效斐然,我对我们之间的合作深为满意:我们双方都有收获,我们都经受住了国际市场的激烈竞争。

**Passage 2**
　　女士们,先生们,我想各位已经看到了有关我集团组织重新调整的那份报告,由此而产生的问题是如何为新组建的集团选择所在地。// 一种设想是将所有的总部机构都迁移到上海,这也是这份报告所提出基本意见。// 另一种设想是继续在两处经营我们两家公司,公司的现址不变,小公司设在上海。// 虽然我对第二种选择的经营效率有所怀疑,但是我想听听各位的高见。

### Part B (C—E)

**Passage 1**
　　A Chinese saying goes like this: "Just as there is a paradise in Heaven, there are Suzhou and Hangzhou on earth." // This saying is no exaggeration about the scenic beauty of the two historic cities near Shanghai which attract millions of tourists from home and abroad every year. // For example, the charming landscaped gardens of Suzhou, typical of China's southern garden architecture, contain numerous created landscape scenes within limited space. // The ponds, water, stones, flowers and trees of these gardens create a poetic mood for tourists and therefore, a visit to these gardens is a must for every tourist visiting Suzhou.

**Passage 2**
　　Ladies and gentlemen, Shanghai of the new century is developing rapidly into one of the world's economic, financial and trade centers. // The development of Shanghai's financial industry is particularly spectacular, with a fairly large and influential system of a financial market coming into shape. // The rise of Pudong

New Area in recent years has turned this most valuable place into a hot destination of overseas investment, with a total investment volume reaching US $ 98 billion. // Shanghai, the brilliant Oriental Pearl with its unique charm, invites financiers and entrepreneurs with broad visions to this city, where they will readily materialize their ambitions.

# Model Test Two

## Part A (E—C)

**Passage 1**

请允许我今晚重申,让我们以相互尊重、互惠互利的原则,以尊严与公正共存的原则为行动指南。// 同中国人民进行贸易往来,同中国人民交朋友,必定符合我国人民的根本利益。// 贵国的现代化建设给我们留下了深刻的印象,这一雄心勃勃的伟业,使我们未来的合作关系前程似锦。// 据我所知,今日中国采取了一种务实的、行之有效的方法。我们祝愿你们取得成功,并愿意在这项伟大的事业中与你们合作。

**Passage 2**

我们知道人脑分为大致相称的两个半球,它们的大小与形状比较相近,而功能则不同。// 人脑的左半球主要负责语言交际活动,也就是说,大多数人的语言中枢位于左半球。// 而人脑的右半球负责与视觉和空间有关的活动,同时也负责对音乐的感知。// 人类与其他动物之间最大的不同在于人类语言的创造性以及人类复杂的认知能力。

## Part B (C—E)

**Passage 1**

Welcome to Shanghai, Mr. and Mrs. Collins. I'm Meng Shiqi, manager of the Overseas Marketing Department of the Shanghai Lianhua Garment Manufacturing (Group) Corporation. // It's my pleasure to meet you and your wife here on behalf of Mr. Chen, general manager of the company. // Mr. Chen would like me to represent the company at our business talks in the next few days. // I will talk with you about the establishment of the company's overseas sales network. Your advice will be very much appreciated.

**Passage 2**

"Distant relatives are not as helpful as close neighbors" is a cherished and time-honored belief in China. // This widely recognized belief indicates quite meaningfully the important role of mutual care in China's communities. // In China there are about three and a half million volunteers who provide service for the aged, sick, handicapped and people who need help. // These community service volunteers, who come from all walks of life, act upon their belief of "All for one and one for all."

# Model Test Three

## Part A (E—C)

### Passage 1

我怀着愉快的心情,以我个人的名义,向光临悉尼农业技术展览会的中国来宾,表示热烈的欢迎。// 我们在这里向中国朋友全面展示我国的农业成就,并介绍我们所能提供的先进的农业技术。// 我对澳中两国在贸易合作中发展起来的友谊和建立起来的信心是非常珍视的。// 我确信,这次展览会将进一步加强我们的经济合作,并直接对扩大我们之间的贸易往来做出贡献。

### Passage 2

作为一名在一家中美合资企业工作了两年的美国经理,我认为中国人和美国人在经营管理中存在着差异,这些差异是我们这些在华工作的美国商务人士应该去理解和尊重的。// 由于我们有着与中国人不同的文化传统,所以我们比大部分中国人来得直率。中国人经常认为我们的经营方式咄咄逼人,而我们却认为他们的决策过程过于冗长。// 我不能说我们的经营之道一定优于中国的同事,毕竟各有各的优点和弊端。// 必须指出的是,近年来越来越多的美国经理人员开始认识到中国人的那种更具人情味的、东方式的管理方法的长处,这正是我们所欠缺的。

## Part B (C—E)

### Passage 1

It gives us great pleasure to play host again to Dr. and Mrs. Green in Beijing University. On behalf of the faculty, students and staff of the university, I wish to extend our warm welcome to Dr. and Mrs. Green and other distinguished New Zealand guests. // The exchange of visits between Chinese and New Zealand educators has facilitated our mutual understanding and academic exchanges. // I am convinced that Dr. Green's current visit to our university will surely make an important contribution to further strengthening the friendly relations and cooperation between our two universities. // Our distinguished guests will leave for Nanjing and Shanghai tomorrow. I wish you all a pleasant journey.

### Passage 2

I am very pleased to be invited to attend this gathering to celebrate the current Sino-foreign Cultural Exchange Festival, and to talk about Chinese calligraphy, mankind's cultural heritage and China's highly valued tourist resources. // The Chinese saying goes that "Any mountain can be famous with the presence of an immortal, and any river can be holy with the presence of a dragon." // The Chinese calligraphic works that you have seen in China's tourist resorts are like an immortal in a high mountain and a dragon in a great river. Many Chinese characters are pictographs and often the meaning of a particular character is apparent in the pictorial form of the character. // Whether done with a knife or brush, Calligraphy can be rendered in ways that exaggerate the form, and consequently yields the inviting effects of artistic beauty. Calligraphy is a subject of artistic study, and the appreciation of ancient calligraphic relics seen in places of tourist attraction is certainly an artistic entertainment.

# 上海市英语高级口译考试的要求、题型及形式

## 考试要求

"上海市英语高级口译资格证书考试"要求凡获得"上海市英语高级口译资格证书"者均具有良好的口语能力和口译技能，可以为政府机构、企业公司、文教单位、社会团体等部门从事诸如外事接待、旅游观光、礼仪活动、参观访问、宣传介绍、文化交流、国情咨询、新闻发布、商务谈判、国际问题研讨等方面的口译工作。

英语高级口译考试旨在测试考生的"英译汉"和"汉译英"的口译能力及技巧，衡量考生口译水平的基本标准为"准确"和"流利"。英语高级口译考试要求考生准确传达原话意思，注意语气、语音、语调、用词、句法的准确与规范，同时以恰当的速度流利通顺地进行口译。

## 考试题型

口译考试采用段落翻译的形式。翻译总量为四篇短文，其中两篇为"英译汉"，两篇为"汉译英"。每篇短文分为两小段，整个考试为八小段。考试题材与本教程的题材大体吻合。每篇短文的篇幅为120～150个词，每段为60～75个词。每个考生的口译考试时间约10分钟。

## 考试形式

口译测试采用个别面试的形式。考生分段听事先录制好的原文，并按段准确而流利地进行口译。通常先考"英译汉"部分，然后再考"汉译英"部分。每个考生可得到一张"口译记录纸"，用以在听录音时做一些必要的笔记。考生听完一段话后约有30～40秒左右的间隙供口译。口译时间的长短均由口译录音信号控制，即考生必须在"始译信号"和"止译信号"之间完成有关内容的口译。

以下为三套口译模拟试卷，其的题材、形式与要求同"上海市英语高级口译资格证书"的口译部分相吻合。

# 英语高级口译模拟考试

## Model Test One

### Part A（E—C）

**Directions**: *In this part of the test, you will hear two passages in English. Each passage consists of two paragraphs. After you have heard each paragraph, interpret it into Chinese. You will start at the signal ... and then stop at the signal... You may take notes while listening. Now let us begin Part A with the first passage.*

**Passage 1**

This is a happy and memorable occasion for me personally and for the members of my delegation. On behalf of all the members of my mission, I would like to take this opportunity to express our sincere thanks to our host for their earnest invitation and the gracious hospitality we have received since we set foot on this charming land.

// In accepting Your Excellency's gracious invitation to this great city, it has provided me with an excellent opportunity to convey to you and to the people of Shanghai the warm greetings and sincere good wishes of the government and people of my town. I would like you to join me in a toast to the health of Your Excellency and to the health of all our Chinese friends present here.

**Passage 2**

In an era dominated by electronics and telecommunications, we can never emphasize too much the importance of change. Motorola defines "change" as both challenge and opportunity. The past decade has seen Motorola seize the opportunities opened up by changes in China and build itself into one of the most successful American investors in the country. // With a firm commitment and substantial investment, we promote technological progress in China. By doing so, Motorola's brand has become a household name in China. We have laid a lot of groundwork, and helped China to implement its own strategy. We will reinvest and bring new technology into China.

### Part B (C—E)

**Directions**: *In this part of the test, you will hear two passages in Chinese. Each passage consists of two paragraphs. After you have heard each paragraph, interpret it into English. You will start at the signal ... and then stop at the signal ... You may take notes while listening. Now let us begin Part B with the first passage.*

**Passage 1**

国际旅游是促进各国人民相互了解的有效途径。有着五千年文明史的中国是各国人民向往的旅游目的地。中国人民创造了世界上无与伦比的灿烂文化，名胜古迹比比皆是，如北京的长城和故宫、杭州的西湖、桂林的山水。// 然而现在展现在您面前的是一整套全新的游览节目，其中大部分以中国传统文化为特色。这些旅游节目集观光、度假和文化活动于一体，使海外游客有机会了解中国文化，尽情观赏所到之地的历史名胜和人文景观。

**Passage 2**

育菁宾馆的是一家高校涉外宾馆。宾馆拥有雅致舒适的标准客房和豪华套房，客房内设有卫星闭路电视系统和中央空调。宾馆还有多功能厅、会议厅、华丽宽敞的宴会厅多座，以及国际标准保龄球馆、桌球房、游艺室、歌舞厅、商场、美容中心、桑拿浴房等设施。// 宾馆曾多次安排国内外重要会议，接待经验丰富，是国内外教育界、科技界、文艺界专家学者以及其他各界人士开展学术研究和文化交流的理想场所。

## Model Test Two

### Part A (E—C)

**Directions**: *In this part of the test, you will hear two passages in English. Each passage consists of two paragraphs. After you have heard each paragraph,* interpret it into Chinese. You will start at the signal ... and then stop at the signal... You may take notes while listening. Now let us begin Part A with the first passage.

**Passage 1**

I'm very happy that the Chinese Provincial Trade Delegation is here attending the opening ceremony of the US Science and Technology Exhibition. My warmest welcome goes to our Chinese friends from the other side of the planet. This exhibition is a display of recent Hi-Tech achievements in the United States. // Please share with us the pride and joy we have that some of exhibits are the products from some US-Chinese joint ventures. Although display of these exhibits is proportionally a mere fraction, less than 5% of the all the exhibits, it is nevertheless a promising sign of our future cooperation. "A good beginning is half the battle," as we always believe it. I wish my Chinese friends a most rewarding visit

**Passage 2**

Information technologies are fundamentally transforming the world in which people live, work, govern, and communicate. In this global Information Revolution, the accelerated development of information and communications technologies is having an increasing impact on virtually all aspects of economic activity and social structures. // More importantly, the nature of technologies is shifting from analog to digital, wired and fixed to wireless and mobile, and from separate transmissions of voice, data, text and image to interactive multimedia. This world of advanced electronic networks will open up an entirely new domain of possibility and progress.

## Part B (C—E)

**Directions**: *In this part of the test, you will hear two passages in Chinese. Each passage consists of two paragraphs. After you have heard each paragraph, interpret it into English. You will start at the signal ... and then stop at the signal... You may take notes while listening. Now let us begin Part B with the first passage.*

**Passage 1**

上海是中国重要的经济、金融、贸易、科技、信息和文化中心。作为一座历史文化名城,上海以她独特的风韵吸引了数以百万计的海内外游客。上海同时也是美食家的乐园,尤其是上海的本邦菜,特别受到海外人士的青睐。// 最引人入胜的建筑物当属黄浦江畔的东方明珠塔。登上观光层,或俯视浦江对岸的外滩万国建筑博览群,或举目鸟瞰全市,无限风光,尽收眼底,令人心旷神怡,流连忘返。

**Passage 2**

欢迎各位游览远东世界公园。远东世界公园是一座集世界名胜之大成的主题公园,其规模为远东同类公园之冠。您置身于100处历史名胜与自然景观之中,一日便可游遍天下景。// 园内各类微型景观的选料大多为优质石料,这些景观的制作工艺精湛无比,独具匠心,其复制程度之精确,形象之逼真,足可以假乱真,令游人叹为观止。

# Model Test Three

## Part A (E—C)

**Directions:** *In this part of the test, you will hear two passages in English. Each passage consists of two paragraphs. After you have heard each paragraph, interpret it into Chinese. You will start at the signal ... and then stop at the signal... You may take notes while listening. Now let us begin Part A with the first passage.*

### Passage 1

The 21st century is a networked age that binds us all together. Whether we like it or not, we're bound tightly together in our life, social or economic. We realize that advanced electronic networks enable us to transcend the barriers of time and distance and take advantage of business opportunities never before imagined. // This world of networks has opened up an entirely new domain of possibility and progress, and bring us into an unprecedented age of networked intelligence. This new age of networked intelligence promises that we are able to combine our knowledge and creativity for breakthroughs in social development and economic growth.

### Passage 2

For most people, almost any place can become a tourist destination as long as it is different from the place where the traveler usually lives. New York may not be a tourist attraction to a New Yorker, but for a Londoner it may have many charms. The famous tourist sites of many big cities offer a unique historic atmosphere, such as the Great Wall and the Palace Museum of Beijing, and the Buckingham Palace and St Paul's Cathedral of London. Tourists will indeed be affected by the unusual atmosphere of those cities. // Smaller towns and rural areas throughout the world have attractions of this kind for tourists. An excellent example is the small village town of Zhou Zhuang in China, known as "the Venice of the Orient". Of course, natural scenery has always been an attraction for tourists. Tens of thousands of people visit Niagara Falls every year, for example. Its reputation as a place for honeymoon is world-famous.

## Part B (C—E)

**Directions:** *In this part of the test, you will hear two passages in Chinese. Each passage consists of two paragraphs. After you have heard each paragraph, interpret it into English. You will start at the signal ... and then stop at the signal... You may take notes while listening. Now let us begin Part B with the first passage.*

### Passage 1

今晚我很高兴能在此设宴招待希尔会长和夫人以及加拿大商会的其他朋友。我此时的心情可以用中国一句古话来表达:"有朋自远方来,不亦乐乎。"我愿借此机会向各位表示热烈的欢迎。// 我深信,两国商界领导人之间的频繁互访不仅有助于我们两国之间经贸关系的改善,而且还有助于亚太地区乃至整个世界的经济发展。会长先生及其代表团将访问我国中西部,会见这些地区的商业界重要人士,我预祝各位旅途愉快!

**Passage 2**

现代化的交通、电信与大众传媒手段使世界变得越来越小,国际社会如同一个地球村,居住在地球村里的各国人民在文化交流中彼此尊重,共求发展。我认为,不同的文化应该相互学习,取长补短。// 文化交流不是让外来文化吞没自己的文化,而是为了丰富各民族的文化。当然,在广泛的文化交流中,一个民族的文化必须保持本民族的鲜明特色,必须对人类文明的发展做出贡献。

# 高级口译模拟考试参考译文

## Model Test One

### Part A（E—C）

**Passage 1**

对我本人以及我的代表团来说,这是一个愉快而难忘的时刻。我愿借此机会,代表我们代表团的全体成员,对我们东道主的诚挚邀请,对我们一踏上这块充满魅力了土地便受到的友好款待,向东道主表示真诚的感谢。// 我接受阁下的盛情邀请,来访问这座伟大的城市,这使我有极好的机会向阁下和上海人民转达我市政府和人民的热烈问候以及诚挚的良好祝愿。请各位与我一起举杯,祝愿阁下身体健康,祝愿出席今晚招待会的所有中国朋友身体健康!

**Passage 2**

在一个电子与电信占主导地位的时代,我们无论怎样强调变化的重要意义都不会过分。摩托罗拉公司对"变化"所下的定义是,变化既是挑战又是机会。摩托罗拉公司在过去十年中抓住了中国的变化带来的机遇,把公司建设成美国在华投资者中最成功的公司之一。// 我们以坚定的参与精神和巨大的投资份额,在中国促进技术进步。正因为如此,摩托罗拉品牌才得以在中国家喻户晓。我们已经做了许多基础工作,同时也帮助中国实施自己的战略。我们将再度投资,向中国引进新的技术。

### Part B（C—E）

**Passage 1**

International travel is an effective way of promoting mutual understanding among the peoples of the world. China, with its history of five thousand years' civilization, is an attractive tourist destination for people of various countries. In its long history of development, China has created a splendid national culture incomparable elsewhere in the world, with numerous scenic spots and historic sites all over the country, such as the Great Wall and the Palace Museum of Beijing, the West Lake of Hangzhou, and the natural scenery of Guilin. // However, a whole new panorama of Chinese destinations awaits you, most of which are characterized by traditional Chinese cultures. The new tour programs, which are so designed as to incorporate sightseeing, vacationing and cultural activities, will give overseas tourists a chance to learn about Chinese culture and enjoy their visits to their hearts' content to places of historic interest and cultural heritage.

**Passage 2**

Yujing Hotel is a university hotel authorized to accommodate overseas guests. The hotel has elegant and cozy standard rooms and luxury suites, all equipped with closed-circuit satellite TV and central air conditioning. The hotel boasts a multi-functional hall, a conference hall, a number of splendid and spacious banquet rooms, in addition to the bowling alleys of international standards, a billiard room, a game room, a ballroom, a shop, a beauty salon, as well as sauna facilities. // The hotel has successfully hosted quite a few important domestic and international conferences. Its recognized experience in providing adequate accommodations for such activities renders the hotel an ideal location for academic and cultural exchange activities for international and Chinese scholars and specialists in such fields as education, science and technology, and literary and art, and for people with other professional backgrounds.

# Model Test Two

## Part A (E—C)

**Passage 1**

我很高兴中国地方贸易代表团能来参加美国科技展览会。我向来自地球另一面的中国朋友们表示最热烈的欢迎。本次展览会展出美国近年来所取得的高科技成就，同时也是反映我国科技进步的一个窗口。// 有些展品是美中合资企业的产品，请各位与我们一起分享这种自豪和快乐。虽然这些展品数量微不足道，仅占所有展品的5％不足，却表明了我们广阔的合作前景。我们始终认为，"良好的开端是成功的一半。"我预祝中国朋友们在参观期间取得丰硕的成果。

**Passage 2**

信息技术正在从根本上改变着世界，改变着人们的居住、工作、管理和交际方式。在这场全球信息革命中，信息技术和通信技术的加速发展正在对经济活动和社会结构的几乎所有方面产生越来越大的影响。// 更重要的是，技术的本质是将模拟技术转变为数字技术，将有线电信和固定电信转变为无线电信和移动电信，将互为独立的声音、资料、文字和图像传播方式转变为交互式的多媒体方式。这个先进的电子网络世界将开辟一个创新与发展的崭新天地。

## Part B (C—E)

**Passage 1**

Shanghai is China's important center of economy, finance, trade, science and technology, information and culture. As a noted historic and cultural city, Shanghai attracts millions of tourists from home and abroad with its unique charm. Shanghai is also a cherished paradise for gourmets; its local cuisine enjoys particular popularity among overseas visitors. //The most attractive work of architecture is no other than the Oriental Pearl Tower standing by the bank of the Huangpu River.

Mounting the observation floor and looking around, you'll admire the view of the famous Bund lined up with a dazzling exhibition of international architecture across the Huangpu River and the charming skyline of the city in the distance, taking delight in the endless soothing vistas that you'll find difficult to turn away from.

**Passage 2**

Welcome to the World Park of the Orient. The largest theme park of its kind unparalleled in the Far East, the World Park of the Orient features a complete collection of famous scenic attractions of the world. Surrounded by 100 sights of historical interest and natural beauty, you will easily fulfill your dream of touring around the world within a day. // These miniature replicas of the original were constructed with top grade stones, boasting an exquisite workmanship and ingenious designs. You'll find yourself engrossed in involuntary admiration of the dazzling arrays of scenic reproductions that are unbelievably true to the original.

# Model Test Three

## Part A (E—C)

**Passage 1**

主席先生,您的国事访问给予我们机会并赋予我们责任为未来制定一条比过去几年里我们两国关系所走过的更积极、更稳定,但愿也是更富有成效的航线。中国是一个伟大的国家,有着辉煌骄傲的历史和前程强劲的未来。// 中国在合作与冲突问题上的走向,对亚洲、美洲乃至全球都将产生数十年的深远影响。一个稳定、开放、非侵略性的强大中国,一个选择了自由市场的中国,一个与我们携手共建安全的国际秩序的中国,是符合我国人民的根本利益的。

**Passage 2**

对大多数人来说,只要不是自己通常居住的地区,几乎任何一个地方都可以成为旅游胜地。纽约对纽约人来说也许不是旅游胜地,而对伦敦人来说却不乏魅力。许多大城市的名胜有一种独特的历史氛围,如北京的长城和故宫,伦敦的白金汉宫和圣保罗大教堂,游客的确可以在那里感受到一种与众不同的氛围。// 世界各地的小城镇和乡村地区也有这类游客趋之如鹜的景点,如被誉为"东方威尼斯"的中国小村镇周庄便是其中的一个典范。当然,自然风光始终吸引着游客。例如,尼亚加拉大瀑布每年吸引着数以万计的游客,其"蜜月巢"之美誉举世闻名。

## Part B (C—E)

**Passage 1**

It gives me great pleasure to host this banquet in honor of President and Mrs. Hill and other friends from the Canadian Chamber of Commerce. As an ancient Chinese saying goes, "It is such a delight to have friends coming from afar!" I would avail myself of this opportunity to extend my warm welcome to you all. // I'm deeply convinced that frequent exchanges between the business leaders of the two countries are beneficial not only to the improvement of our economic and trade relations, but also to the economic development of the Asian-pacific region and the world as a whole. Mr. President and his delegation will visit China's central and western areas and talk with important personalities of the business community in these areas. I wish you all a pleasant journey!

**Passage 2**

Modern means of transportation, telecommunication and mass media have shortened the geographical distance of the world. The international community appears to be no more than a global village, in which people of different nations engage in cultural exchange, while seeking common development in a harmonious and respectful relationship. I think different cultures should learn from each other's strengths to offset their own weaknesses. // Cultural exchange is by no means a process of losing one's own culture to a foreign culture, but a process of enriching each other's national cultures. Of course, the culture of a nation must withhold its own distinctive national characteristics in its extensive exchange with other cultures, and make contributions to the development of human civilization.

# 附录一:常用国名(地区名)速记方法

| | | | | | | |
|---|---|---|---|---|---|---|
| A | Austria | 奥地利 | B | Belgium | 比利时 |
| AL | Albania | 阿尔巴尼亚 | BM | Burma | 缅甸 |
| AUS | Australia | 澳大利亚 | BN | Bahrain | 巴林 |
| BD | Bangladesh | 孟加拉国 | BV | Bolivia | 玻利维亚 |
| BG | Bulgaria | 保加利亚 | CA | Canada | 加拿大 |
| BR | Brazil | 巴西 | CL | Chile | 智利 |
| BRU | Brunei | 文莱 | CO | Colombia | 哥伦比亚 |
| C | Czech | 捷克 | CU | Cuba | 古巴 |
| CH | Switzerland | 瑞士 | D | Germany | 德国 |
| CN | China | 中国 | DK | Denmark | 丹麦 |
| CR | Costa Rica | 哥斯达黎加 | E | Spain | 西班牙 |
| CY | Cyprus | 塞浦路斯 | EL | Ireland | 爱尔兰 |
| DZ | Algeria | 阿尔及利亚 | ET | Egypt | 埃及 |
| ED | Ecuador | 厄瓜多尔 | BK/UK | Great Britain | 英国 |
| ES | El Salvador | 萨尔瓦多 | GM | Gambia | 冈比亚 |
| F | France | 法国 | HK | Hong Kong | 中国香港 |
| FLD | Finland | 芬兰 | I | Italy | 意大利 |
| GH | Ghana | 加纳 | IK | Iraq | 伊拉克 |
| GO | Gabon | 加蓬 | IN | India | 印度 |
| H | Hungary | 匈牙利 | IS | Iceland | 冰岛 |
| HN | Honduras | 洪都拉斯 | J | Japan | 日本 |
| IA | Indonesia | 印度尼西亚 | JO | Jordan | 约旦 |
| IL | Israel | 以色列 | KE | Kenya | 肯尼亚 |
| IR | Iran | 伊朗 | KT | Kuwait | 科威特 |
| IV | Ivory Coast | 象牙海岸 | LI | Liberia | 利比里亚 |
| JA | Jamaica | 牙买加 | LY | Libya | 利比亚 |
| K | Korea | 韩国 | MA | Malaysia | 马来西亚 |
| KA | Kampuchea | 柬埔寨 | MC | Monaco | 摩纳哥 |
| KN | Cameron | 喀麦隆 | MO | Mozambique | 莫桑比克 |
| LE | Lebanon | 黎巴嫩 | NL | Netherlands | 荷兰 |
| LS | Laos | 老挝 | NZ | New Zealand | 新西兰 |
| LU | Luxemburg | 卢森堡 | OMN | Oman | 阿曼 |
| M | Morocco | 摩洛哥 | PA | Panama | 巴拿马 |
| AF | Afghanistan | 阿富汗 | PH | Philippines | 菲律宾 |
| AN | Angola | 安哥拉 | PL | Poland | 波兰 |
| AR | Argentina | 阿根廷 | R | Russia | 俄罗斯 |
| RM | Romania | 罗马尼亚 | P | Portugal | 葡萄牙 |
| S | Sweden | 瑞典 | PE | Peru | 秘鲁 |
| SD | Sudan | 苏丹 | PK | Pakistan | 巴基斯坦 |
| SGP | Singapore | 新加坡 | PY | Paraguay | 巴拉圭 |

| | | | | | |
|---|---|---|---|---|---|
| SJ | Saudi Arabia | 沙特阿拉伯 | RW | Rwanda | 卢旺达 |
| TN | Tunis | 突尼斯 | SA | South Africa | 南非 |
| TW | Taiwan | 中国台湾 | SG | Senegal | 塞内加尔 |
| U | Uruguay | 乌拉圭 | SL | Sri Lanka | 斯里兰卡 |
| VE | Venezuela | 委内瑞拉 | SO | Somalia | 索马里 |
| YE | Yemen | 也门 | SY | Syria | 叙利亚 |
| ZA | Zambia | 赞比亚 | TA | Tanzania | 坦桑尼亚 |
| MEX | Mexico | 墨西哥 | TH | Thailand | 泰国 |
| MS | Mauritius | 毛里求斯 | TR | Turkey | 土耳其 |
| MLT | Malta | 马耳他 | US | United States | 美国 |
| N | Norway | 挪威 | UG | Uganda | 乌干达 |
| NG | Nigeria | 尼日利亚 | V | Vatican | 梵蒂冈 |
| NIC | Nicaragua | 尼加拉瓜 | VN | Vietnam | 越南 |
| NP | Nepal | 尼泊尔 | YU | Yugoslavia | 南斯拉夫 |
| OM | Macao | 中国澳门 | ZR | Zaire | 扎伊尔 |
| RC | Central African Republic | 中非共和国 | | | |

# 附录二:常用国际机构名称英汉对照表

| | |
|---|---|
| Arab Monetary Fund (AMF) | 阿拉伯货币基金组织 |
| Asian Development Bank (ADB) | 亚洲开发银行 |
| Association of Southeast Asian Nations (ASEAN) | 东南亚国家联盟 |
| Atlantic Treaty Association (ATA) | 大西洋公约组织 |
| Bank for International Settlement (BIS) | 国际清算银行 |
| Council of Ministers for Asian Cooperation | 亚洲合作部长理事会 |
| Committee for European Economic Cooperation | 欧洲经济合作委员会 |
| Committee on Development and International Economic Cooperation | 发展和国际经济合作委员会 |
| Committee on Economic Cooperation among Developing Countries | 发展中国家经济合作委员会 |
| Committee on Technical Cooperation among Developing Countries | 发展中国家技术合作委员会 |
| Customs Cooperation Council (CCC) | 海关合作委员会 |
| Economic and Social Council of Asia and Pacific (ESCAP) | 亚太经社理事会 |
| European Cooperation Organization (ECO) | 欧洲经济合作组织 |
| European Common Market | 欧洲共同市场 |
| European Community (EC) | 欧洲共同体 |
| European Economic Community (EEC) | 欧洲经济共同体 |
| European Free Trade Area (EFTA) | 欧洲自由贸易区 |
| European Foundation for Management Development (EFMD) | 欧洲管理开发基金会 |
| European Monetary System (EMS) | 欧洲货币体系 |
| European Monetary Union (EMU) | 欧洲货币联盟 |
| European Political Union (EPU) | 欧洲政治联盟 |
| First National City Bank | 美国花旗银行(万国通宝银行) |
| General Agreement on Tariffs and Trade (GATT) | 关税及贸易总协定 |
| Geneva Conference on Disarmament | 日内瓦裁军谈判会议 |
| International Agricultural Development Bank | 国际农业开发银行 |
| International Association for the Protection of Industrial Property | 国际保护工业产权协会 |
| International Atomic Energy Agency (IAEA) | 国际原子能机构 |
| International Bank for Reconstruction and Development (IBRD) (World Bank) | 国际复兴开发银行(世界银行) |
| International Chamber of Commerce (ICC) | 国际商会 |
| International Committee of the Red Cross (ICRC) | 红十字国际委员会 |
| International Convention on Patents | 国际专利协定 |
| International Cooperation Administration | 国际合作总署 |

| | |
|---|---|
| International Copyright Agreement | 国际版权协定 |
| International Criminal Police Organization (INTERPOL) | 国际刑事警察组织 |
| International Development Association (IDA) | 国际开发协会 |
| International Investment Bank (IIB) | 国际投资银行 |
| International Labor Organization (ILO) | 国际劳工组织 |
| International Monetary Fund (IMF) | 国际货币基金组织 |
| International Olympic Committee (IOC) | 国际奥林匹克委员会 |
| International Organization of Journalists (IOJ) | 国际新闻工作者协会 |
| International Rules for the Interpretation of Trade Names | 国际商会国际贸易术语解释通则 |
| International Standard Organization (ISO) | 国际标准化组织 |
| International Telecommunications Union (ITU) | 国际电信联盟 |
| Non-Aligned Movement | 不结盟运动 |
| North America Free Trade Area (NAFTA) | 北美自由贸易区 |
| North Atlantic Treaty Organization (NATO) | 北大西洋公约组织 |
| Organization for Economic Cooperation and Development (OECD) | 经济合作与发展组织 |
| Organization for Petroleum Exporting Countries (OPEC) | 石油输出国组织 |
| Organization of African Unity (OAU) | 非洲统一组织 |
| Organization of American States (OAS) | 美国国家组织 |
| Organization of Islamic Conference (OIC) | 伊斯兰会议组织 |
| United Nations Advisory Committee on the Application Of Science and Technology to Development | 联合国科学与技术应用与发展咨询委员会 |
| United Nations Children's Fund (UNICEF) | 联合国儿童基金会 |
| United Nations Commission on International Trade Law | 联合国国际贸易法委员会 |
| United Nations Commission on Transnational Corporations | 联合国跨国公司委员会 |
| United Nations Conference on Trade and Development (UNCTAD) | 联合国贸易和发展会议 |
| United Nations Development Program (UNDP) | 联合国开发计划署 |
| United Nations Economic Commission for Asia and the Far East | 联合国亚洲及远东经济委员会 |
| United Nations Economic Commission for Europe | 联合国欧洲经济委员会 |
| United Nations Educational, Scientific and Cultural Organization (UNESCO) | 联合国教科文组织 |
| United Nations Environment Program | 联合国环境规划署 |
| United Nations Food and Agricultural Organization (FAO) | 联合国粮农组织 |
| United Nations General Assembly | 联合国大会 |
| United Nations High Commissioner for Refugees (UNHCR) | 联合国难民事务高级专员公署 |
| United Nations Industrial development Organization | 联合国工业发展组织 |

## 附录二 常用国际机构名称英汉对照表

| | |
|---|---|
| United Nations Monetary and Financial Conference | 联合国货币金融会议 |
| United Nations Relief and Rehabilitation Administration | 联合国救济总署 |
| United Nations Security Council | 联合国安理会 |
| United Nations Special Fund | 联合国特别基金 |
| United Nations Standards Coordinating Committee | 联合国标准协调委员会 |
| United Nations Statistical Office | 联合国统计局 |
| Universal Post Union(UPU) | 万国邮政联盟 |
| World Assembly of Youth (WAY) | 世界青年大会 |
| World Data Center | 世界资料中心 |
| World Environment and Resources Council | 世界环境和资源委员会 |
| World Federation of Trade Union | 世界工会联盟 |
| World Health Organization (WHO) | 世界卫生组织 |
| World Meteorological Organization (WMO) | 世界气象组织 |
| World Trade Center Association (WTCA) | 世界贸易中心协会 |
| World Trade Center (WTO) | 世界贸易组织 |

# 附录三：常见企业英文译名

**1. 工厂**

|  |  |
|---|---|
| 半导体器械厂 | semi-conductor apparatus plant |
| 包装材料厂 | packaging materials plant |
| 保温瓶厂 | thermos flask factory |
| 被单厂 | bedsheet factory |
| 变压器厂 | transformer factory |
| 玻璃制品厂 | glassware factory |
| 柴油机厂 | diesel engine plant |
| 船舶修理厂 | ship repair yard |
| 灯具厂 | lighting equipment factory |
| 低压开关厂 | low-voltage switch factory |
| 电动工具厂 | electric tool works |
| 电机厂 | electrical machinery plant |
| 电讯器材厂 | telecommunication apparatus factory |
| 电子管厂 | electronic tube factory |
| 电子设备厂 | electronic equipment factory |
| 发电厂 | power plant |
| 纺织机械厂 | textile machinery plant |
| 服装厂 | garment factory |
| 钢铁公司 | iron and steel company |
| 罐头食品厂 | canned food plant |
| 光学仪器厂 | optical instrument factory |
| 广播器材厂 | broadcasting equipment factory |
| 锅炉厂 | boiler factory |
| 化肥厂 | chemical fertilizer plant |
| 化工厂 | chemical works |
| 化学纤维厂 | chemical fiber plant |
| 化妆品厂 | cosmetics plant |
| 机械修理厂 | machine repair plant |
| 家具厂 | furniture factory |
| 建筑机械厂 | construction machinery plant |
| 金属工艺制品厂 | metal handicraft plant |
| 晶体管厂 | transistor factory |
| 绝缘材料厂 | insulating materials plant |
| 炼油厂 | oil refinery |
| 粮油加工厂 | grain and cooking oil processing factory |
| 毛纺厂 | woolen mill |
| 民族乐器厂 | folk music instrument factory |
| 木材厂 | timber mill |
| 农药厂 | insecticide factory |

| | |
|---|---|
| 皮革制造厂 | leather goods factory |
| 啤酒厂 | beer brewery |
| 汽车修配厂 | motor-car repair and assembly plant |
| 汽车制造厂 | automobile works |
| 乳品加工厂 | milk processing plant |
| 石油化工机械厂 | petro-chemical machinery plant |
| 水泥厂 | cement plant |
| 塑料厂 | plastics plant |
| 搪瓷厂 | enamel plant |
| 陶瓷厂 | pottery and porcelain factory |
| 通用机械厂 | general machinery plant |
| 玩具厂 | toy factory |
| 无线电器材厂 | radio alliances factory |
| 五金厂 | hardware factory |
| 橡胶厂 | rubber plant |
| 羊毛衫厂 | woolen sweater mill |
| 冶炼厂 | metallurgical plant |
| 医疗器械厂 | medical apparatus factory |
| 仪表厂 | instrument and meters factory |
| 饮料厂 | soft drinks plant |
| 印染厂 | printing and dyeing mill |
| 油漆厂 | paint factory |
| 有机化工厂 | organic chemical plant |
| 造船厂 | shipbuilding plant |
| 造纸机械厂 | paper making machinery plant |
| 针织厂 | knitwear mill |
| 制药厂 | pharmaceutical factory |
| 铸造厂 | foundry works |

## 2. 公司

| | |
|---|---|
| 电力机械制造公司 | electrical machinery manufacturing company |
| 电信发展公司 | telecommunications development co. |
| 电子技术开发公司 | electric technology development co. |
| 电子器材公司 | electronic equipment & materials corporation |
| 对外服务公司 | foreign service company |
| 对外经济发展公司 | foreign economic development company |
| 对外贸易公司 | foreign trade company |
| 饭店集团服务公司 | hotel group, ltd. |
| 房产投资有限公司 | realty & investment company |
| 纺织企业集团 | textile enterprise group |
| 工程承包有限公司 | project contracting co., ltd. |
| 工艺美术品公司 | arts and crafts corporation |
| 广告公司 | advertising company |
| 国际工程集团 | international engineering group |
| 国际租赁公司 | international leasing company |
| 国际广告展览有限公司 | international advertising and exposition co., ltd. |

| | |
|---|---|
| 国际经济技术合作公司 | international economic and technological cooperation corporation |
| 国际经济开发公司 | international economic development corporation |
| 国际科技咨询公司 | international scientific and technological consulting corporation |
| 国际信息处理公司 | international information processing company |
| 化纤工业集团公司 | chemical fiber industry group |
| 计算机技术服务公司 | computer technology service corporation |
| 技术开发咨询公司 | technical development and consultancy co. |
| 家用电器有限公司 | household electrical appliances co., ltd. |
| 建筑工程公司 | construction engineering co. |
| 建筑工程咨询公司 | construction project consulting corporation |
| 建筑设计合资公司 | building design joint venture corporation |
| 交通进出口服务公司 | communications import & export service company |
| 旅游公司 | travel corporation / tourism company |
| 能源开发公司 | energy development corporation |
| 农资公司 | agricultural materials company |
| 水产品有限公司 | aquatic product company ltd. |
| 讨债公司 | debt collecting company |
| 新型建筑材料供应公司 | new building materials supply company |
| 实业集团公司 | industrial group corporation |
| 饮料有限公司 | beverage company limited |
| 制衣实业公司 | garments industrial company |

如需参考译文和听译练习录音稿，请联系北京大学出版社外语编辑部郝妮娜：bdhnn2011@126.com